IMAGES
of America

FREEBORN COUNTY

MINNESOTA

IMAGES
of America

FREEBORN COUNTY
MINNESOTA

Freeborn County Historical Society

ARCADIA
PUBLISHING

ISBN 978-0-7385-0303-5

Published by Arcadia Publishing
Charleston, South Carolina

Printed in the United States of America

Library of Congress Catalog Card Number applied for.

For all general information contact Arcadia Publishing at:
Telephone 843-853-2070
Fax 843-853-0044
E-mail sales@arcadiapublishing.com
For customer service and orders:
Toll-Free 1-888-313-2665

Visit us on the Internet at www.arcadiapublishing.com

Contents

ACKNOWLEDGMENTS

The Freeborn County Historical Society is proud to present *Images of America: Freeborn County, Minnesota.*

We wish to acknowledge Bev Jackson, FCHS Executive Director, for weaving these threads of history into narratives that educate and entertain, and for coordinating this project; and Linda Evenson, FCHS Librarian, for the archival research that provided the interesting images and little known bits of history, and for the assembly of the final product. Kathy Freese, FCHS Administrative Assistant, supplied unending patience as she processed our ideas, revised, and revised again. We also thank Georges Denzene, museum volunteer, who provided limitless hours in the photo selection process, valuable information, and editing skills; and Jonathon Green, member of FCHS Board of Directors, who assisted in the planning of the book, in photo selection, and with proofreading.

Equally as appreciated are the following: Irv Sorenson, whose *Hi-Lites & Shadows* entertained readers of the *Albert Lea Tribune* for many years; Grace Haukoos, owner of The Constant Reader, who encouraged us to tackle this project; Roger Lonning, FCHS member, who provided his copious notes of Freeborn County's history for our use; Ed Shannon, of the *Albert Lea Tribune*, for informative columns; Kathy Jensen, author of "*Clarks Grove…A Place We Call Home;*" Bidney Bergie, Freeborn County historian; Michael Cotter, farmer and storyteller; Freeborn County residents who donated photographs; and the numerous authors of the publications—*Histories of Freeborn County* (1882, 1911) and *Freeborn County Heritage* (1988); *The Hollandale Story 1918–1950*; *Historiography*; and *The Community Magazine*.

Each of these people, with their own significant contribution, has made possible this publication, and for this we are grateful.

INTRODUCTION

The history of Freeborn County, Minnesota is the story of people—their dreams, their hard work, their joys, and their disappointments.

Our history is: Lieutenant Albert Miller Lea of the First United States Dragoons, who surveyed and mapped these beautiful prairies; and it is Elizabeth Stacy, the first woman to graduate from the University of Michigan Medical School. It is George Ruble, the stubborn gentleman who built the dam and the lumber mill for the town he dreamed would become the county seat; and it is the indomitable spirit of the pioneers, who could not speak the English language, but knew they would make their homes on this fertile Minnesota soil. It is the child who lies buried in a shallow grave, and the mother who dried her tears and then prepared supper for her family.

In this book, we will introduce to you these ethnically diverse people, and we will attempt to explain the human natures that braved the hot, sticky summers and the sub-zero winters. In earlier years, Native Americans had built mounds and lived in villages along the shores of the lakes. The Europeans arrived later in covered wagons, and some of these earliest settlers lived in dugouts until they could build better homes. Then came the merchants, who believed in the future of these small farming communities; and the entrepreneurs, who platted sites for the villages. This complicated mix defines our history.

Many books have been written about Freeborn County. Most of them focus on Albert Lea, the largest city and the county seat. We have chosen a broader view for this work.

We have selected prints and photographs from each of the twenty townships that make up the county. In these townships, many communities have developed over the years. Some of them lived only a short time, and died because they were bypassed by the railroads that criss-crossed Southern Minnesota, providing transportation for new settlers and shipping for agricultural products. Other villages could not attract settlers. Those that survived grew, and to this day provide homes for descendants of the earliest pioneers, as well as newer residents, who were attracted by industry or the beauty of Southern Minnesota.

A history of Freeborn County could not be written without an emphasis on agriculture. Farming has been the mainstay of the area. Early records describe fertile fields, the abundance of crops, and numerous creameries. For many years the largest industry in the county, the meat packing industry, provided jobs for the townspeople as well as a market for the cattle, hogs, and sheep raised in the rural areas.

Albert Lea is the county seat—a picturesque community surrounding Fountain Lake and touching the shores of Albert Lea Lake. It is a city of a legend—the horse race that determined its position as the county seat, and the mysterious man whose body was found hanging in the courthouse clock tower. It is the only city in Minnesota that was named after the United States Army Officer who served with the Dragoons out of Fort Des Moines; and then almost thirty years later, who fought on the side of the Confederacy during the Civil War.

The county's namesake was William S. Freeborn, who served in the Territorial Legislature from 1854 to 1857. He was a politician with an interest in land development, and with whose support neighboring counties were also created.

Most of the photographs in this book are from the files of the Freeborn County Historical Society. The others have been donated in an effort to further define the communities, past and present, that make up our rural Southern Minnesota landscape.

Historical research for the photo captions was done in the FCHS library and archives. This library contains an abundance of information—original accounts, as well as other articles written many years after the actual incidents occurred. Research efforts were based on the earliest information possible, keeping in mind that later accounts were often affected by misinterpretation, personal bias, and the prevailing public attitudes. Sometimes only the later information was available.

Although dates, locations, and names are occasionally missing from photo identification, the editors felt that some pictures were simply too good to be omitted. We ask the readers to provide their own interpretations, knowing that this particular situation did take place sometime in the history of Freeborn County.

This book, *Images of America: Freeborn County, Minnesota*, has been designed as a guide for an afternoon's drive through one of the quadrants of the county, or a visit to the county seat. Whether you are in your car, or in an easy chair, and no matter which section of the county you choose, in these pages you will find photos that represent the people, the landscape, the economic purpose, and the lifestyles of each area.

We hope you enjoy your trip!

One

The Southeast

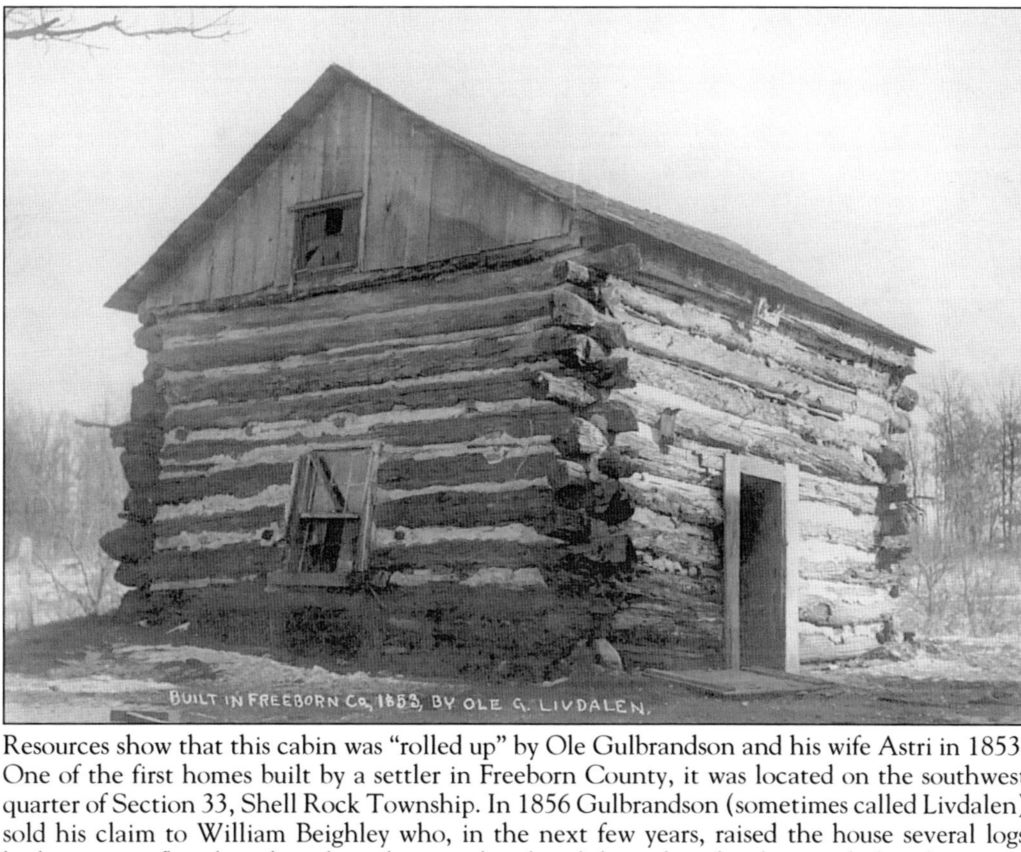

Resources show that this cabin was "rolled up" by Ole Gulbrandson and his wife Astri in 1853. One of the first homes built by a settler in Freeborn County, it was located on the southwest quarter of Section 33, Shell Rock Township. In 1856 Gulbrandson (sometimes called Livdalen) sold his claim to William Beighley who, in the next few years, raised the house several logs higher, put in floor boards and windows, and replaced the sod roof with cut oak shingles.

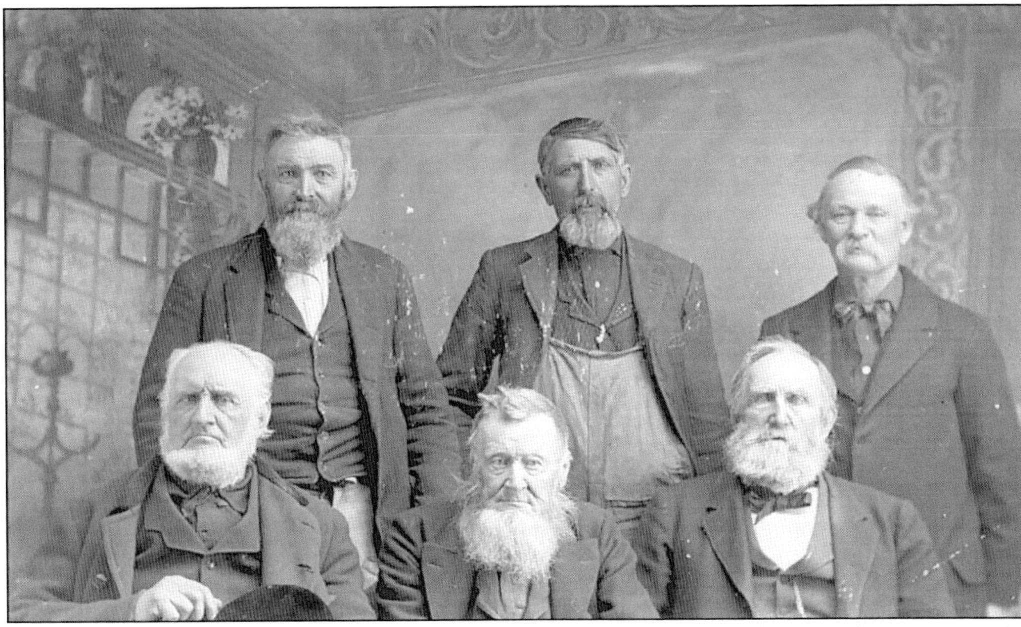

These distinguished early Freeborn County settlers pose for a group photograph in 1890 at the J.O. Booen Studio in Glenville. They are, from left to right, Charles T. Knapp (first to use a breaking plow in the county), Jacob Hostetter (spokesman at the funeral of two men found frozen during the blizzard of 1856), George Gardner (hotel owner), Mark Freeman (farmer), Henry Cottrell (who hauled supplies from McGregor, Iowa), and Edward Budlong (who farmed 230 acres).

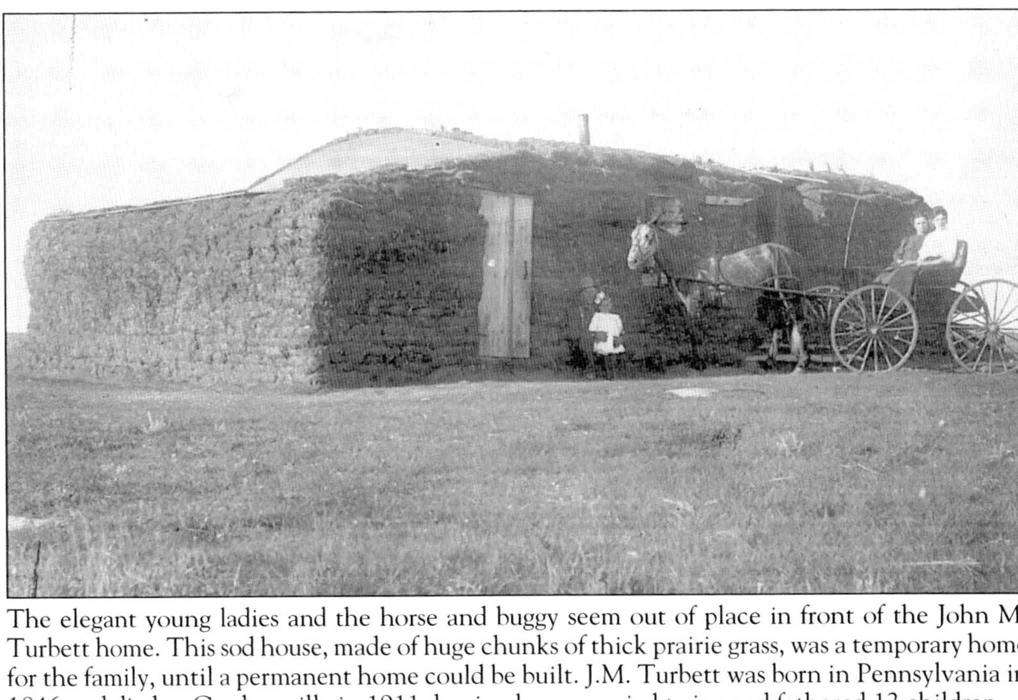

The elegant young ladies and the horse and buggy seem out of place in front of the John M. Turbett home. This sod house, made of huge chunks of thick prairie grass, was a temporary home for the family, until a permanent home could be built. J.M. Turbett was born in Pennsylvania in 1846 and died at Gordonsville in 1911, having been married twice and fathered 12 children.

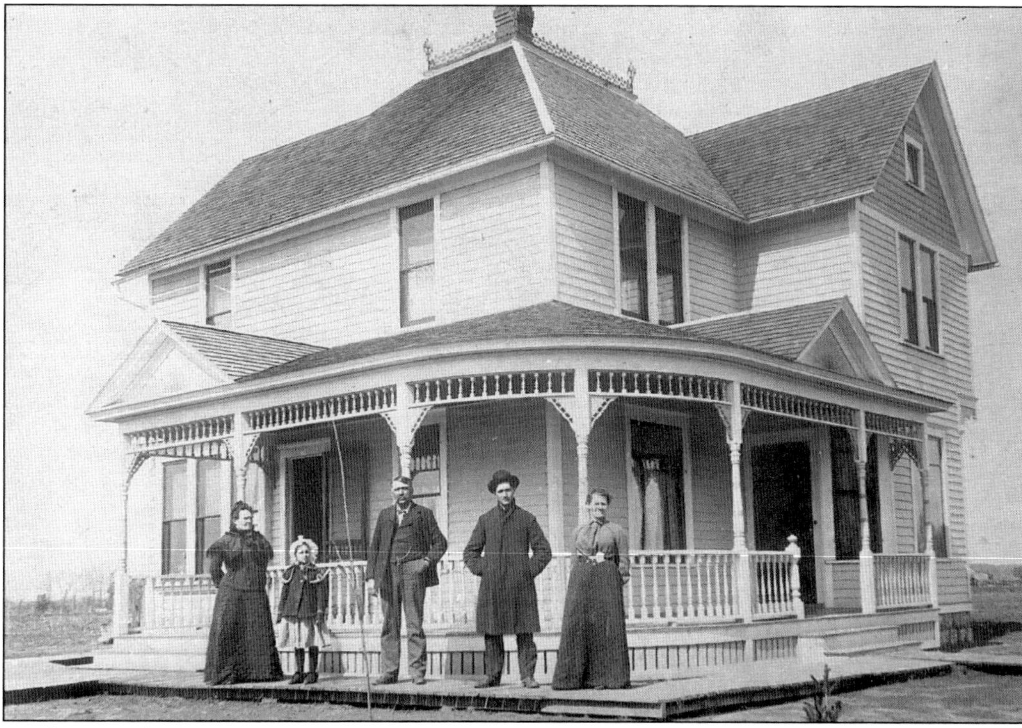

A photograph from the FCHS archives lists this beautiful Victorian home as the Lackey residence, on Skinner Street in Glenville. Shown here, from left to right, are: Ida Hull, Ida Lackey, Fred Morrison, Harry Morrison, and Mrs. Fred Morrison. No date is given. Other records show that Harry Morrison died in 1957, after several years of illness, remaining "strong in spirit, alert mentally, and interested in family and world news."

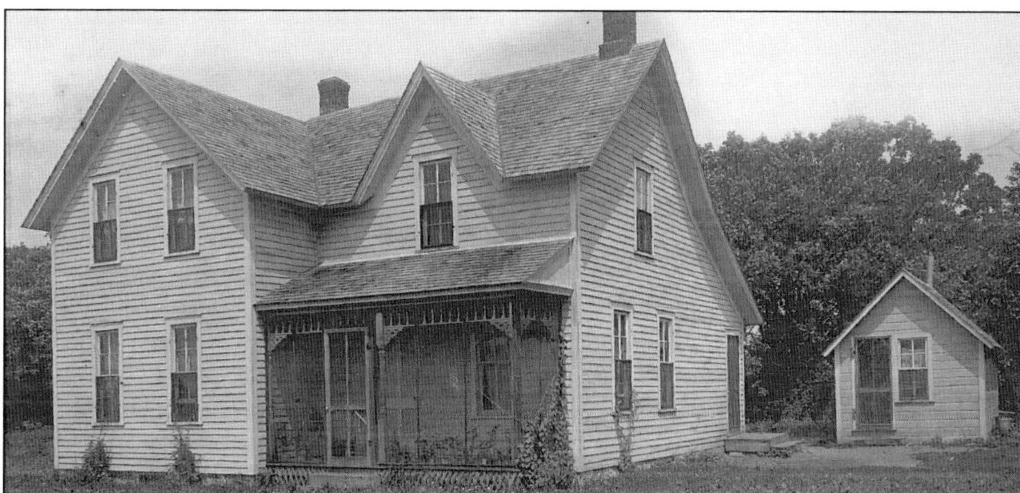

This typical 19th-century Minnesota farmhouse, with its steep-gabled roof and decorative porch, was the home of the Martin Nelson family from Gordonsville. For 40 years the Nelsons farmed, until Martin's death. He "sank quietly down in death," (*Albert Lea Tribune*, September 1930) while attending the funeral of an old friend, Aleck J. Lee, at Shell Rock Lutheran Church west of Northwood, Iowa.

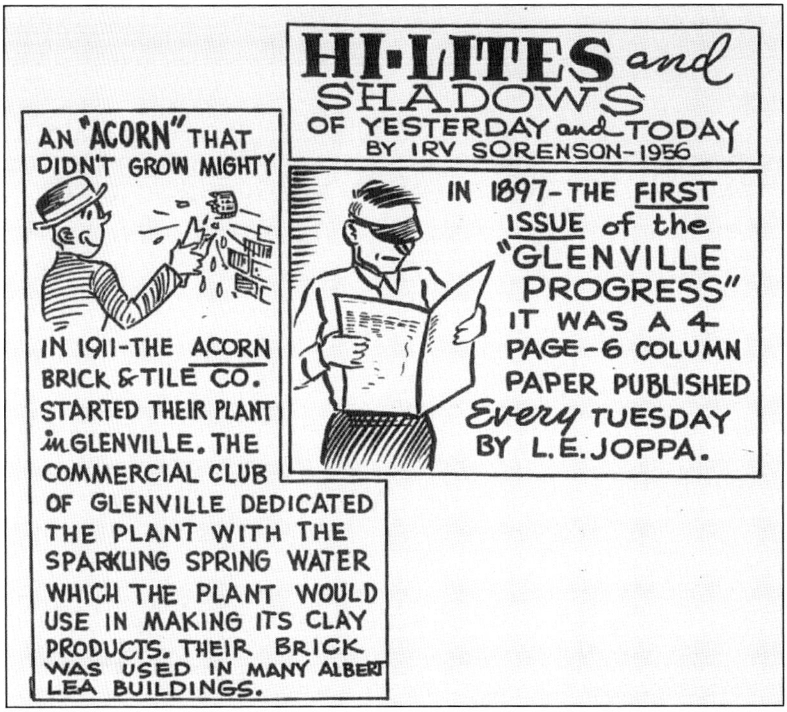

Hi-Lites and Shadows of Yesterday and Today, drawn by Irv Sorenson in 1956, is pictured here.

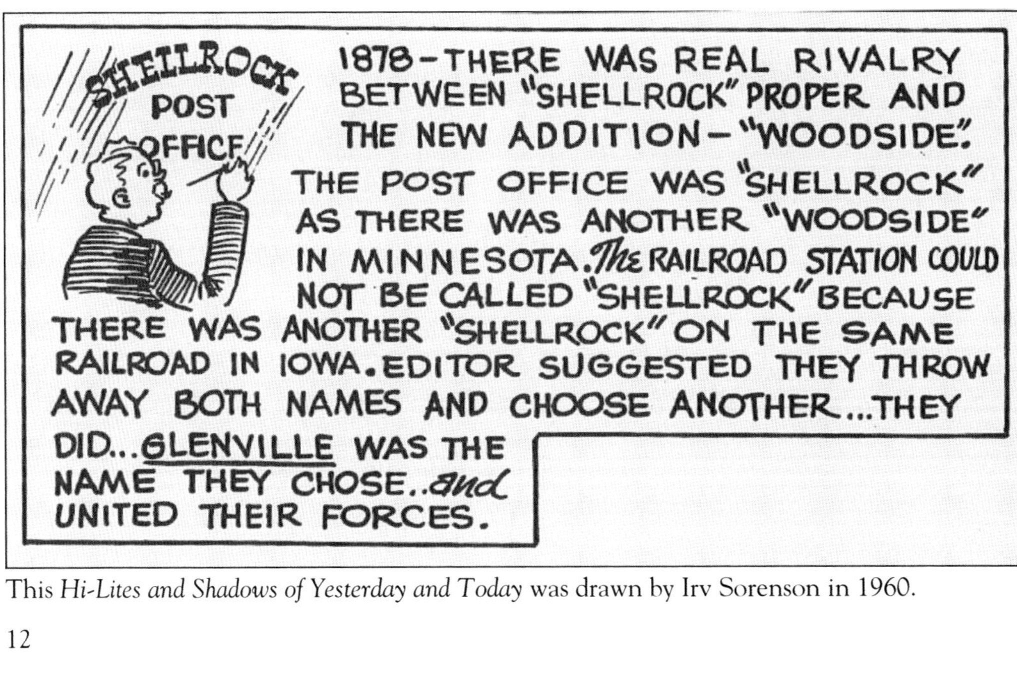

This *Hi-Lites and Shadows of Yesterday and Today* was drawn by Irv Sorenson in 1960.

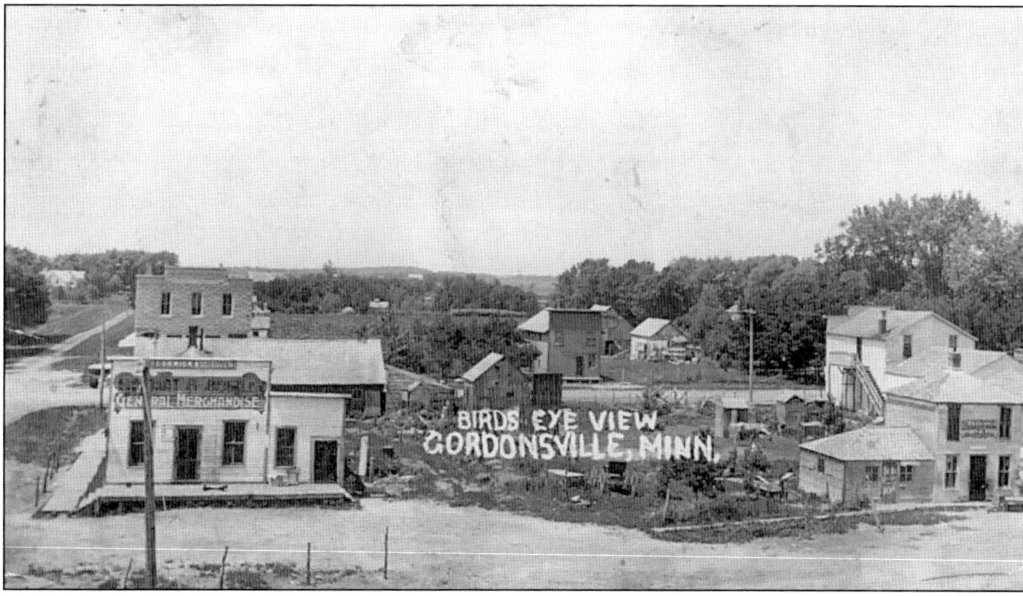

This 1910 view of Gordonsville shows the old bank building, one of the city's general stores, the Larson Cement plant, and the original home of the Pierce Harrows. The icehouse and the Methodist Parsonage are also shown. The 1904 city directory lists Samuel Beighley as the manager of the Long Distance Telephone Company. He also sold cigars, gum, and candy, with special attention given to oysters and ice cream when in season.

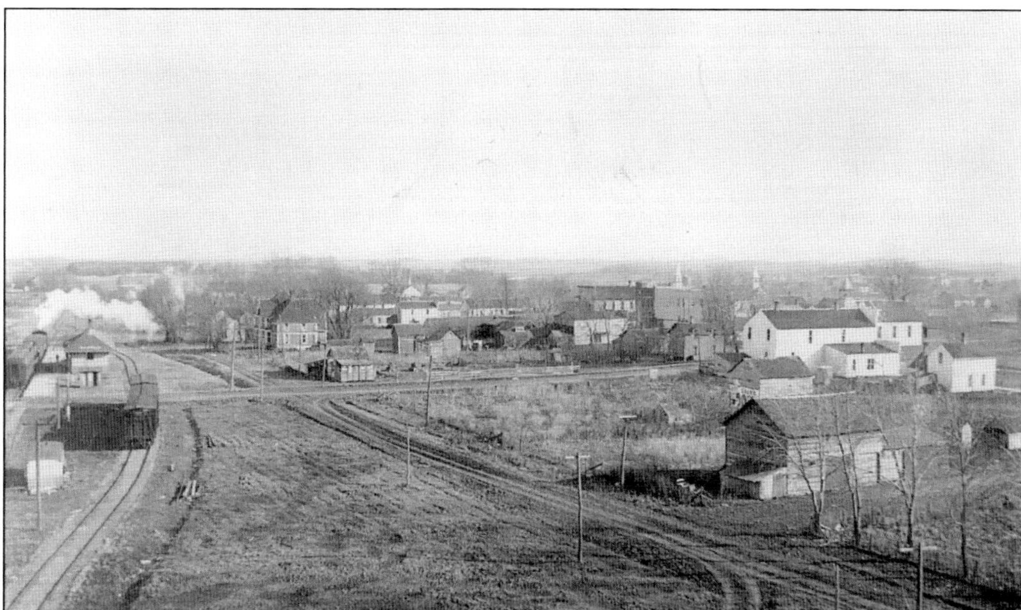

The village of Glenville was incorporated in 1898, and was a combination of two villages—Shell Rock and Woodside. By 1911, Glenville could boast of "four churches (Methodist Episcopal, Free Methodist, United Brethren, and Norwegian Methodist), a creamery, school, telephone system, a fine city hall, two banks, a fire company, a newspaper, and the usual business houses and residences." (*History of Freeborn County* [1911].)

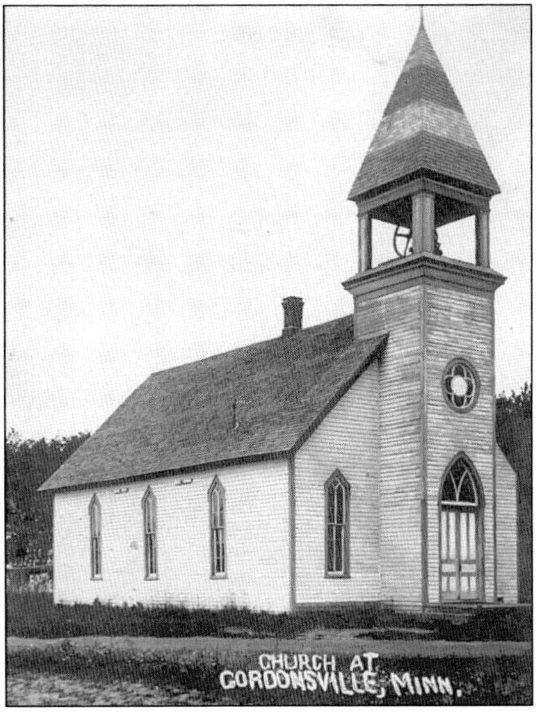

In 1857, an itinerant preacher, the Reverend Moses Mapes of the Methodist Episcopal Church, walked from Austin to what was known as Beighley Grove, to preach the first sermon—the service being held in a log home. A year later he organized the first congregation of the Gordonsville Methodist Church, and services were held in homes, and then in the schoolhouse, until this white-frame church was built in 1883.

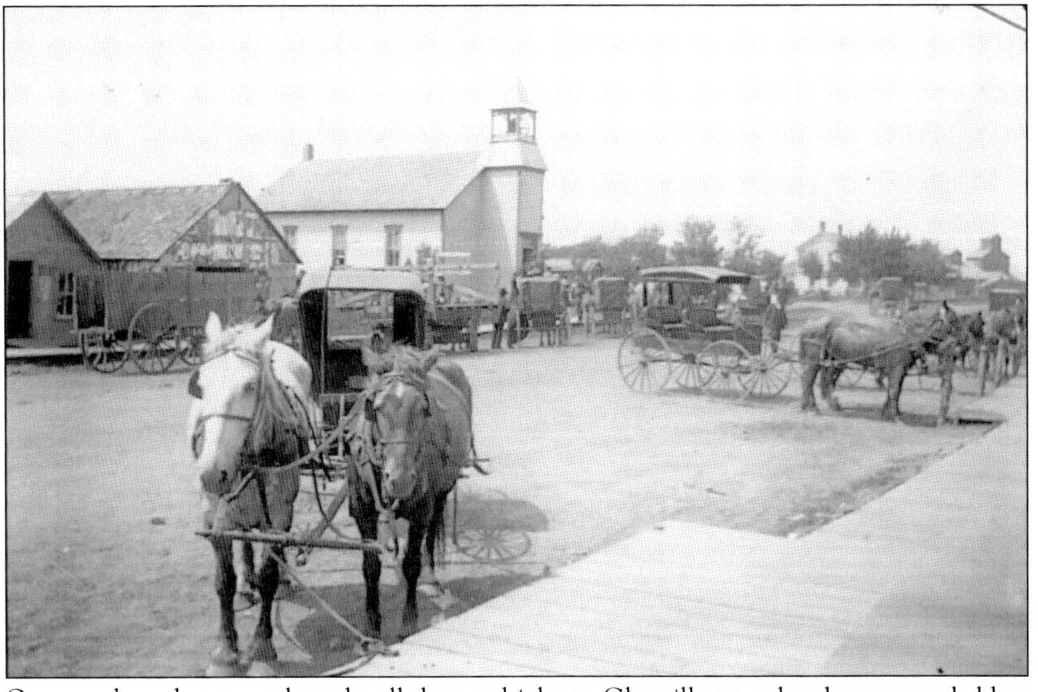

One wonders what event brought all these vehicles to Glenville on a day that was probably a weekday. In addition to the Glenville Free Methodist Church being open, Gillard's Blacksmith Shop also seemed to be busy. Note the iron rings on the sidewalk for tying horses, the single-seated buggies, the double-seated surreys, and the double-grain box and hay rack in front of the blacksmith shop.

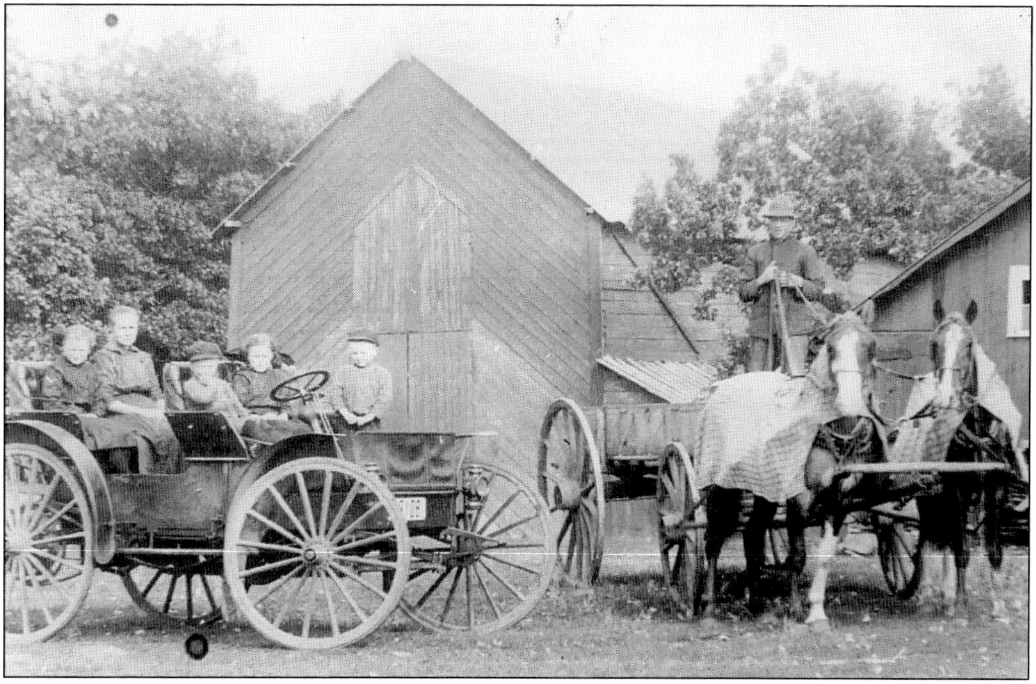

John P. Larson (standing in the wagon), his wife Inger, and their children (in the auto) pose for the camera in 1906. Their farm, Shell Valley Farm, was located west of Gordonsville. He was born in Telemarken, Norway and immigrated to Freeborn County when he was 16 years old. The Larsons and their nine children were well known for their involvement in the church and the community.

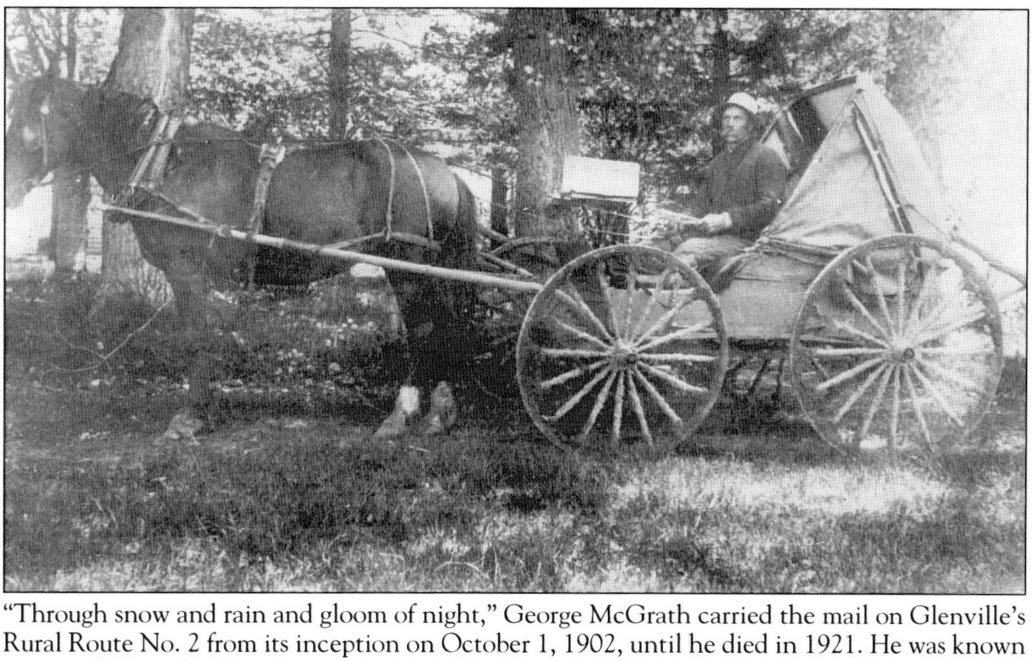

"Through snow and rain and gloom of night," George McGrath carried the mail on Glenville's Rural Route No. 2 from its inception on October 1, 1902, until he died in 1921. He was known as one of Glenville's best citizens, a genial mail carrier who was a friend to those on the route, especially the children.

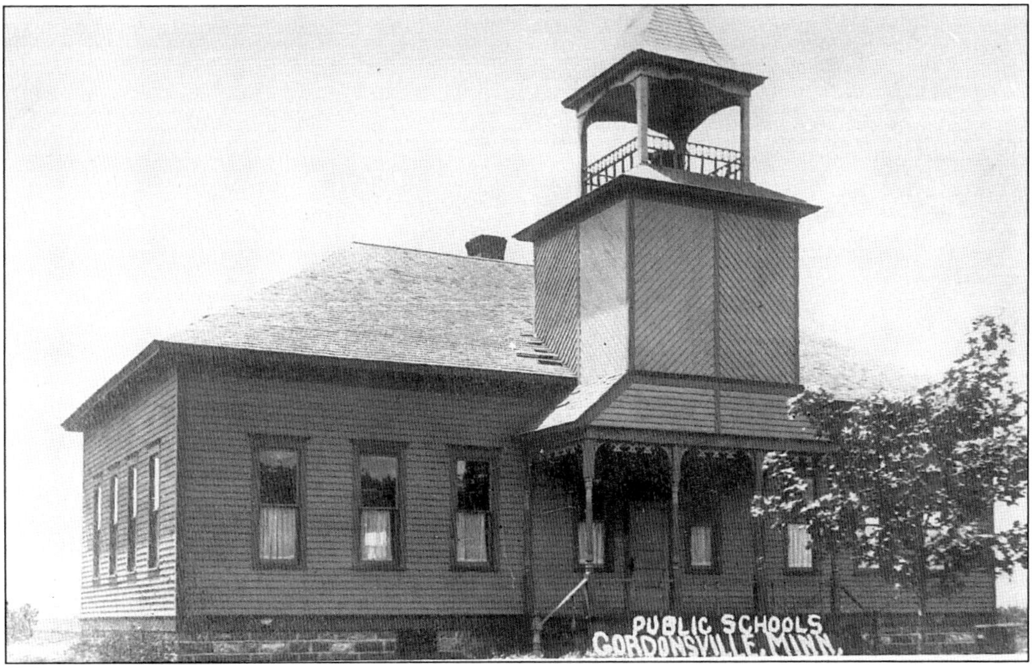

When this Gordonsville District 50 school was built in 1883, it was considered one of the best school buildings in the county. It contained two classrooms, a hallway, and a library with 150 volumes. Heat was provided by coal, which was kept in the basement and carried upstairs by the teachers and students to the two coal heaters. The building had no electricity or running water. It was destroyed by fire in 1900.

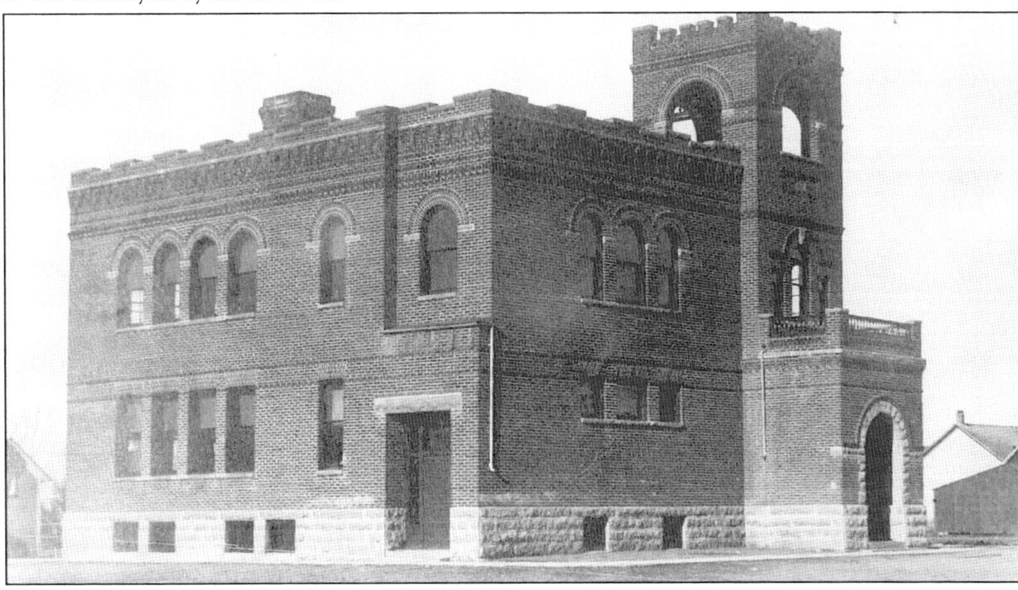

Glenville's third school was built in 1899, at a cost of $6,500. On a Monday morning in May, 1916, pupil Roy McGrath was working at the blackboard when he saw a puff of smoke and fire. He yelled, "fire," and then ran to the town hall to ring the fire bell. In less than three minutes, all the students were outside. They helped the firemen and neighbors with the bucket brigade, carrying water from nearby wells. Only the building interior was damaged.

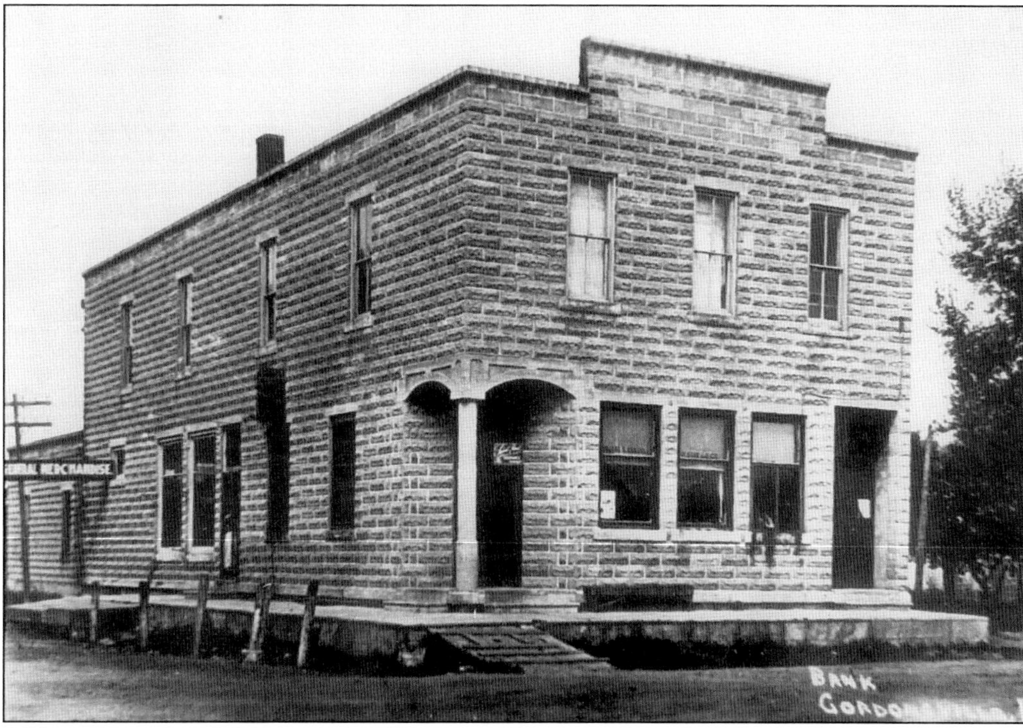

Old-timers spoke of the Gordonsville City Hall with pride and nostalgia. It not only served as an election site, but also a meeting place for organizations and the center for all community events, prize fights, dances, school programs, traveling shows, and church dinners. Built in the early 1900s from cement blocks made on the site, the building also housed the bank and the D.L. Klovis general store.

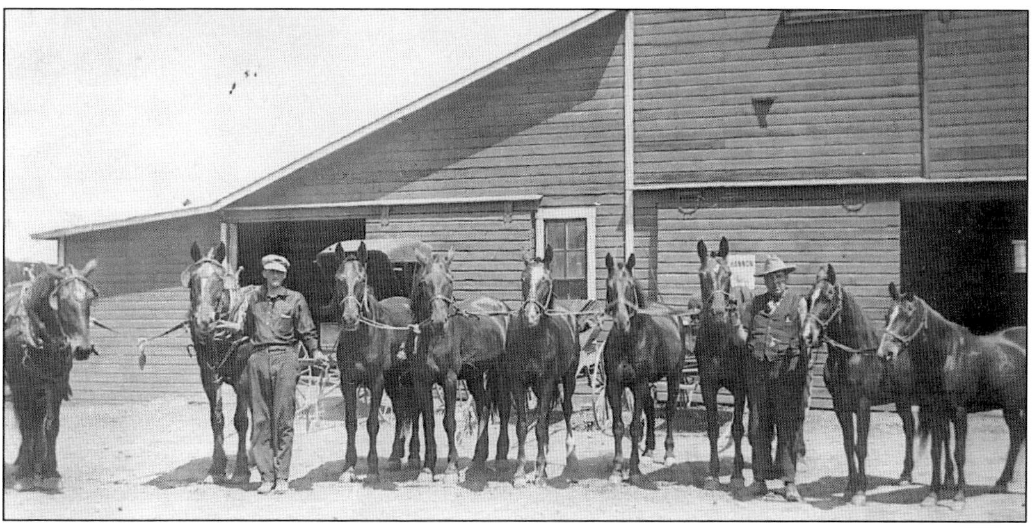

In 1910, George Pfiefer and Fred Holman sold the Glenville livery barn to S.T. Kirkpatrick, who modernized the building with a cement floor and force pump. The business was leased by Lester Abbott and Pardon "Pard" H. Cottrell. "Pard" later purchased Abbott's interest, and he is shown in this photograph with Con Olson. The livery was located one block north of Main Street, near the Illinois Central Railroad depot.

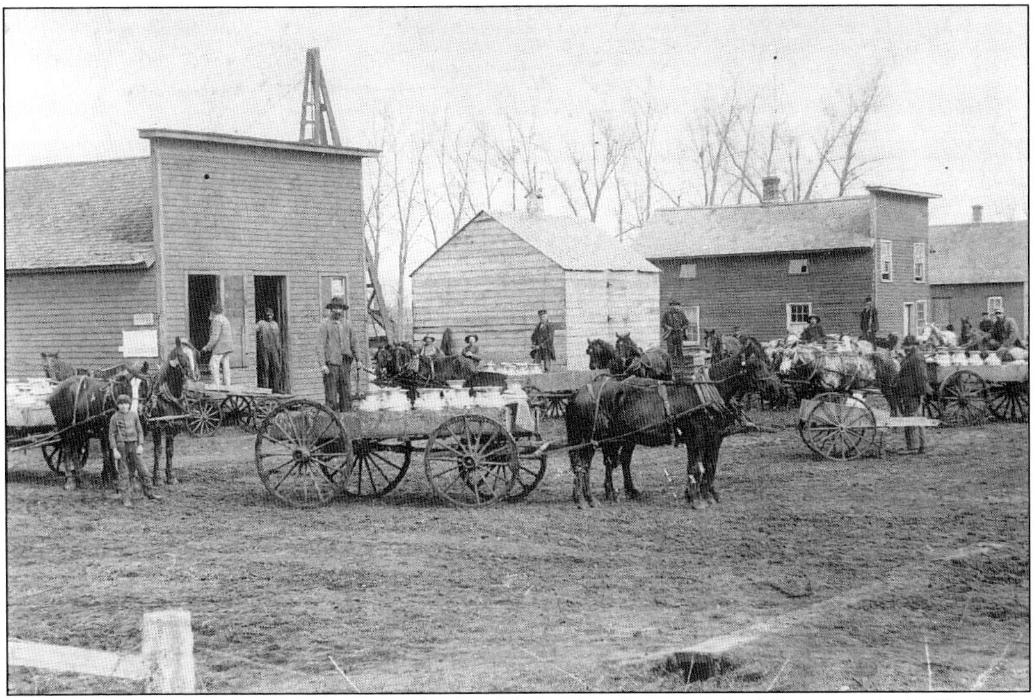

In this 1898 photograph, John C. Buley stands in the doorway (building on the left) of the milk skimming station of Gordonsville. Skimmed-off cream was hauled from this station to the Glenville Creamery to be churned. The second building was the icehouse, then the Forseth Hotel, and then the home of Fred Pierce, the blacksmith, whose business was across the street.

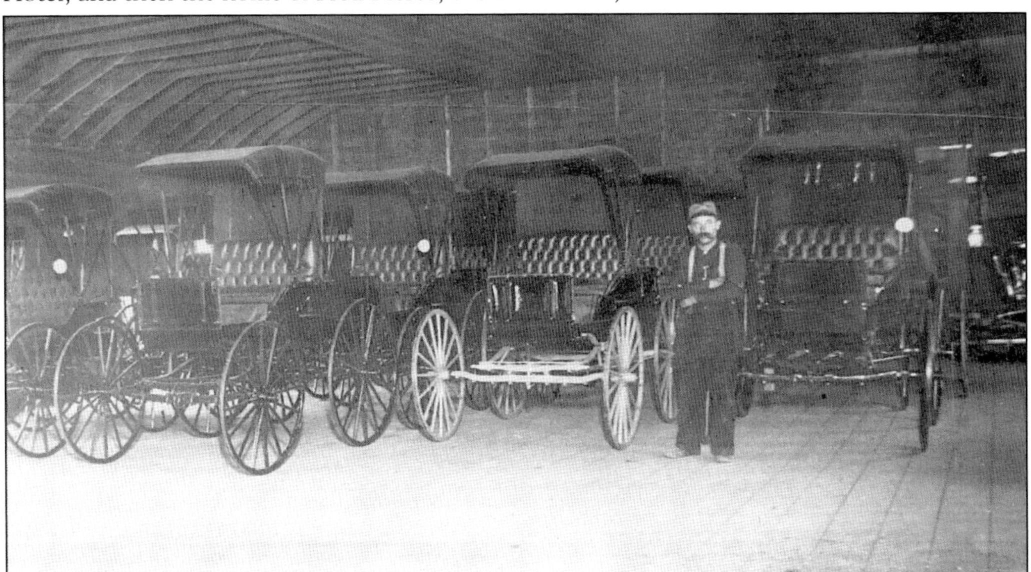

Walter Knutson is shown in the buggy display area of his farm implement business in Glenville. He was born in Denmark, came to the U.S. when he was 22, settled first in Austin, Minnesota, and a year later opened a blacksmith shop and implement business in Glenville. Twelve years later he moved to Albert Lea, going into a similar business. He was well known for his "right methods."

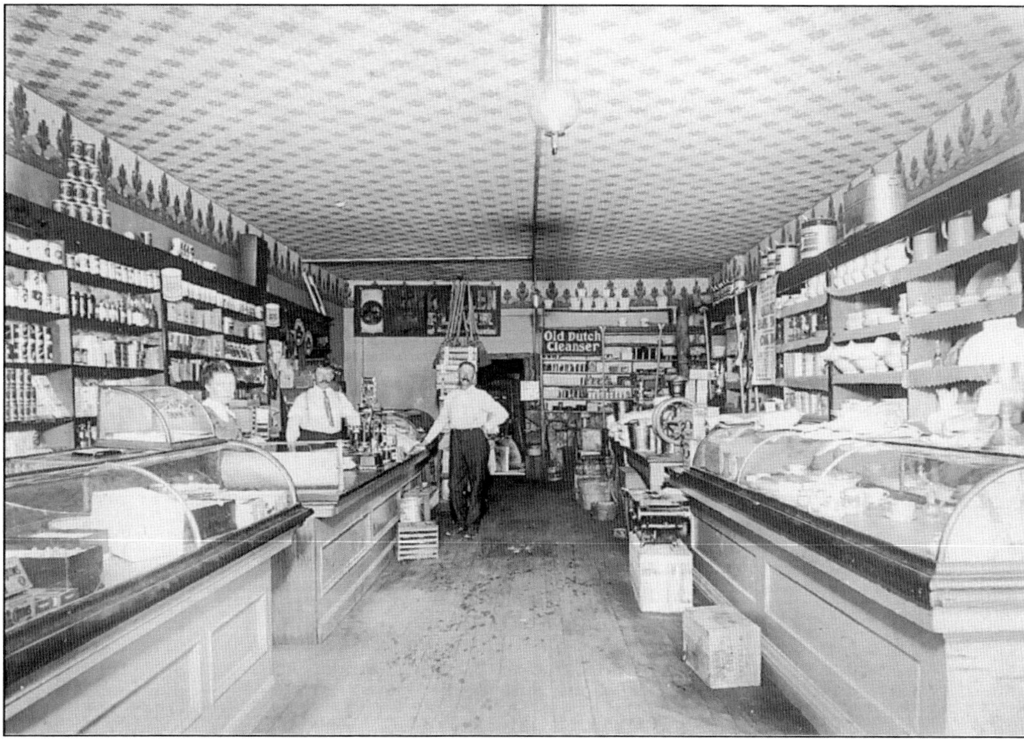

For many years, David J. Roberts owned the general store in Glenville. This photograph shows Roberts and his wife behind the counter and Anton Fields, the store clerk. The patterned tin ceiling, wooden floor, single electric light, wood counters with glass-domed display cases, and floor-to-ceiling shelving were typical of general store interiors in the years following the turn of the century.

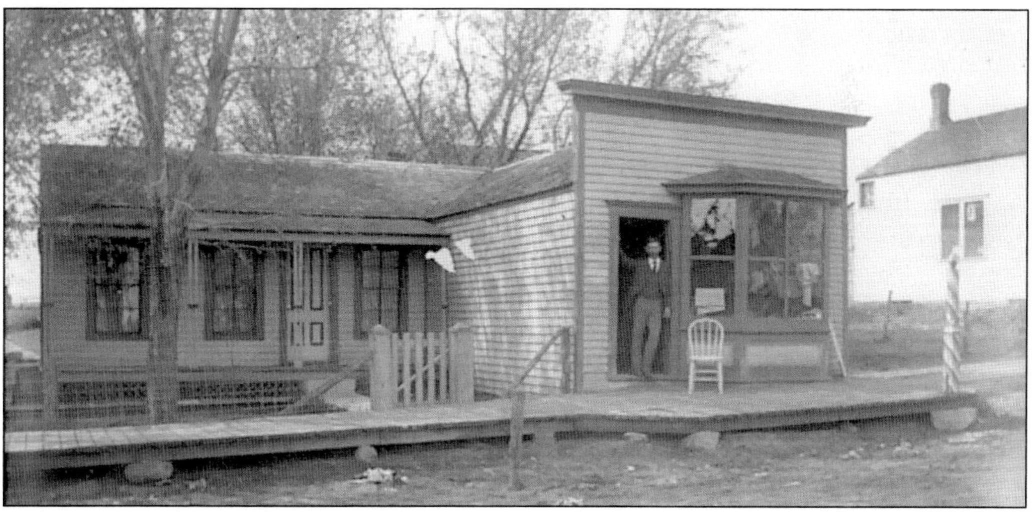

Incorporating his business and his home, James J. Egland's barber shop was located on the south side of Main Street in Glenville in 1896. Note the wooden sidewalks and the muddy streets. An 1890 listing of Glenville businesses also shows dry goods and machinery merchants, a hardware and lumber dealer, shoemaker, milliner, blacksmith, harness maker, butcher, grain and coal dealer, and a hotel owner.

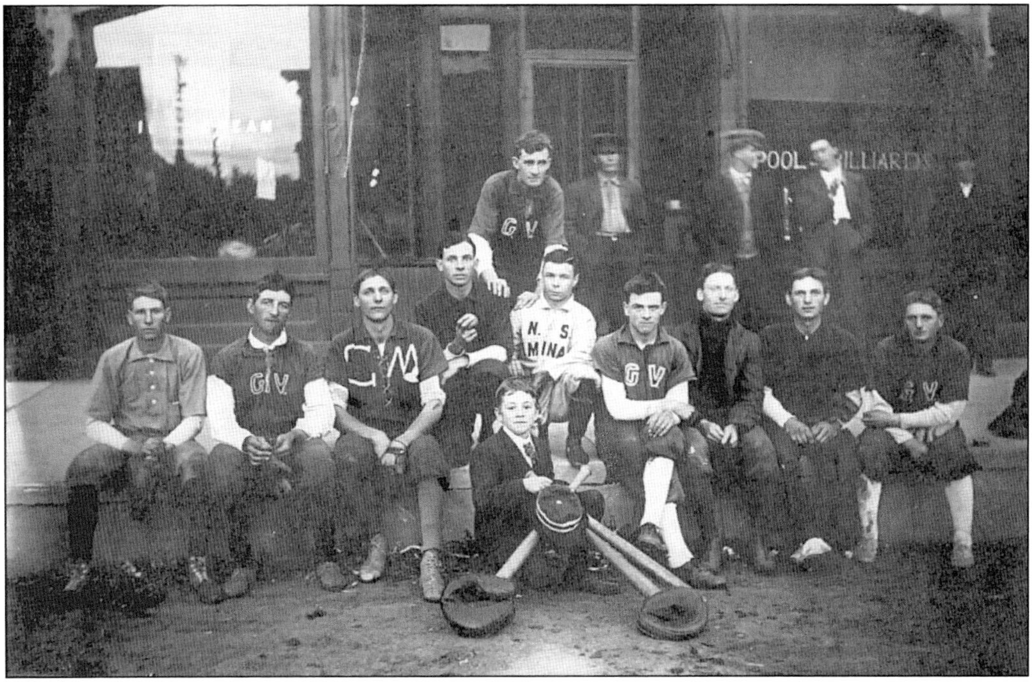

As four gentlemen stand near the Billiards Hall viewing the proceedings, the Glenville baseball team poses for a photograph. This picture, taken in 1908, shows, from left to right: Harry Kirkpatrick, Frank Brown, ? Franke, Gay Seuser, Mort Marcy, Ben Miller, Jess Seuser, unidentified, Jim Garner, George Lundberg, and Wendell "Pat" Seuser. For many years, almost every community had a baseball team that competed with teams from nearby towns.

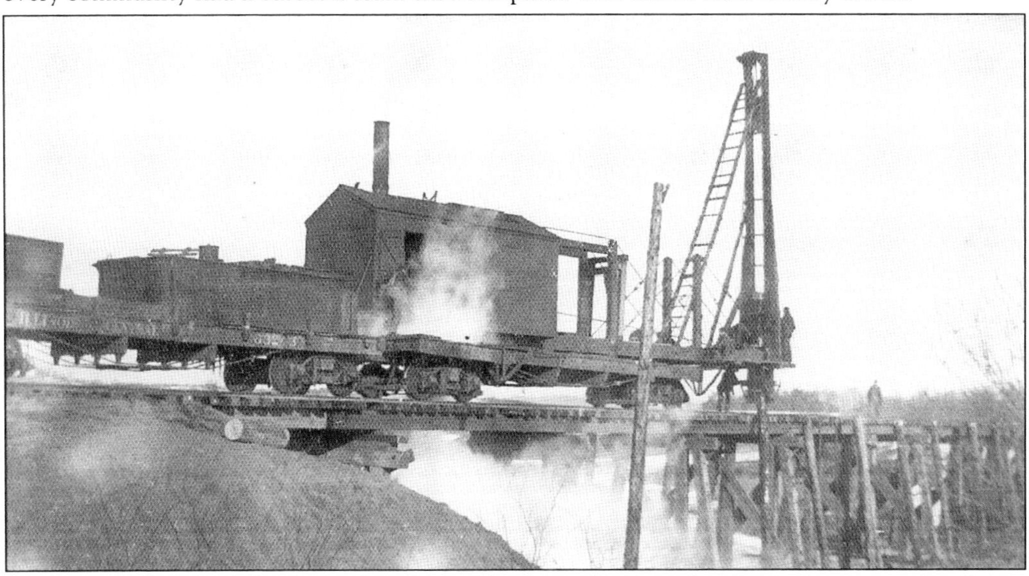

A steam-powered pile driver is being used in this 1900 photograph of bridge repair on the Illinois Central Railroad trestle over the Shell Rock River. In 1910, half of the bridge was destroyed by a fire, which was probably ignited by sparks from a train. The fire company and other citizens worked to prevent the fire from spreading to a nearby home. Both mail and passenger traffic were disrupted until repairs were made.

The Myrtle Post Office has had several locations, beginning at the H.N. Lane farm and operated by Miss Myrtle Lane, who became the town's namesake. In 1906, the post office was moved to the Hanson General Merchandise Store, operated by brothers Carl W. and Bill, where Carl W. Hanson served as postmaster until the store burned in 1927.

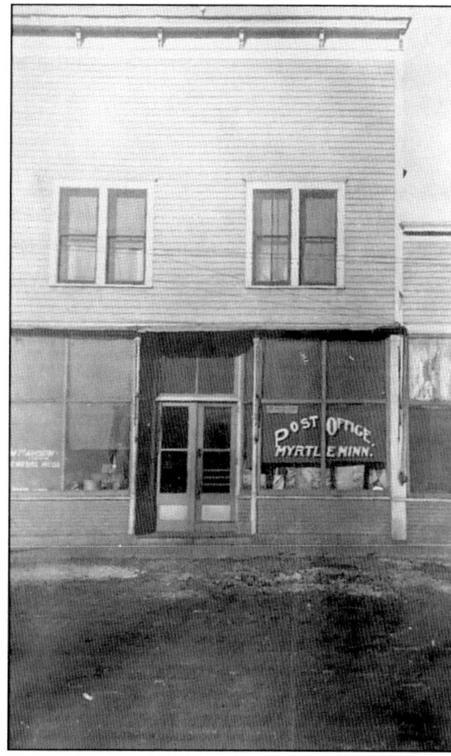

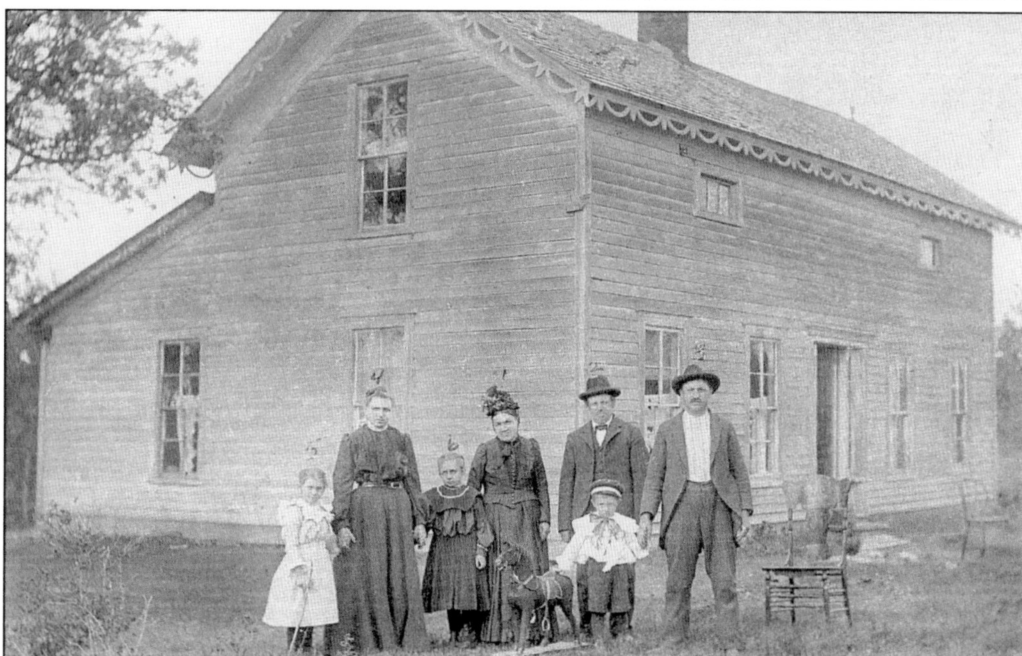

The Harrison Hotel and Grocery Store was located one mile east of Myrtle, and was operated by Frank Flusek from 1901 to 1907. This photograph shows his daughter Ella, wife Josefa, daughter Rose, parents Mr. and Mrs. John Flusek, and Frank Flusek Sr. His son, Frank Jr., is shown with the hobby horse.

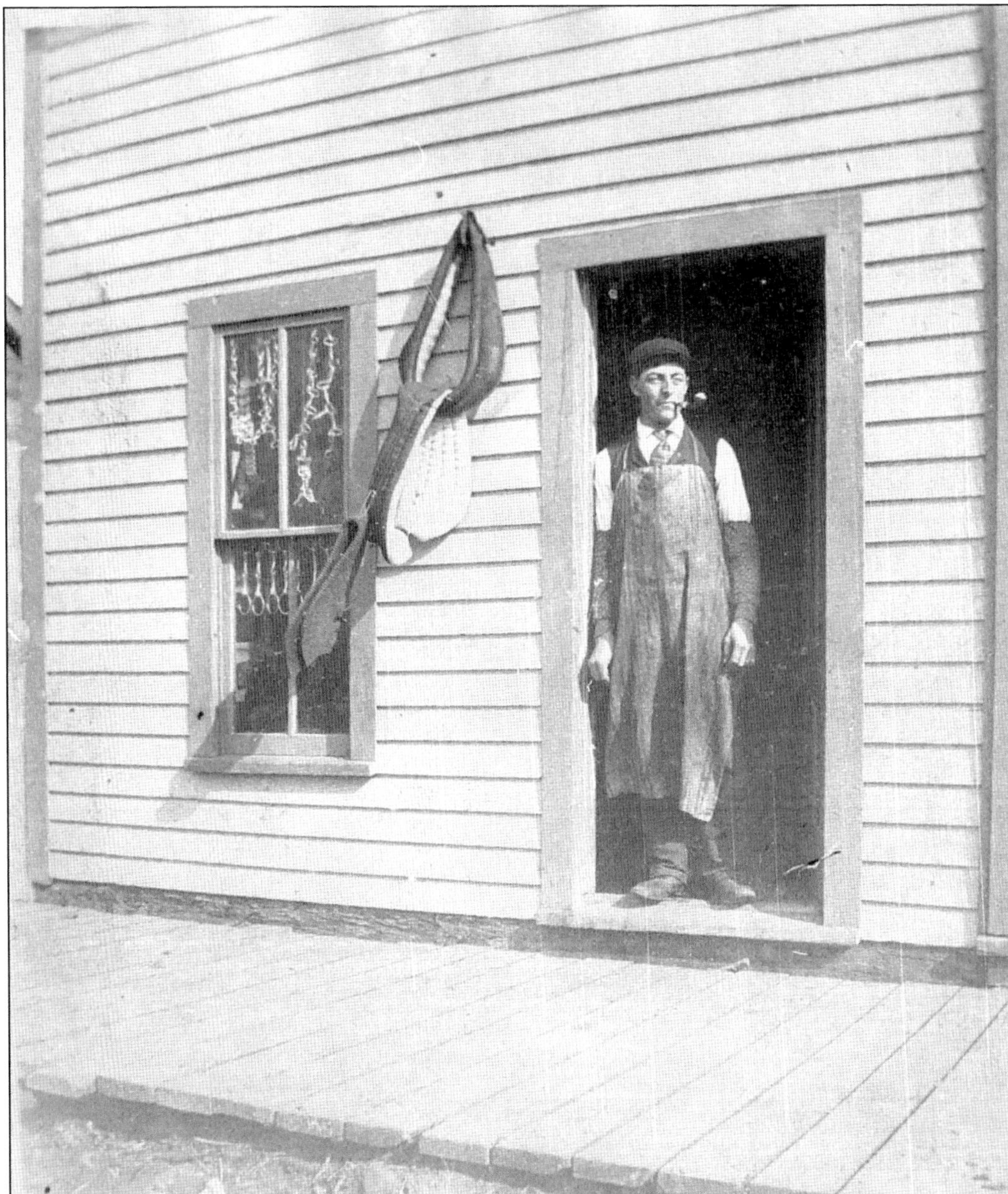

"John Belshan was born in London Township, Freeborn County, Minnesota on August 15, 1876, the son of John and Josefin Belshan. With the exception of four years spent in Wisconsin, he lived in this vicinity all his life. He grew to manhood at the old John Belshan homestead, north of Myrtle. He learned the trade of harness making in Glenville, where he established his shop in the spring of 1900. He was married to Anna Kral on March 27, 1901. To this union one child, Johnnie, was born on January 9, 1900. He passed away one year and 15 days later. Mr. Belshan came to Myrtle in 1909, where he resided until his death. A stroke, on July 23, 1937, incapacitated him to some extent, and he was later unable to continue his vocation. Besides his wife, he is survived by a sister, Mrs. Frank Kral, Route 1, Glenville, and two brothers, Albert J. and Louis J. of Austin, Minnesota. He passed away October 4, 1945, aged 69 years, 1 month, and 19 days. Peace be with him." (*Albert Lea Tribune*, October 22, 1945.)

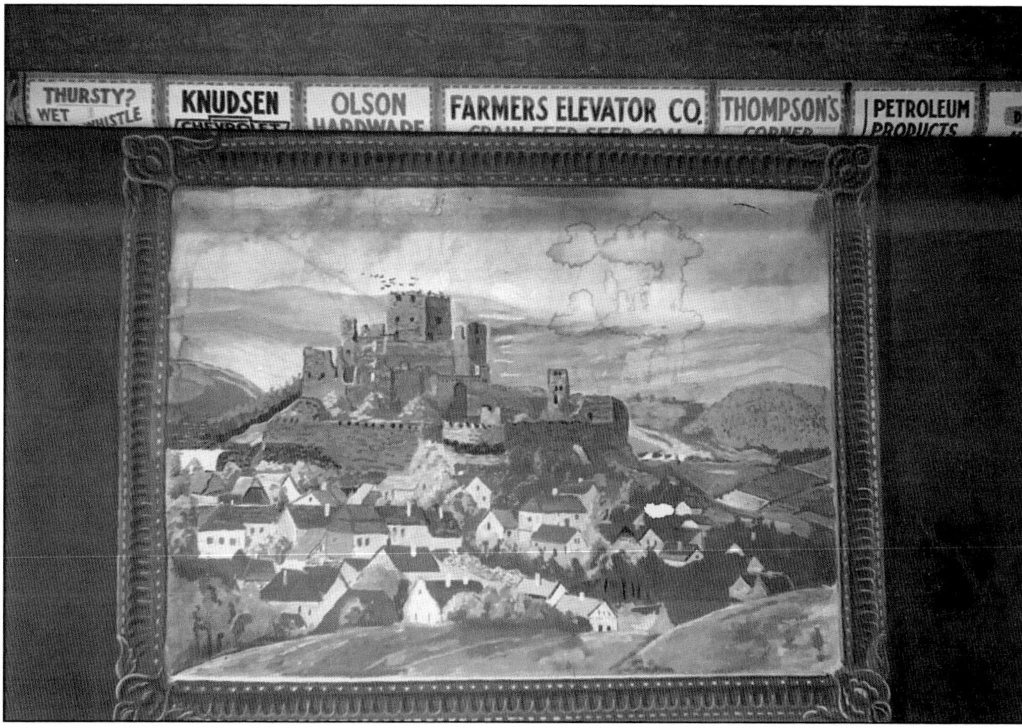

A castle in Bohemia, overlooking and protecting the village, is painted on one of the backdrops in Lodge Zare Zapadu No. 44 in Hayward Township. This painting, by a Mr. Avery, must have brought memories to many of the members of the Lodge fraternity, which, at one time, only admitted Czech people. The other backdrop, partially hidden, is bordered by advertisements of local businesses and products.

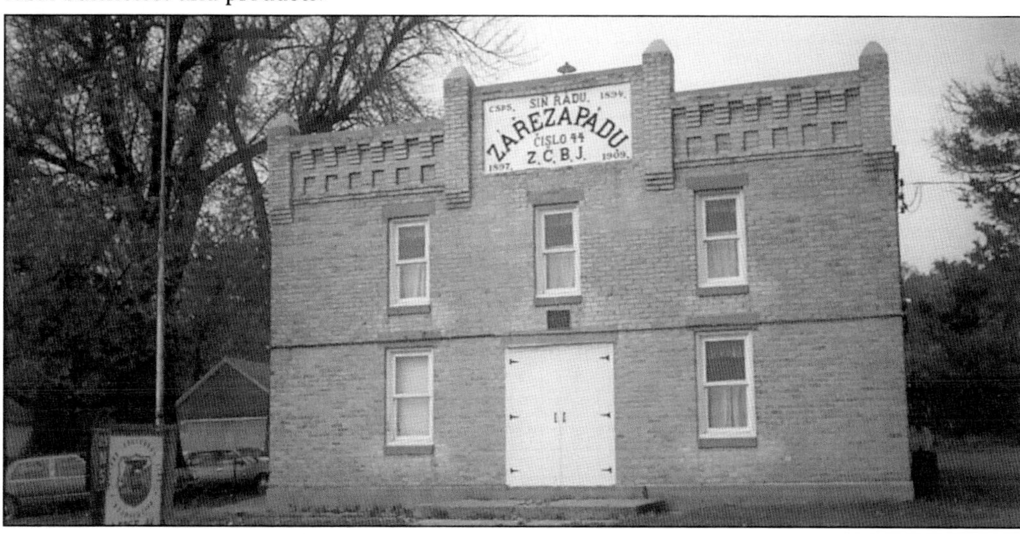

Lodge Zare Zapadu #44, Z.C.B.J., a fraternal organization in the Czech community, was organized in 1894. The name means the "Glow of the West." It has had three homes: two wooden buildings in 1878 and 1896, and the "Brick Hall" built in 1909. They have been the site of countless meetings, dances, reunions, festivals, and theatrical productions. The "Brick Hall" was placed on the National Register of Historic Places in 1986.

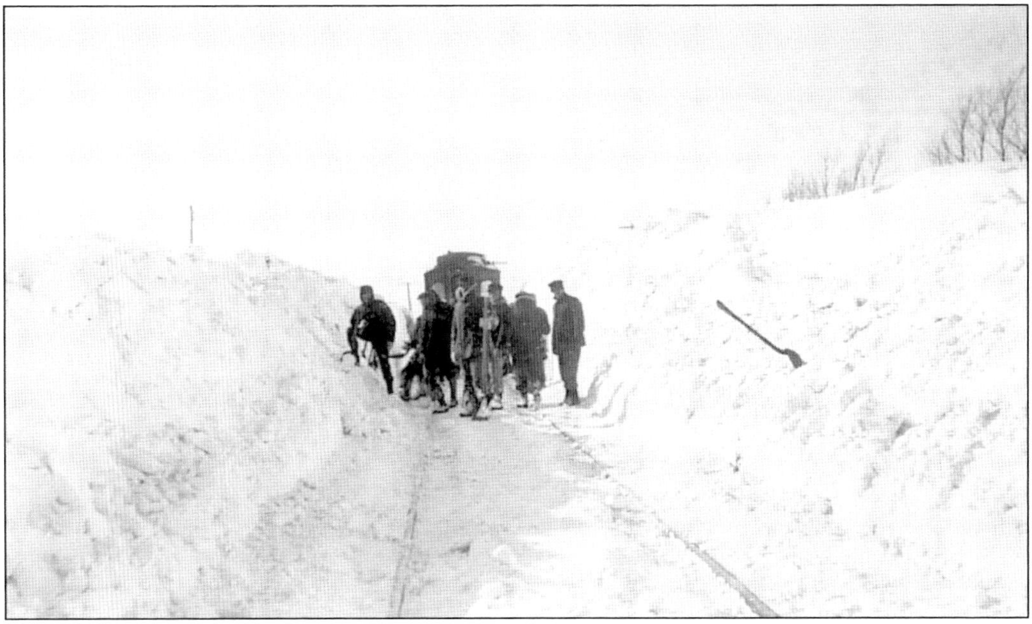

The blizzard of 1916 halted train service until this crew of men was able to shovel out one of the huge snow drifts that blocked the tracks of the Illinois Central Railroad west of Myrtle. Passengers, businessmen, and farmers all appreciated the resumption of service and the gang's hard work in the extreme February cold.

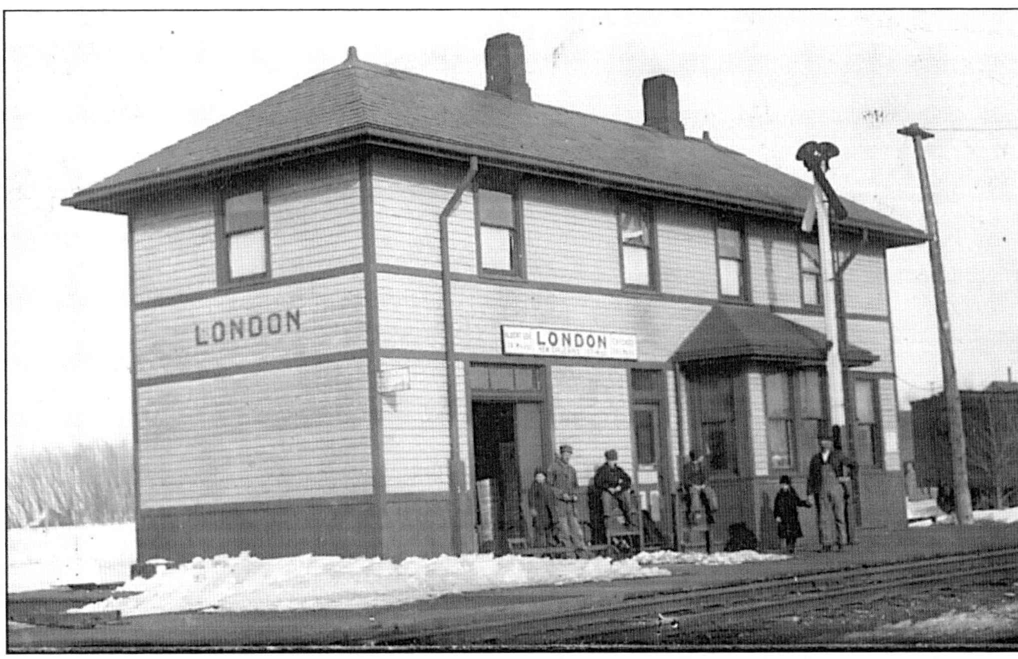

The Village of London was originally constructed about 2.5 miles north of its present location, but it moved when the Albert Lea & Southern Railroad was built across London Township in 1900. The Illinois Central took over ownership, connecting the village with Chicago, and it operated until 1984, when it became the Cedar Valley Railroad.

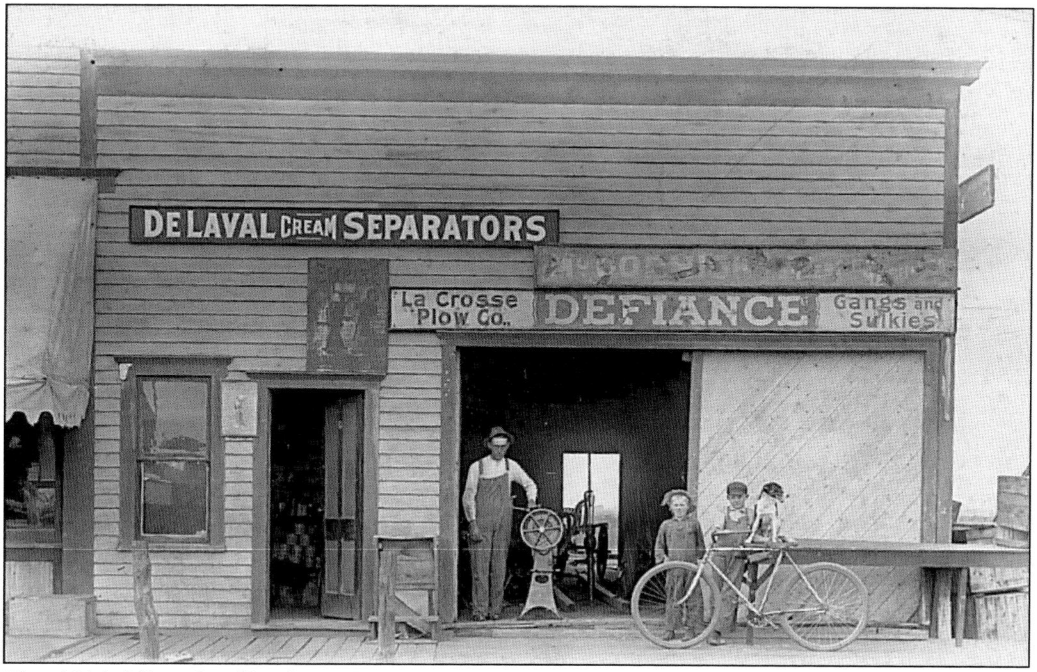

The 1906 Albert Lea/Freeborn County City Directory lists several businesses in the Village of London, among them Haldorson Implement (Christie and Haldorson). Swan H. Haldorson stands in the doorway of his business. The village also included the American Express Co., a bank, creamery, hotel, hardware store, railroad depot, general store, lumber company, blacksmith, and elevator.

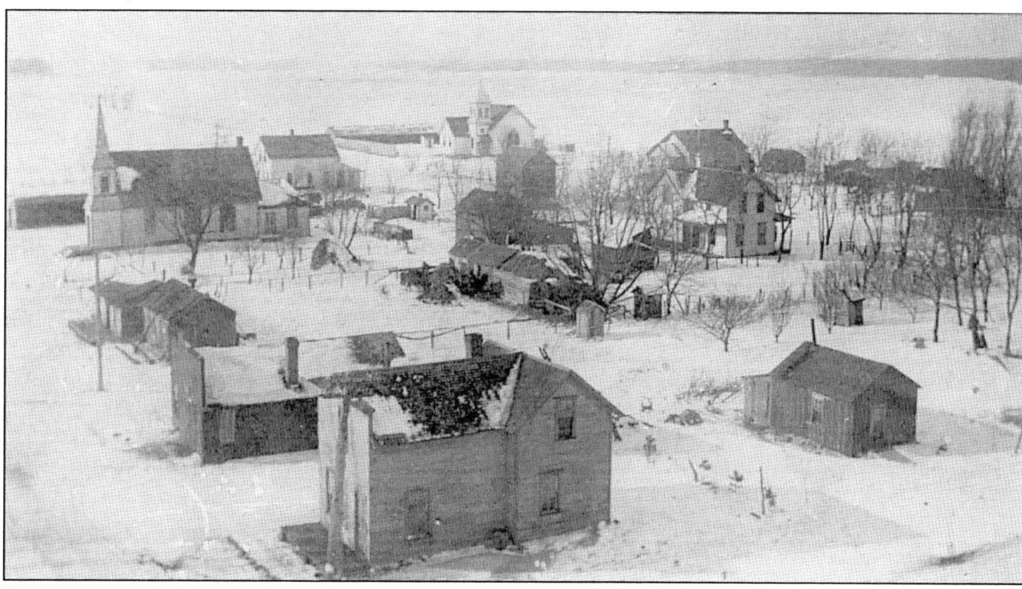

At one time Oakland, shown here around 1910, was considered Freeborn County's Tow Head settlement. It was so named because of the tow, or cottony substance, from the poplar trees, and because of the white hair on the children who came with their families from Illinois. The first years were very difficult, with "An early Thanksgiving dinner containing only cracked corn, milk, one sweet cake, and rye coffee." (*Glenville Progress*, February 4, 1937.)

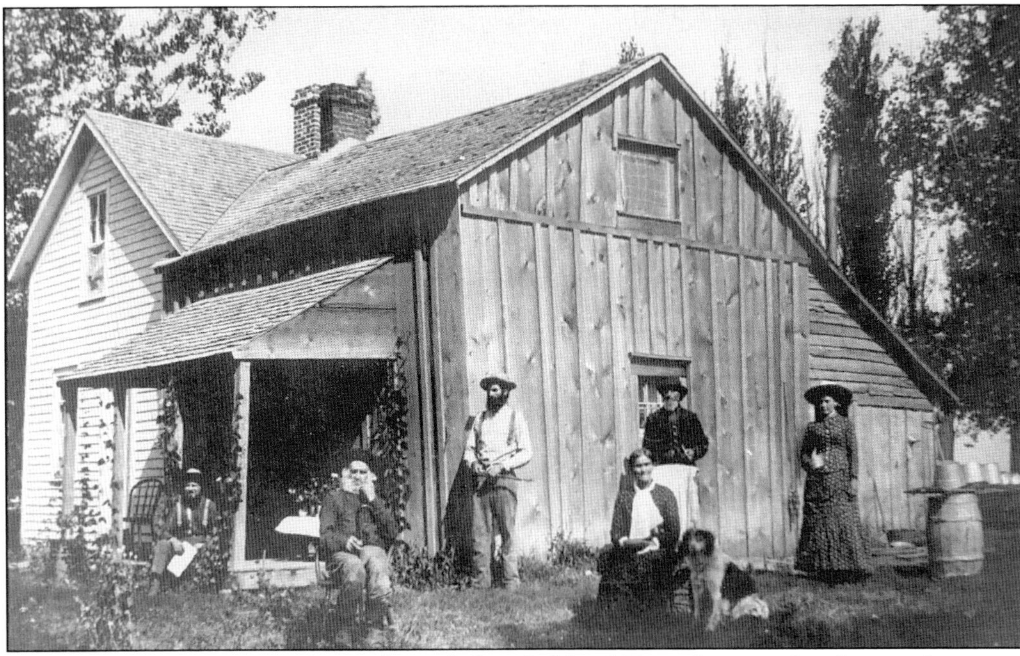

In 1861, the John W. Lightly family settled in Oakland Township on what became known as the "old homestead," as several generations of Lightlys farmed the land. His obituary stated, "He was highly respected by all who knew him, a man possessing an exalted sense of honor." (*Albert Lea Enterprise*, November 7, 1895.) Note the variety of materials used to build this farmhouse.

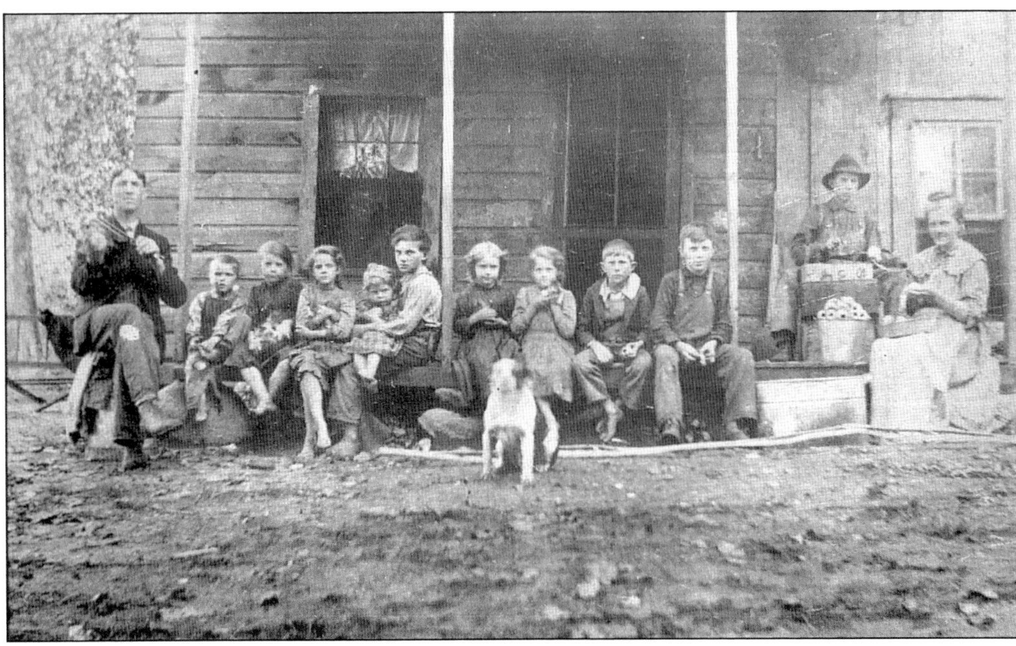

This unusual photograph was taken at the Hayes (possibly Lowry) place near Oakland around 1897. The couple on the right are coring apples, and the gentleman on the left is serenading the group with violin music. Are the children from one family, or are they neighbors or students? The only person identified in the picture is the third child from the left, Grace Lowry.

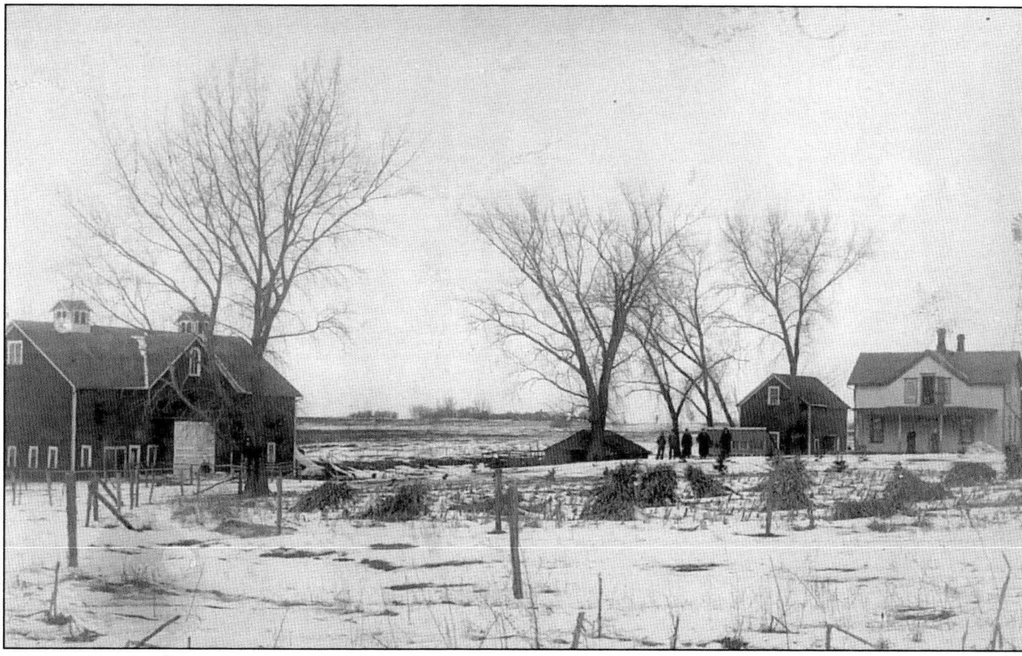

The Endre Gulbrandson farm, near Hayward, wears an air of quietude as it waits for the spring thaw and the busy season of preparation and planting. Gulbrandson was 40 years old and married when his family came from Norway, stopping in Wisconsin, and then moving on to Southern Minnesota and living in a dugout, until their log home was built in 1863.

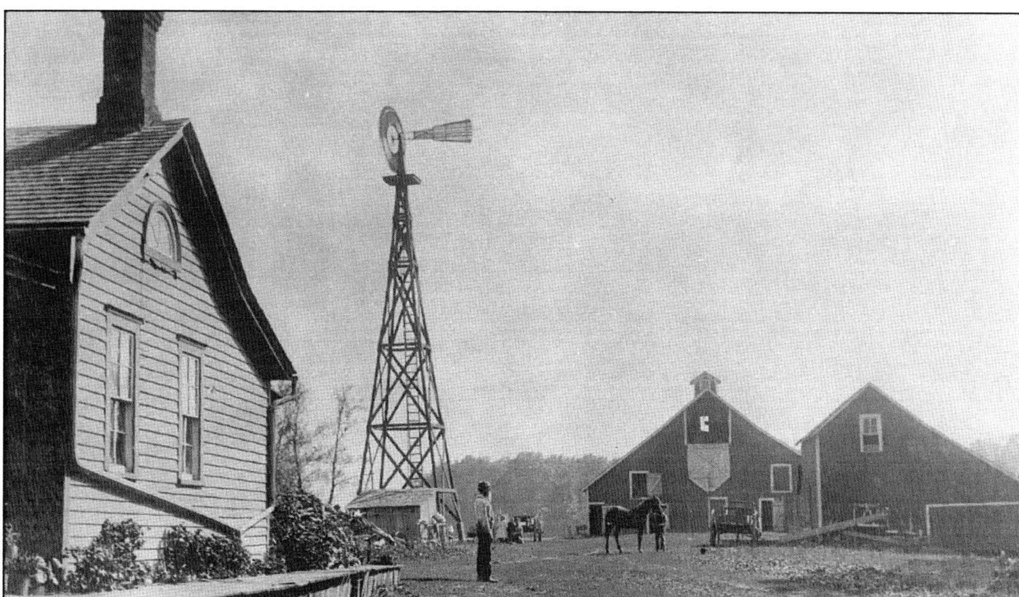

This farm place was located south of the Village of Hayward and typifies the pride and the care shown in the farming community in Hayward Township. Statistics for the year 1882 show that there were 87 farms under cultivation, growing wheat, oats, corn, barley, rye, buckwheat, potatoes, beans, sugar cane, hay, flax, apples, and grapes. There were also 243 milch cows and 135 sheep.

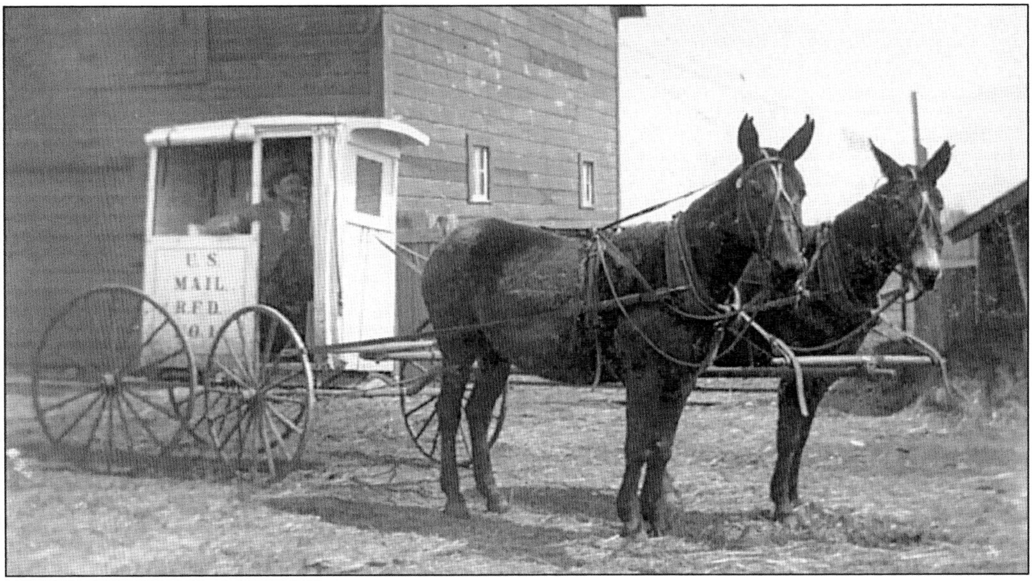

Henry Anderson, as the first rural mail carrier out of Hayward, made his first trip on January 2, 1905. The very first postmaster in Hayward was Nehemiha W. Campbell, who came to this township in 1858. The post office, which was in his home on the stage coach route between Austin and Blue Earth, was moved into the Village of Hayward in 1870.

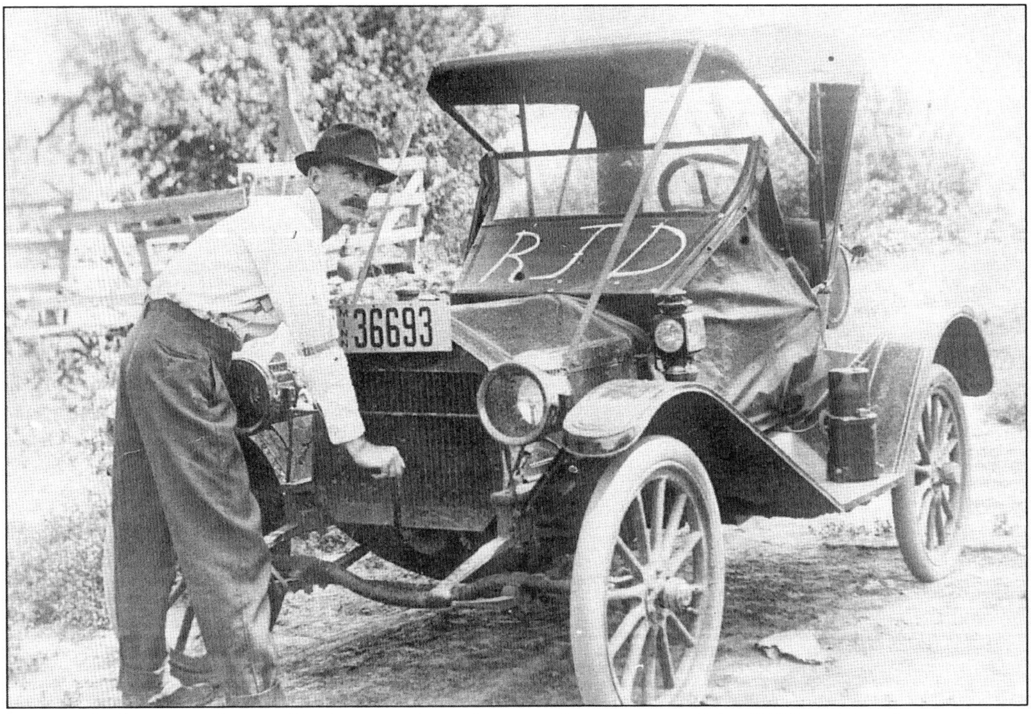

Henry Anderson, Hayward's first rural mail route driver, started in 1905, with a horse-drawn buggy. As rural routes expanded, and autos became the accepted method of transportation, he continued as mail carrier until 1931, serving also in the Lerdal area. An interesting note: On November 2, 1917, a war tax on letters went into effect, and it was repealed on July 1, 1919.

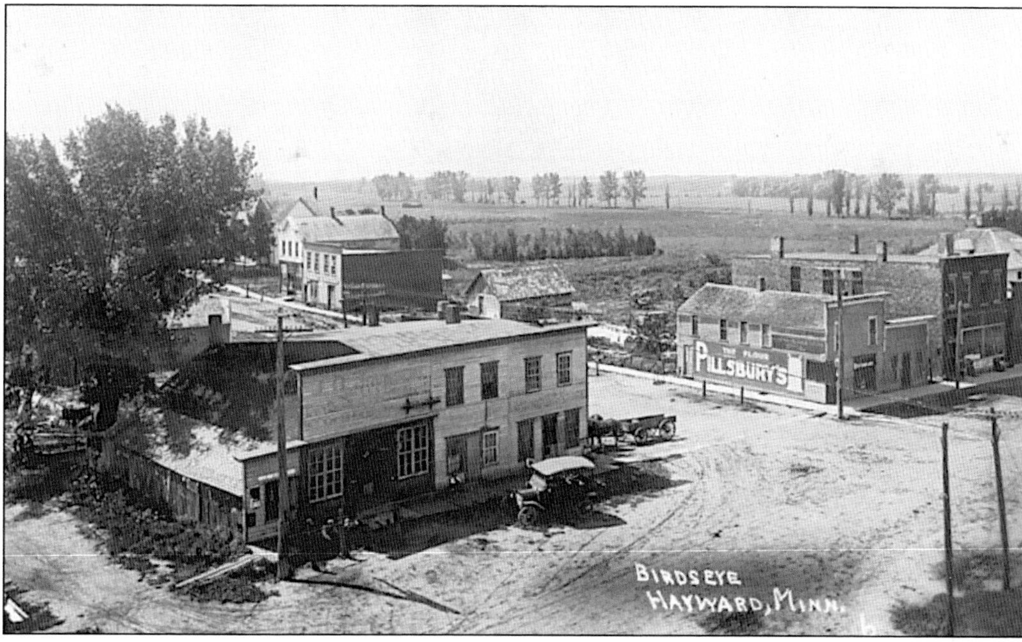

This view of the Hayward business district, in 1910, shows the blacksmith shop and Henry Anderson's store, which were both destroyed by fire in 1918. "The fire had gained considerable headway when discovered and was soon beyond control. . . . Albert Lea was called upon and the Fire Co. and engine made a record trip of six miles in 15 minutes, but not having sufficient water supply, could not do much." (*Glenville Progress*, October 3, 1918.)

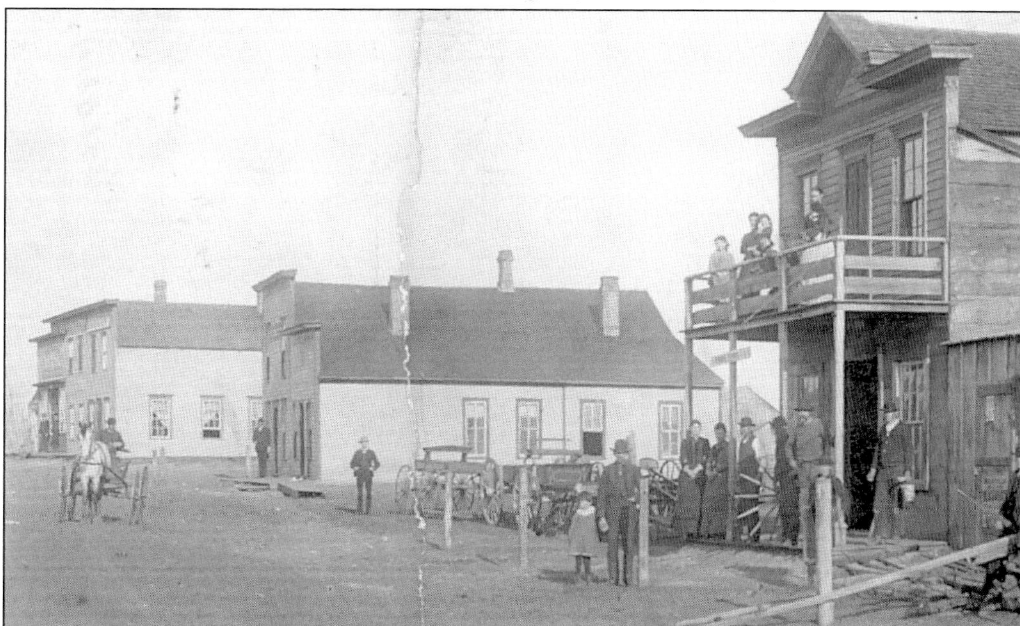

In 1880, Anton and Haakon Hanson purchased the General Store, but over the years it had several owners and was eventually destroyed by fire. The blacksmith and wagon shop was built by Halvor Halvorson in 1878, with living quarters upstairs. His family is on the balcony, and other townspeople are standing near the wagon wheel that is under construction.

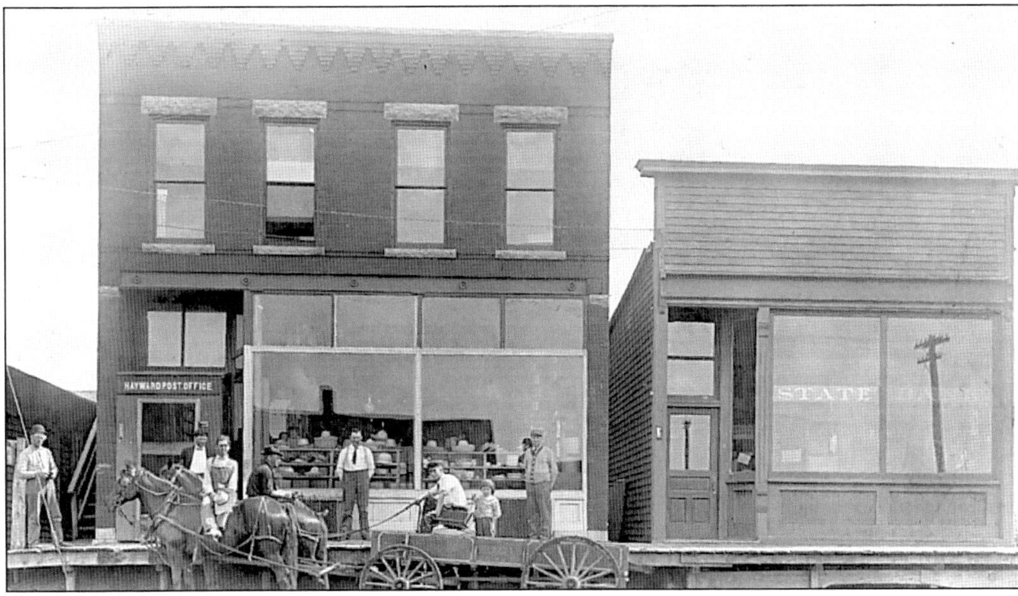

The Savre and Skaug General Store was in operation from 1909 to 1913, and then Elling Savre sold out to his partner Gilbert Skaug, who continued to operate the store until 1929. The post office was in the rear of the store. The wooden sidewalk was built at wagon-bed height, a handy convenience for customers. The State Bank was located next to the general store.

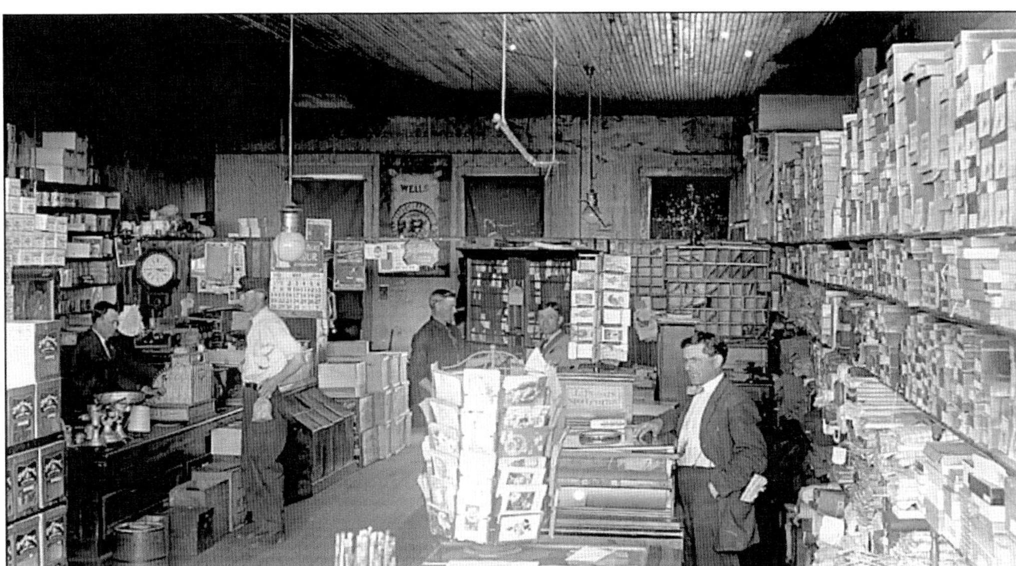

The Savre and Skaug General Store, 1909–1913, offered something for everyone—fabrics, greeting cards, shoes, kitchen wares, groceries, clothing—almost everything needed to provide for home and family. Four of the men in this photo are identified: G. Skaug, Elling Savre, Rolf Gulbrandson, and R.E. Dewey, who was postmaster. The town of Hayward and the township are named after David Hayward, who settled on Section 6 and remained there only two years.

Marie Jensen earned $30 per month as operator for the Hayward Telephone Exchange. Switchboards similar to this one were often located in private homes, so the operator was on duty 24 hours a day. Every telephone family had its own sequence of long and short rings, but because the phones rang in every home on the exchange, listening in on neighbors' calls (rubbering) was a popular pastime.

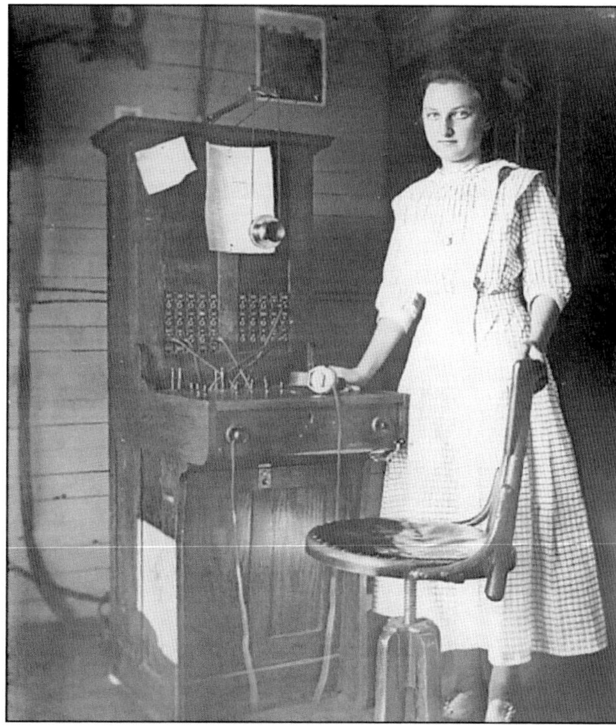

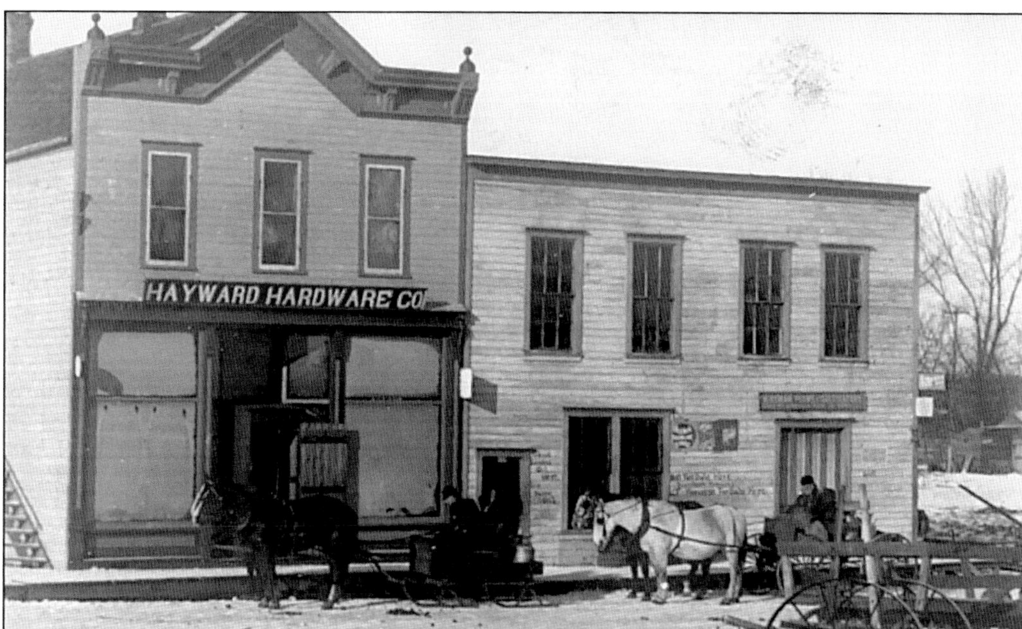

There were no buildings on the Hayward site until the railroad came through in 1869. The Hayward hardware store was built in 1906 by Vegger Gulbrandson. The building on the right advertises gasoline, kerosene, and fishing bait for sale. The teams belong to Vegger Gulbrandson and Lars Lunde. ("Platted 1886 by Morin and registered," *Centennial History of Hayward*, and "Platted 1869 by H.C. Lacey and recorded December 20," *History of Freeborn County* [1882].)

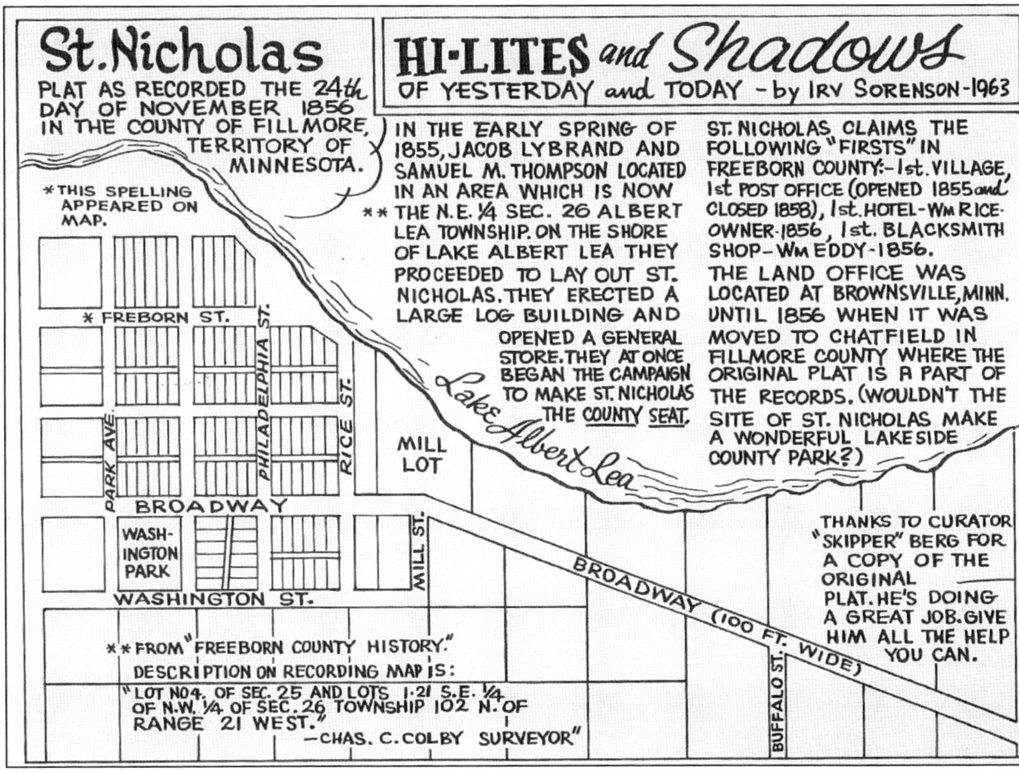

Hi-Lites and Shadows of Yesterday and Today was drawn by Irv Sorenson in 1963.

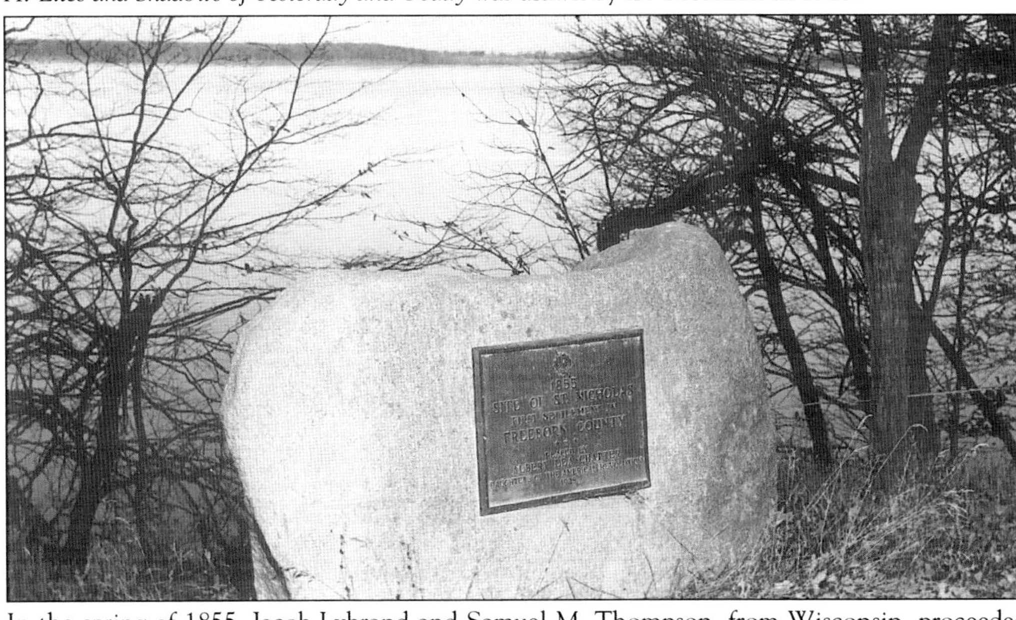

In the spring of 1855, Jacob Lybrand and Samuel M. Thompson, from Wisconsin, proceeded to lay out the village of St. Nicholas on the western shore of Lake Albert Lea. The location was beautiful, at the point of the broadest sheet of water in the county and with a fine gravel beach. Their dreams of attaining county-seat status for the village, however, were dashed by the powerful political machine in Albert Lea.

Two

The Southwest

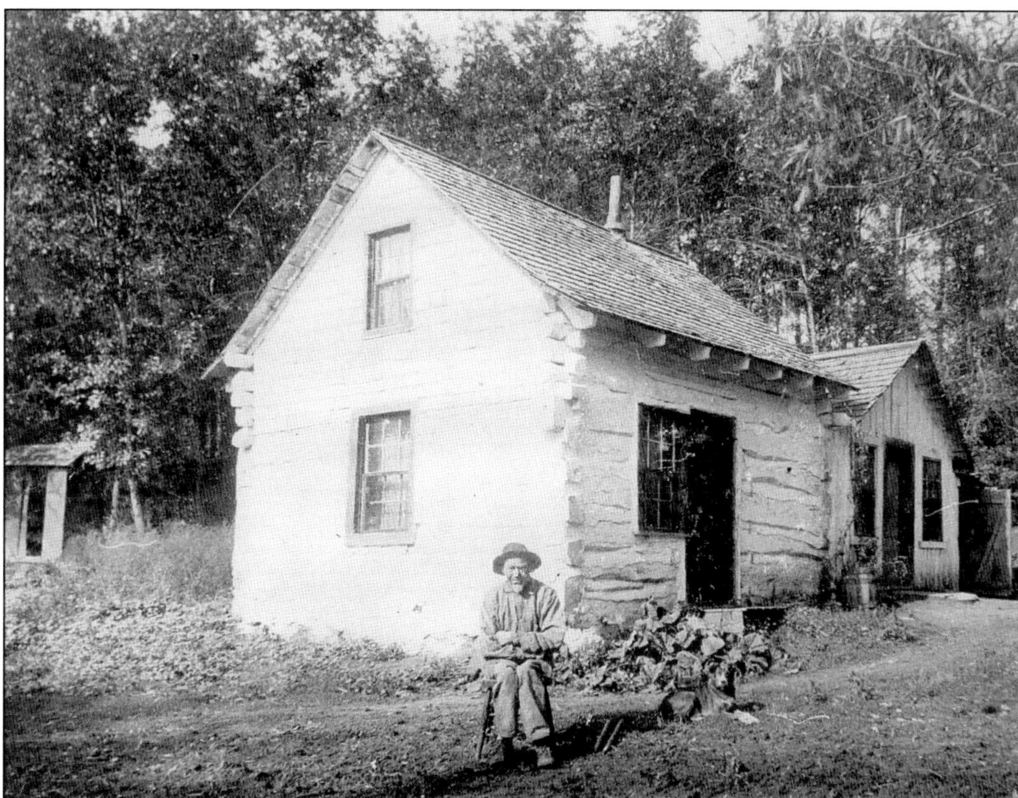

Olaf Torgeson, an early settler in Freeman Township, is shown sitting in front of his log home near Grass Lake. The lake was named for the grasses and sedges growing in its shallow water. The lake was eventually drained for farming. Notice the mortise and tenon cut of the lower logs on the building, and the rudimentary cut of the upper logs.

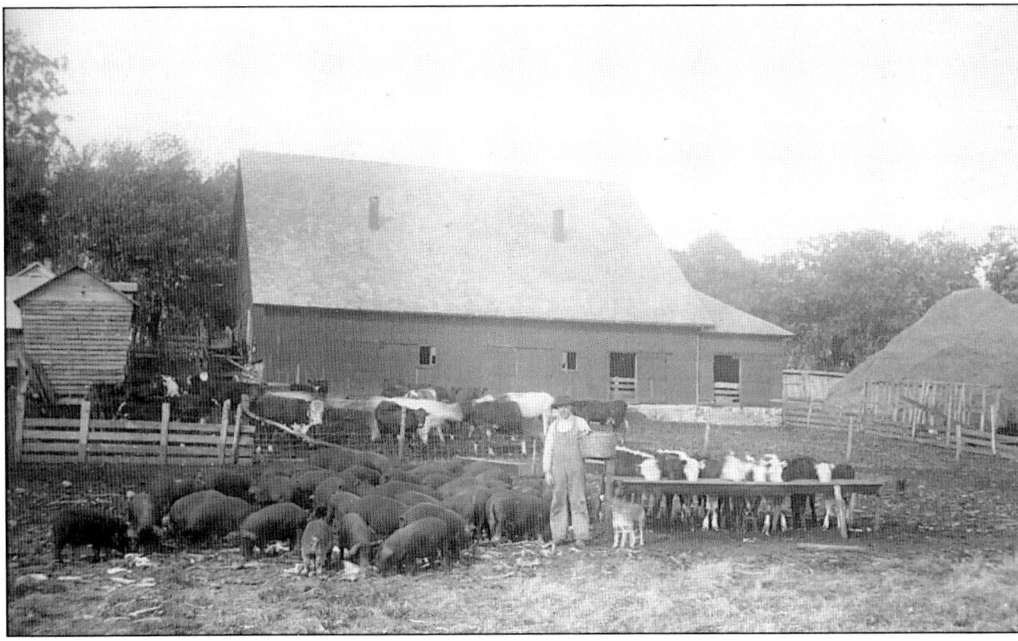

Early Southern Minnesota farms were almost totally self-sufficient. A variety of crops was grown, providing feed for the livestock. Cattle, hogs, chickens, ducks, sheep, and goats were not uncommon. A large vegetable garden was planted, and numerous fruit trees were tended—everything a family needed. This farm place was an example of that diversity. Lars Landaas is shown doing chores.

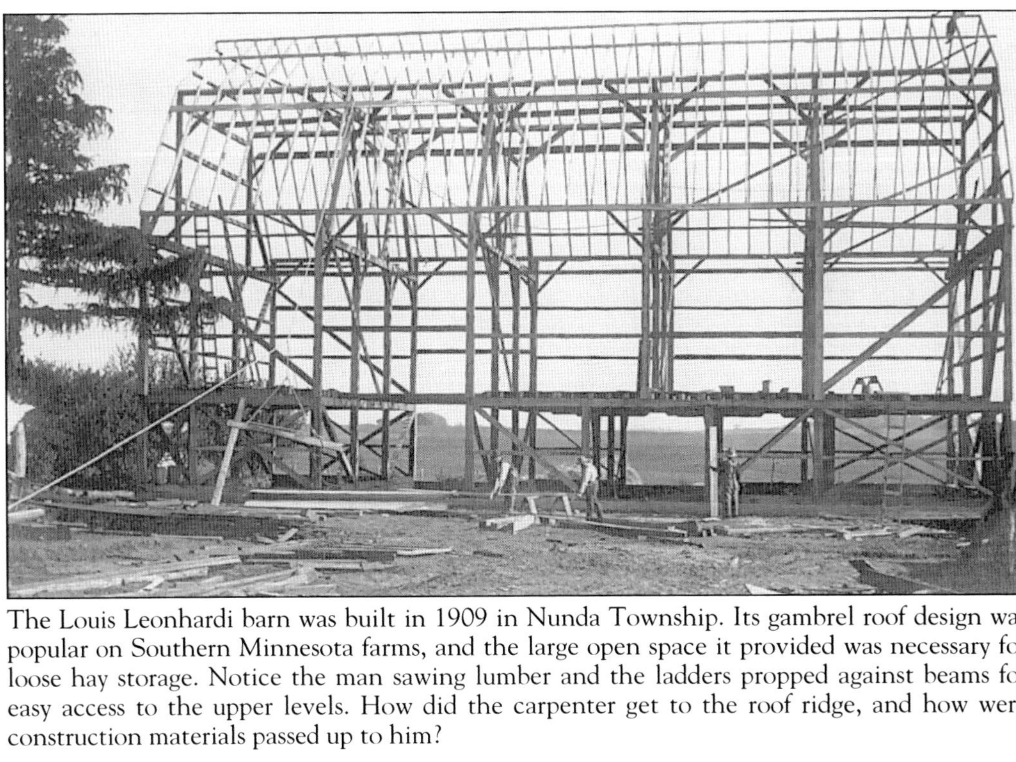

The Louis Leonhardi barn was built in 1909 in Nunda Township. Its gambrel roof design was popular on Southern Minnesota farms, and the large open space it provided was necessary for loose hay storage. Notice the man sawing lumber and the ladders propped against beams for easy access to the upper levels. How did the carpenter get to the roof ridge, and how were construction materials passed up to him?

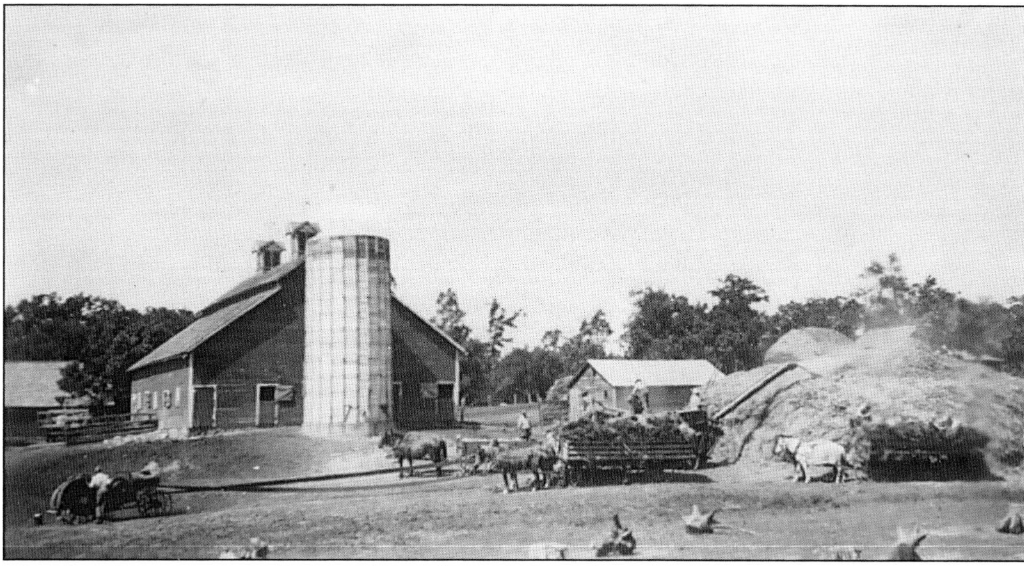

This threshing scene on the Joseph Wadsworth farm shows the manpower and the horsepower needed to operate the farm in Freeman Township. Wadsworth raised 60 acres of crops with the balance of his farm in pasture, and he was very proud of his thoroughbred Shorthorns and Poland China hogs. He and his wife Katherine had three children, he was active in several community organizations, and he was a staunch Republican.

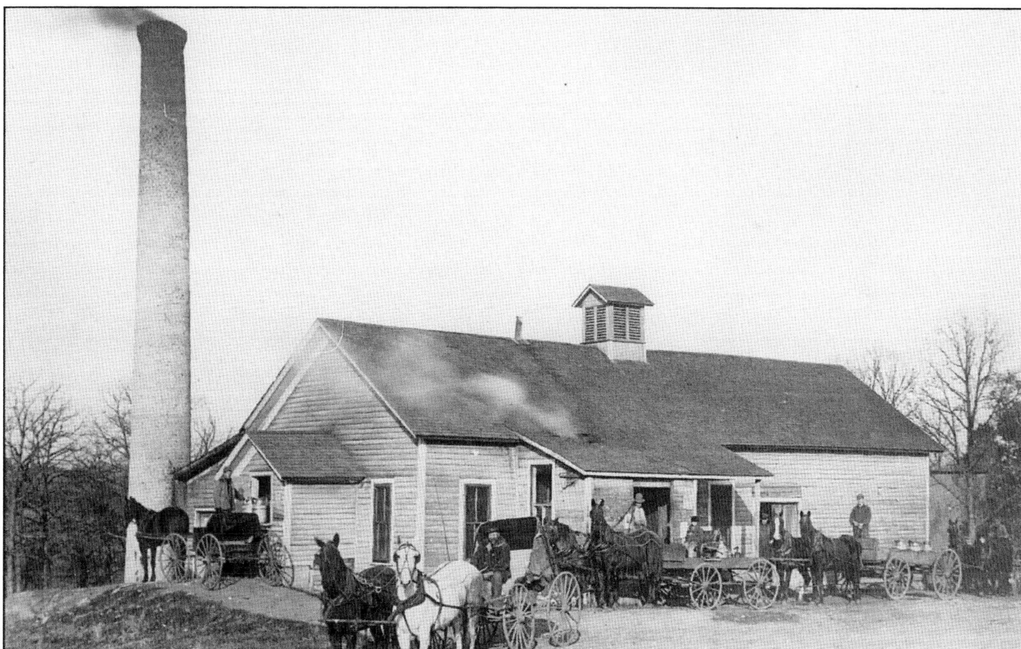

The Knatvold Creamery was operated from 1900 to 1914 by the Freeman Cooperative Creamery Association. The creamery first had a metal stack, which did not draw properly, and it was replaced with a brick chimney. Milk was brought in on Mondays, Wednesdays, and Fridays, and on busy days there might be 25 teams in the yard. Each creamery patron was responsible for two loads of ice for the icehouse.

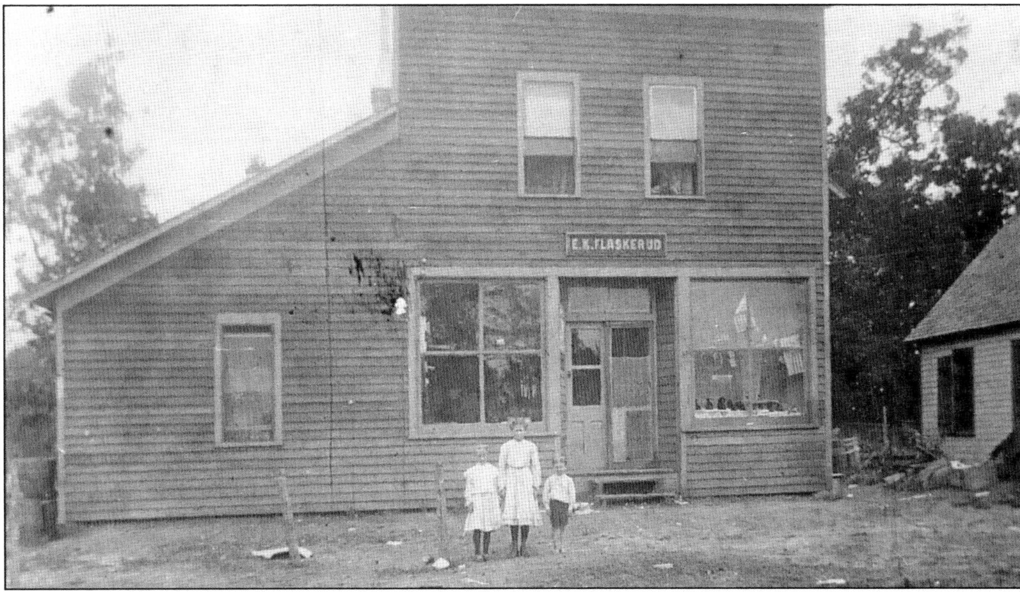

According to the *Freeborn County Standard*, January 3, 1900, it was decided that the new post office in Freeman would be changed to Knatvold in honor of Senator Knatvold. Thomas E. Flaskerud was commissioned as postmaster. The post office was in the H.Q. Angel General Store, which was later owned by Erick K. Flaskerud. The store had family living quarters upstairs and was in operation from 1900 to 1918.

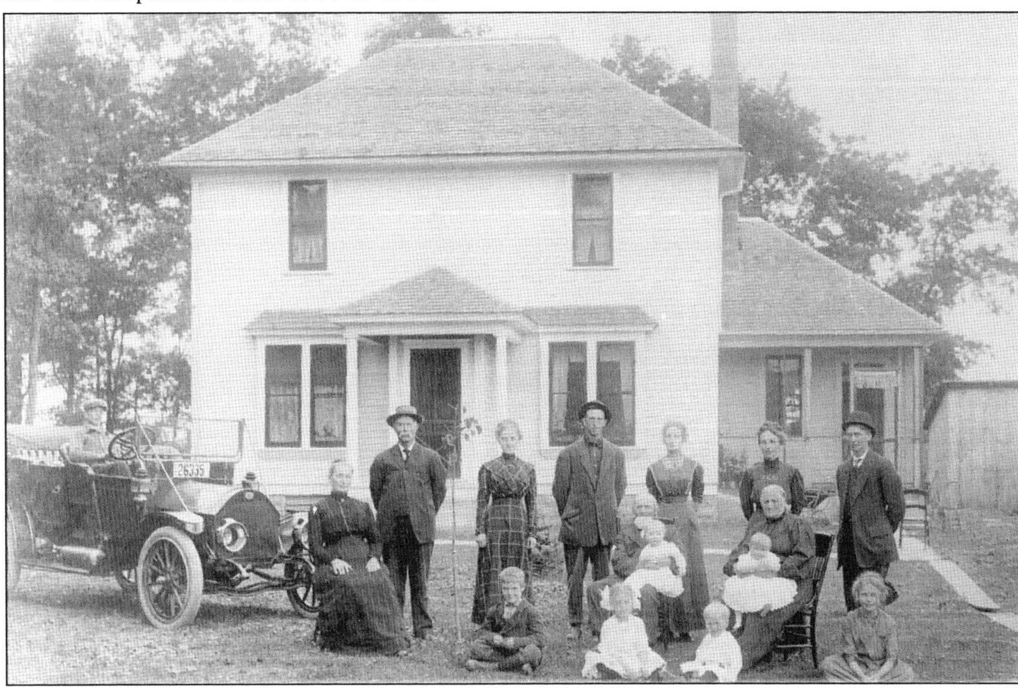

Everyone turned out for this intergenerational family photograph in the front yard of a home near Knatvold. While we cannot identify any of the people, it is interesting to speculate as to the reason for the gathering—a reunion perhaps? A chance to show off the new car? This photograph must have become a family treasure. Note the boardwalk leading to the side door.

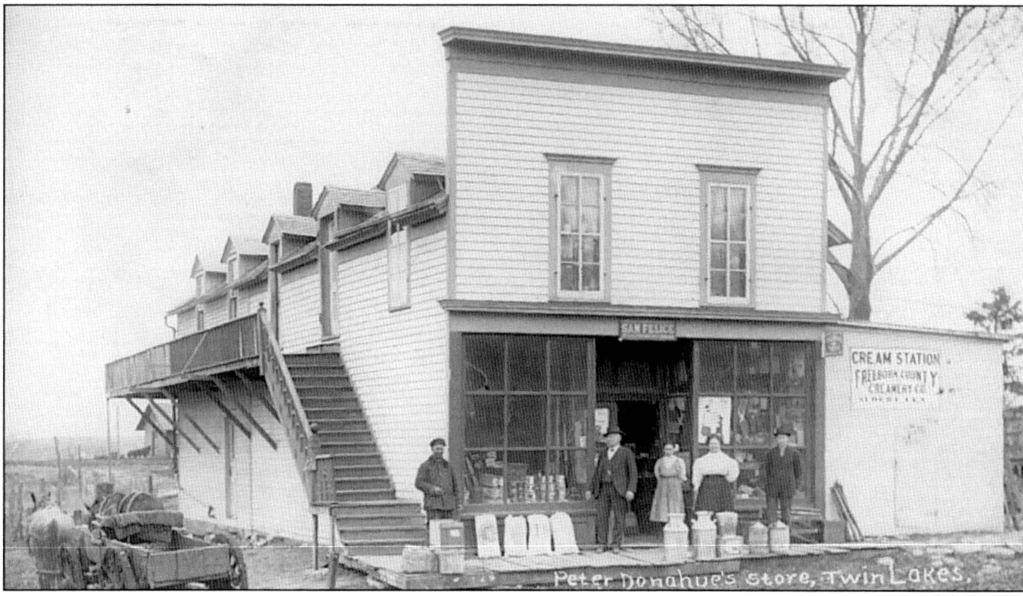

Peter Donahue is pictured here with his wife and daughter in front of their general store in Twin Lakes in 1908. The new addition to the building served as a cream station for the Freeborn County Creamery in Albert Lea. Donahue moved into this building in 1879 and operated the store for 50 years, until his death in May 1929. The man at the left is believed to be Alfred Olson.

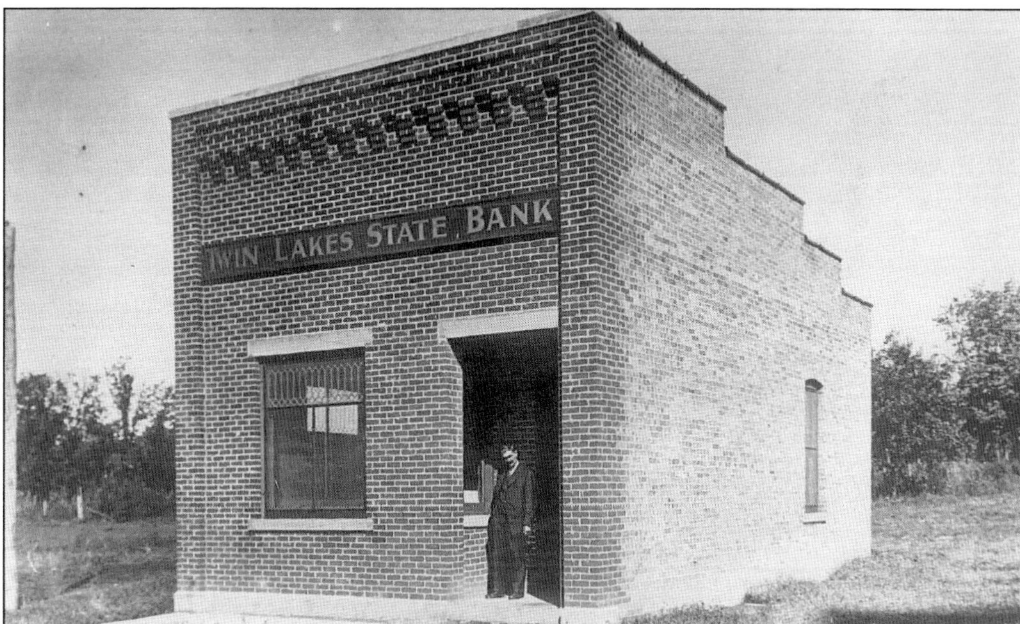

Constructed of brick, with ornate leaded-glass windows, the Twin Lakes State Bank was built in 1912, and was a valuable addition to the community. It was made a member of the Federal Deposit Insurance Corporation in 1933. The bank's interesting history includes a bank robbery in 1935, and another in 1938, with all but one of the 1938 "Milk Can Robbers" being captured.

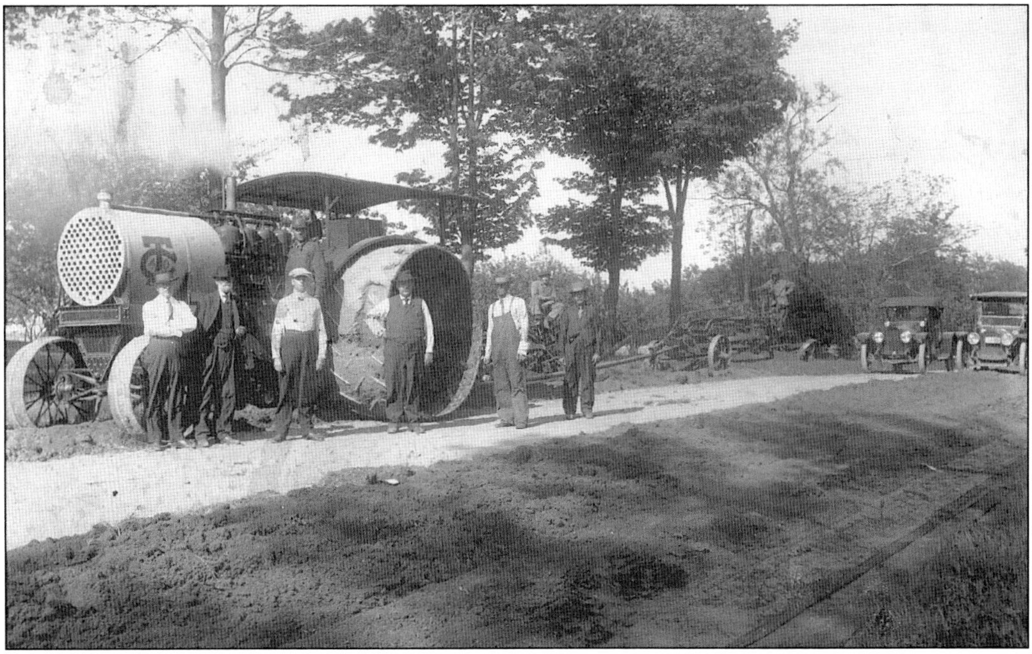

Road work near Emmons, around 1913, required some formidable equipment. This TC gas-powered tractor had four cylinders and one speed, forward and reverse (2 miles per hour). It had 84-inch rear wheels and weighed 23,700 pounds. The gentlemen in the picture are Carl Emmons, Ole Hammer, H.H. Emmons, Carl Olson, and ? Fitzgerald. The three members of the road crew are unidentified.

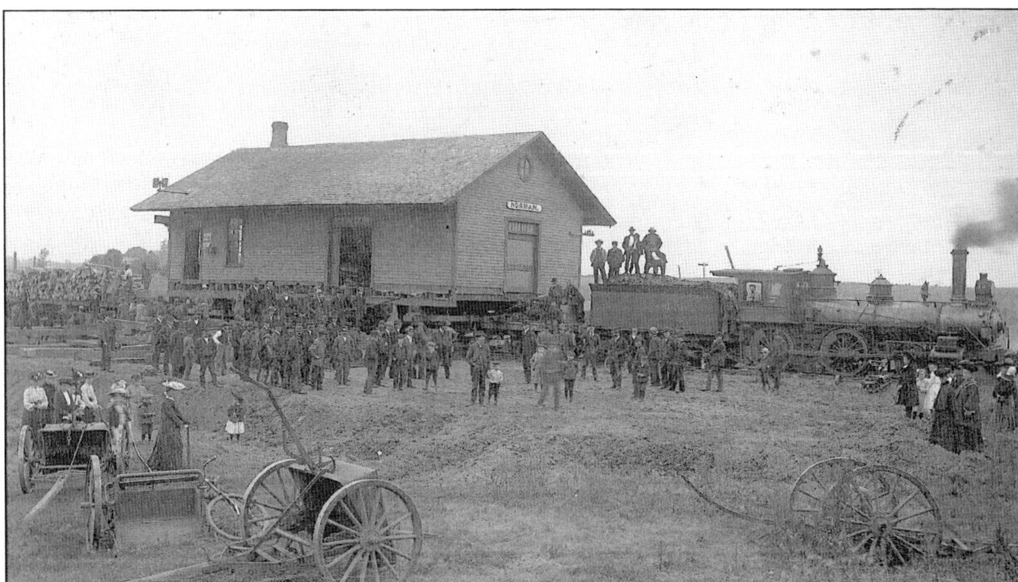

The people of Emmons had cause to celebrate in 1904. The Minneapolis & St. Louis Railroad had originally built its depot in Norman, Iowa, because the people of Winnebago County voted a 5% tax to aid in the cost of road construction. Emmons officials battled the decision all the way to the Supreme Court, and in 1904 the station was moved one mile north, just to the state line, where it was easily accessible.

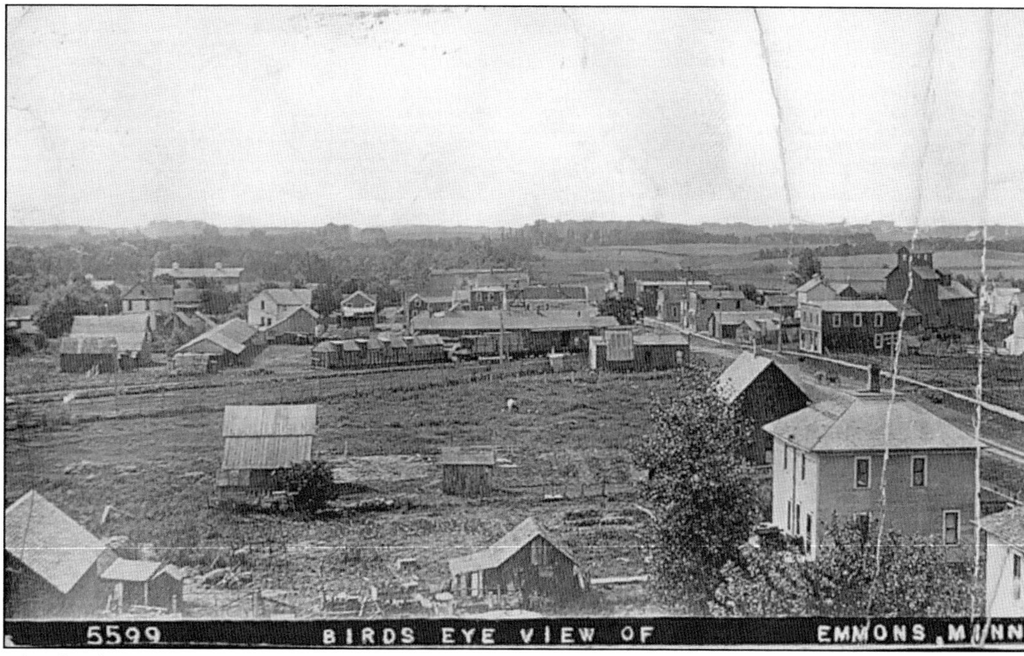

This bird's-eye view of Emmons was taken from the top of the schoolhouse in 1901. According to the 1899 city directory, Emmons is situated "exactly on the state line of Iowa and Minnesota. . . . The business men were all wide awake and prosperous and are always subordinating their own interests to those of the town. Emmons has a phenomenal record of growth and enterprise which cannot be equaled or surpassed."

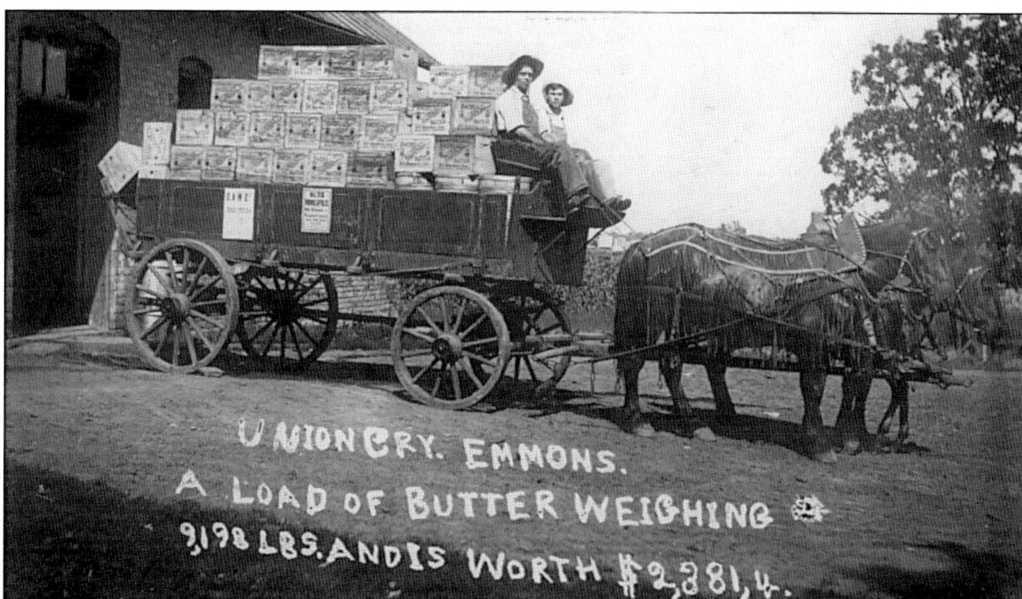

Doing greater business than any other creamery in the county, the Union Creamery Company received 3,075,269 pounds of milk and 498,800 pounds of cream in 1910. It produced 276,194 pounds of butter. Patrons were paid $69,145.06 for the milk and cream produced by their more than 1,500 cows. The creamery building was constructed with brick in 1903 at a cost of $8,000.

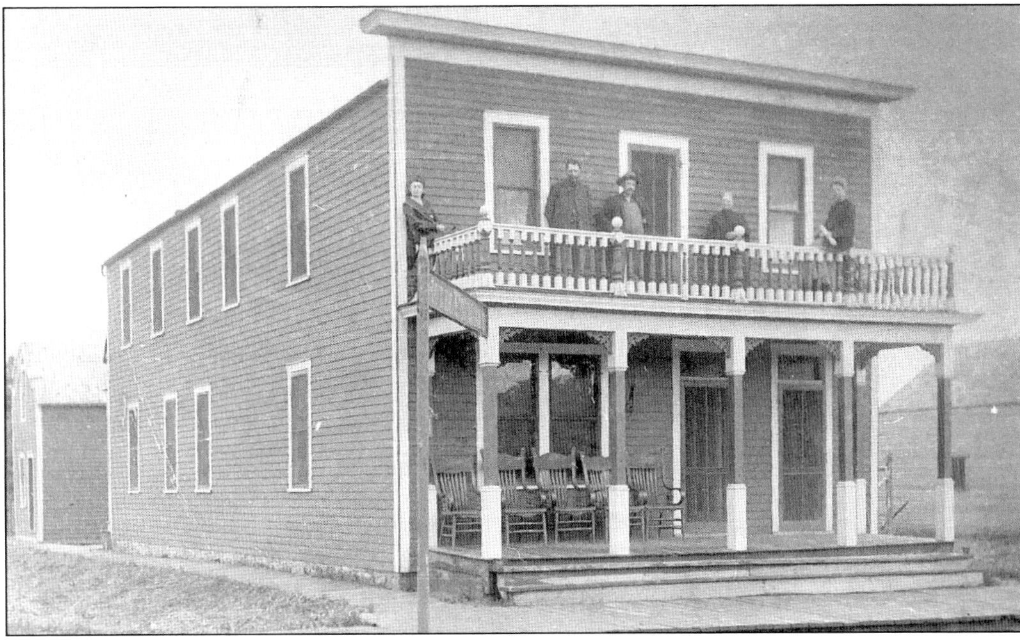

The Hotel Emmons received very little notice in articles on the history of the community; however, we do know the names of the people standing on the balcony. They are, from left to right: Hattie White, Mr. White, Bill Torry, Mrs. White, and Laura Lee. The name "White" surfaces often during research as a family prominent in the community, with service in the Union Army during the Civil War and involvement in many area organizations.

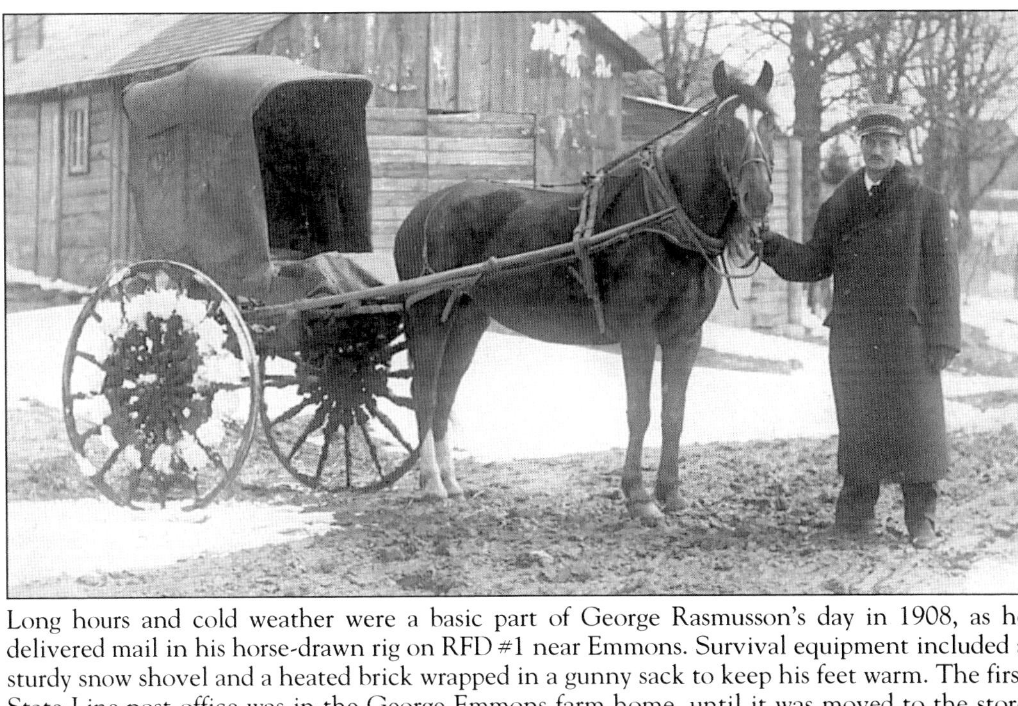

Long hours and cold weather were a basic part of George Rasmusson's day in 1908, as he delivered mail in his horse-drawn rig on RFD #1 near Emmons. Survival equipment included a sturdy snow shovel and a heated brick wrapped in a gunny sack to keep his feet warm. The first State Line post office was in the George Emmons farm home, until it was moved to the store in Emmons.

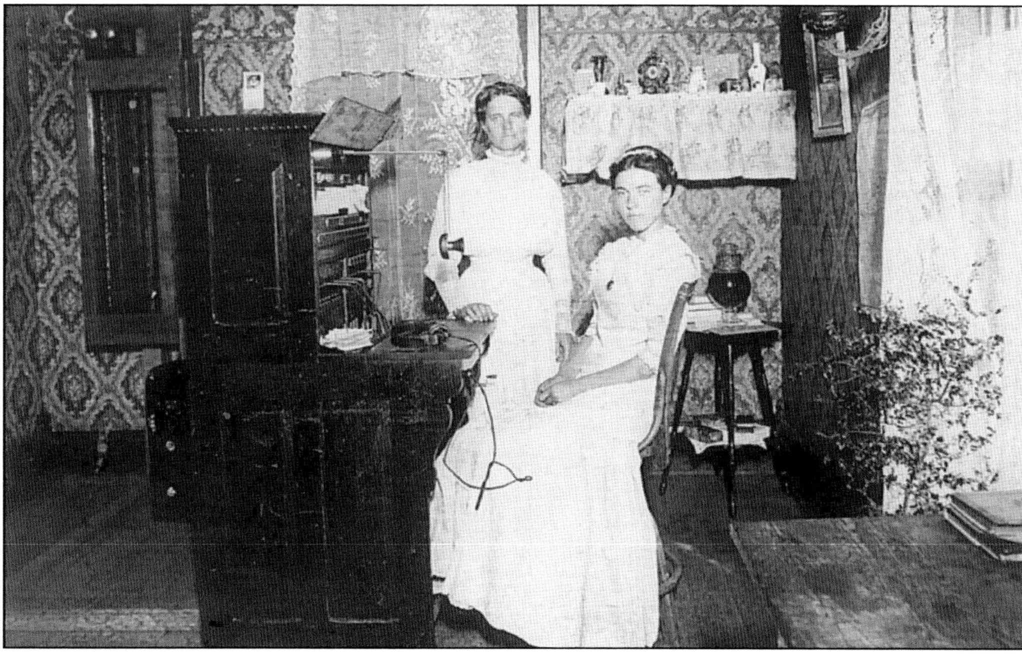

In 1908, Emmons telephone exchange operators were Bettie Engelsrud, seated, and Betsy Rasmusson, standing. At that time the telephone office was on the second floor of the barber shop. There were 15 farm lines, and the calls came in on different sounding rings, each needing to be memorized by the operator for efficient service. In 1910 Bettie Engelsrud and Andrew Rasmusson, the barber, were married.

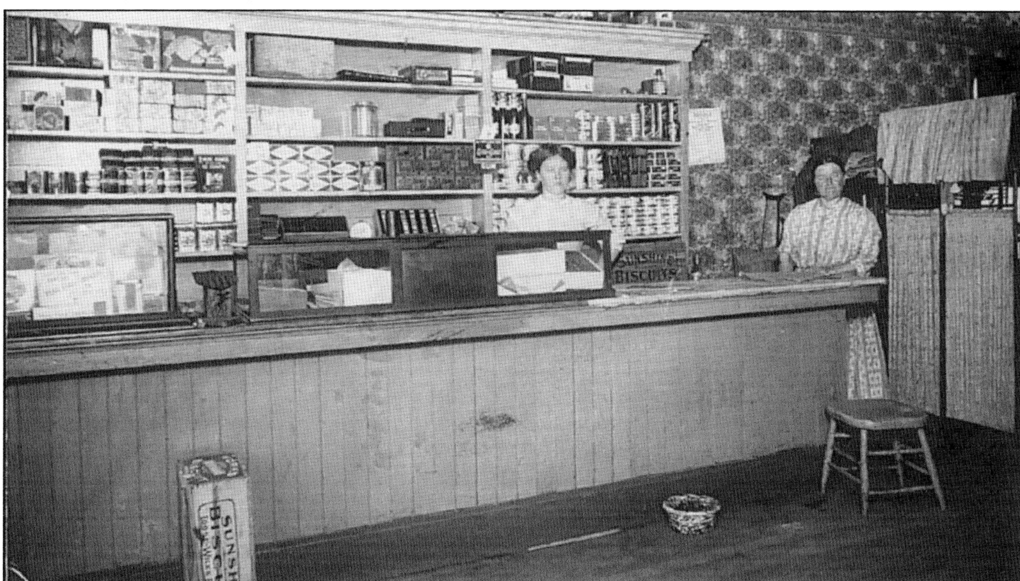

The enterprising Mrs. John Egland operated a cafe/boarding house/rooming house in Emmons in 1914. She is shown here with her daughter, who later became Mrs. Joe McGuire. Some of the other businesses in the community at that time were: a millinery run by Clara Kelly, a furniture and undertaking store owned by Gunder and Henry Clemmetson, and the Emmons Auto Company, Olson and Rasmussen owners.

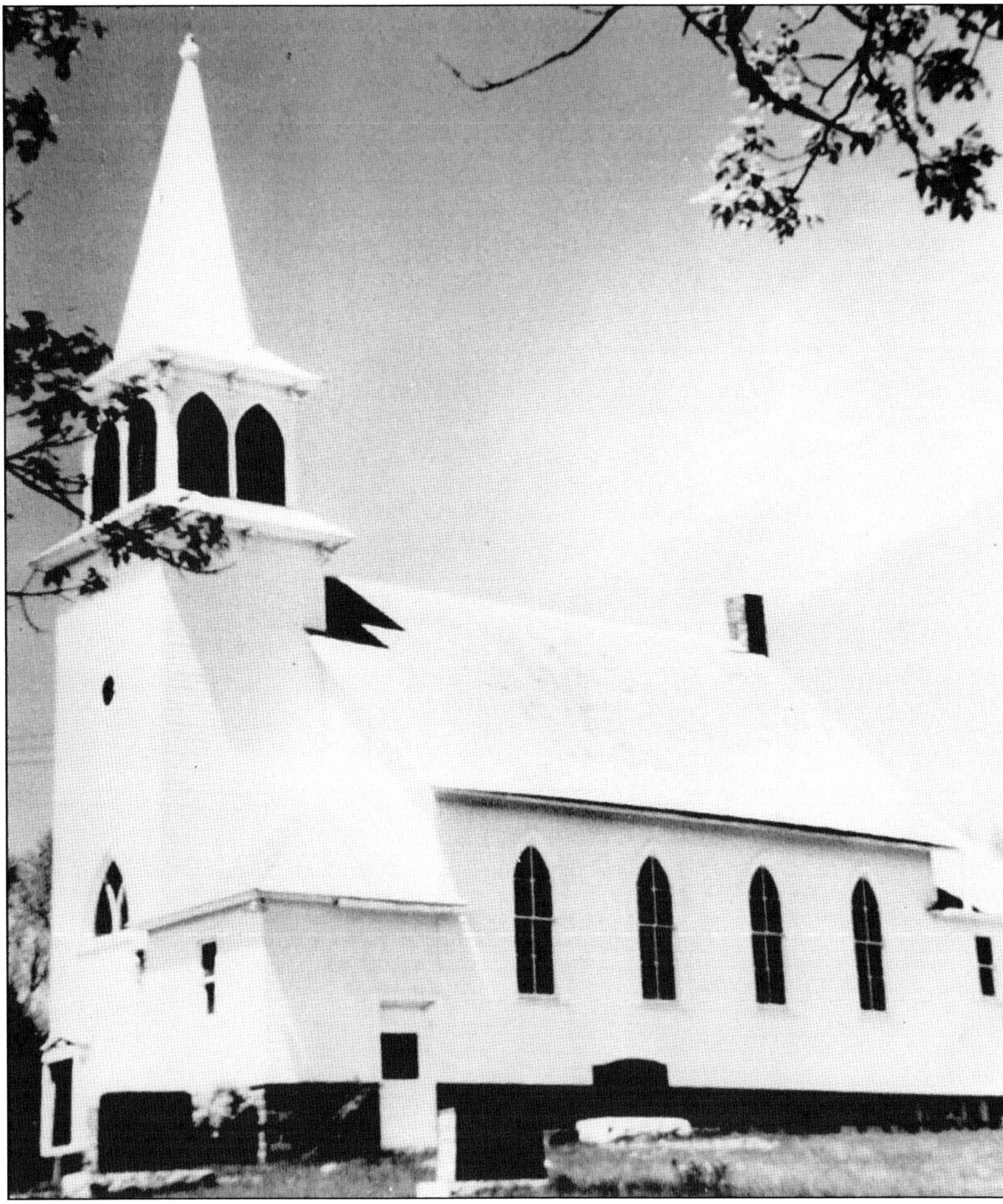

"The Mansfield Congregation of the Augustana Synod, a Swedish Evangelical Lutheran Church, was organized by Rev. S. Anderson in 1893, the first meetings being held and organization perfected at the home of Nels Johnson. . . . In 1894 the congregation was incorporated and a church built in the southeast corner of the southwest quarter of Section 20." In an unrelated article, an early pioneer family experienced difficult times. "The first settlers in Mansfield were the Tunell brothers, John and Henry, who came from Illinois by the way of Iowa with their families and with teams arriving June 23, 1856. . . . These brothers brought with them about one hundred head of cattle, and shortly after their arrival commenced putting up hay, securing enough to carry them safely through the winter; but a prairie fire destroyed it. . . . They finally managed to purchase enough hay from parties in Iowa to tide them over the winter, without a loss of more than half their stock." (*History of Freeborn County* [1911].)

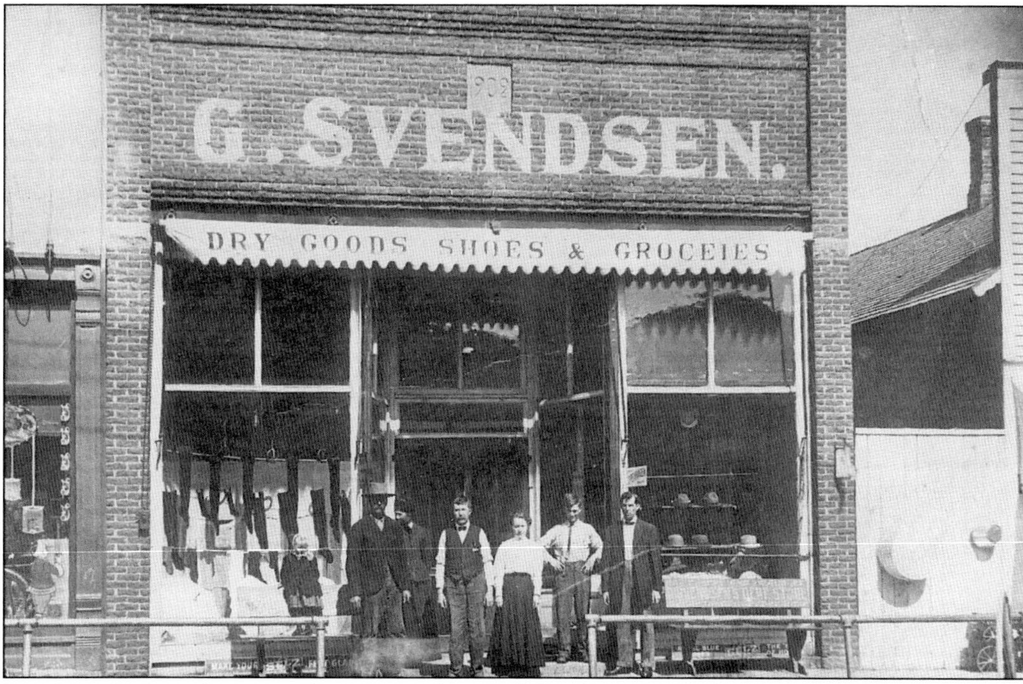

In 1911, G. Svendsen was the owner of one of the three general stores in Alden. The others being A.G. Hall & Son and the Cash Store, with J.E. Clayton as proprietor. Did the misspelled word on the awning help him to draw business from his competitors? The people standing in front of the store are, from left to right: unidentified, Nels Peterson, Gerhart Svendsen, Sadie Yates, unidentified, and Frank Wendt.

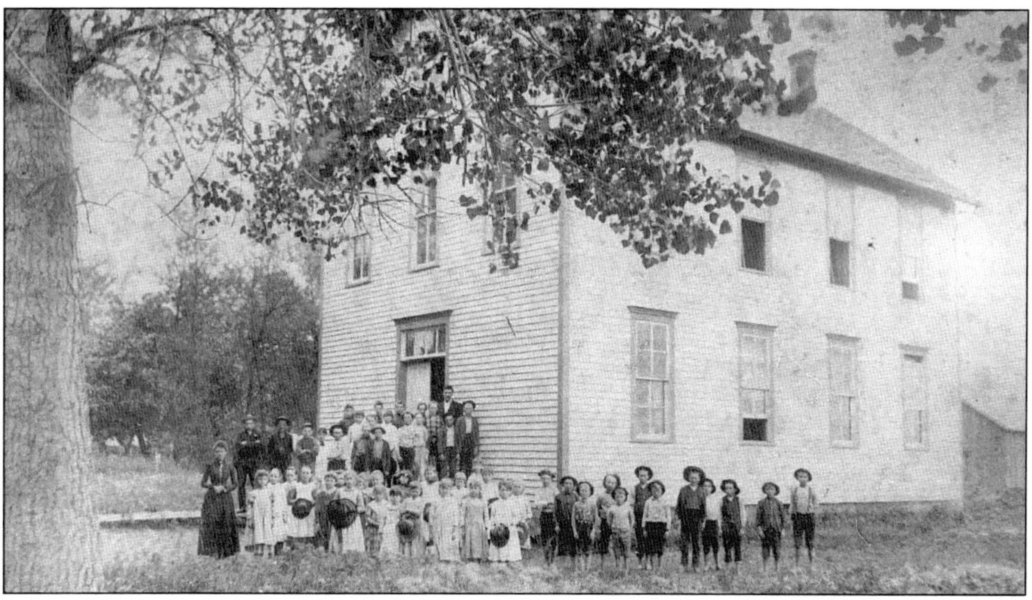

A Seventh Day Adventist School was located on the second story of the Henry Ernst home on the west shore of Gem Lake. The school started on December 15, 1870, with approximately 50 students, each paying $5 to $7 per term. Teachers were Henry Ernst and his sister Minnie. The house was later enlarged and became a residence after 1900.

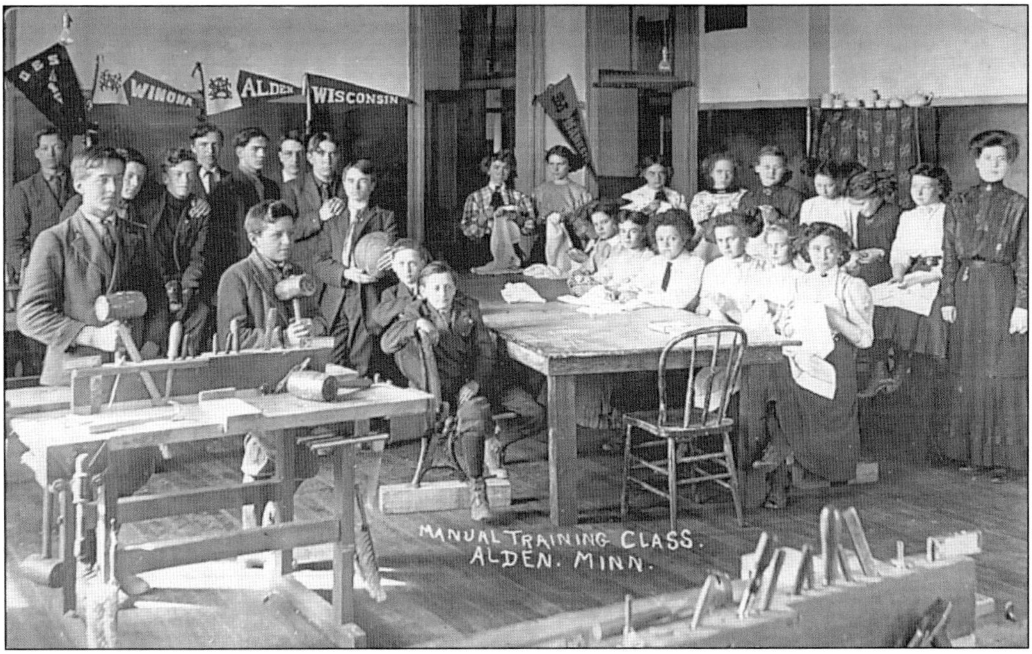

The Alden High School stressed not only the usual academic classes, but emphasized agriculture and manual training, "the institution being thoroughly modern in every respect." (*History of Freeborn County*.) Notice the carpentry tools held by the boys, and their work benches, and the girls learning the fine skills of sewing. Everyone in the picture seems to have dressed in their finest—probably not regular school-day wear.

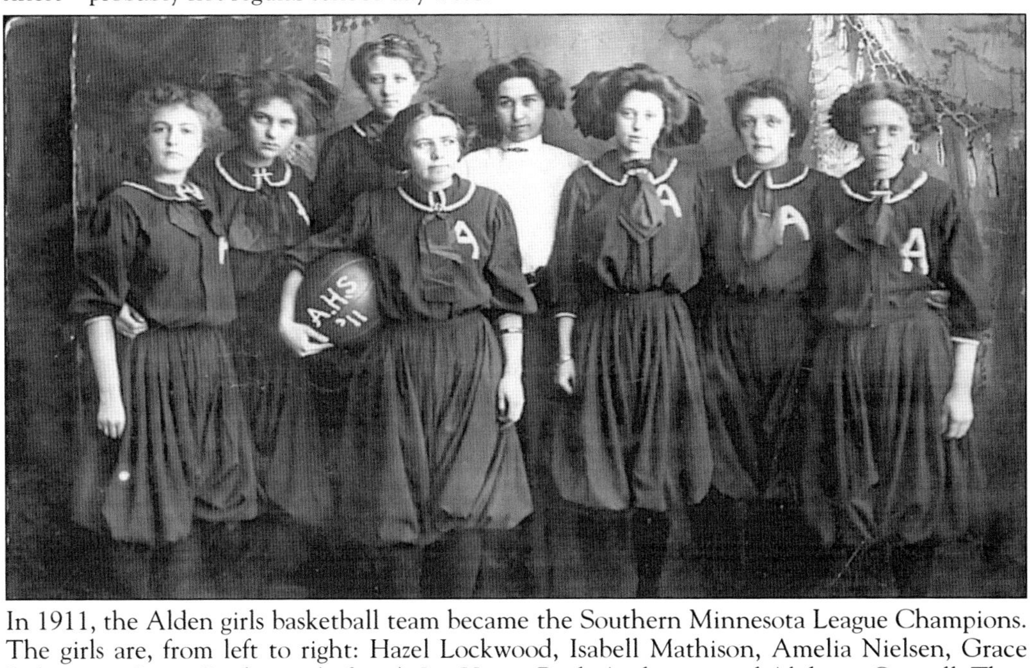

In 1911, the Alden girls basketball team became the Southern Minnesota League Champions. The girls are, from left to right: Hazel Lockwood, Isabell Mathison, Amelia Nielsen, Grace Robertson, Grace Sinderson (referee), Iris Howe, Ruth Anderson, and Alphreta Cottrell. They played against teams from Albert Lea, Jackson, Hartland, and Blue Earth. Their uniforms were dark blue, with white trim and red silk ties.

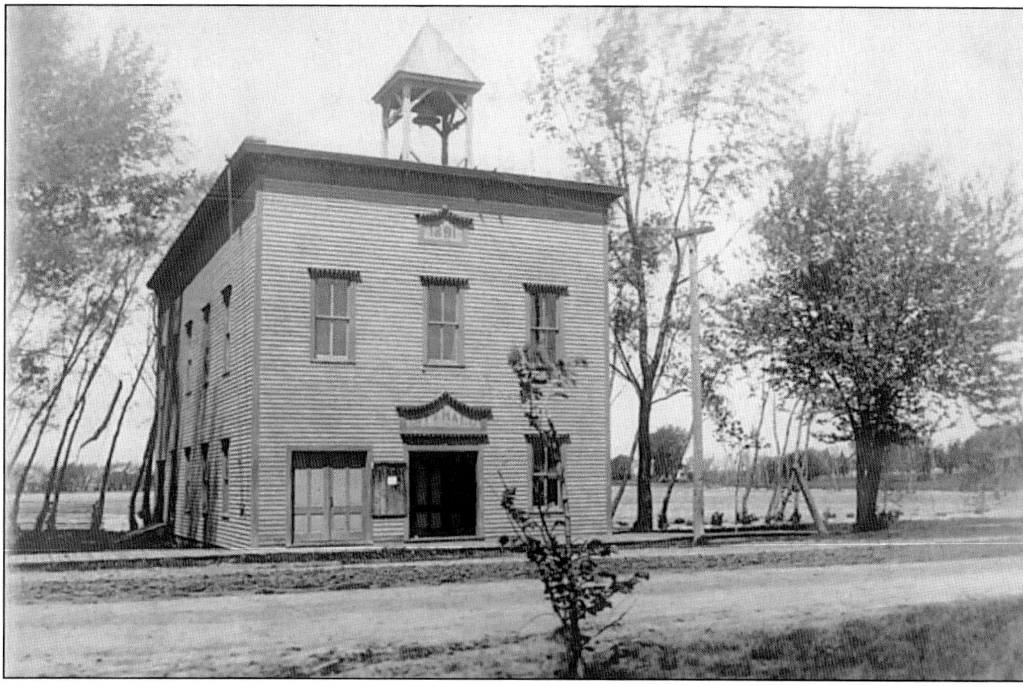

The Alden City Hall was erected in 1891. It was a two-story building, housing the fire department and the council chambers, and featuring a fine hall for entertainment and lectures. The Village of Alden was incorporated by a special act of the legislature in 1879, and the first meeting of the council was held on March 14th of that year.

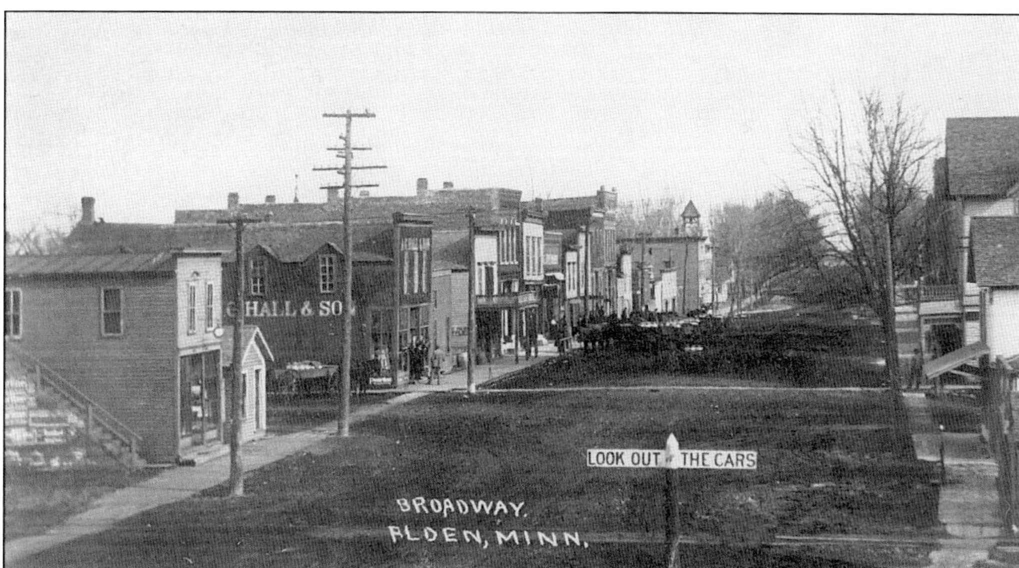

According to the *History of Freeborn County*, "Alden is called the ideal small village. It is situated on a beautiful body of water in the midst of a rich farming country, with neat buildings and well-kept streets, exceptional school opportunities and adequate church facilities. The village has advantages which make it an ideal place of residence." This 1900 Broadway photograph certainly shows this to be true.

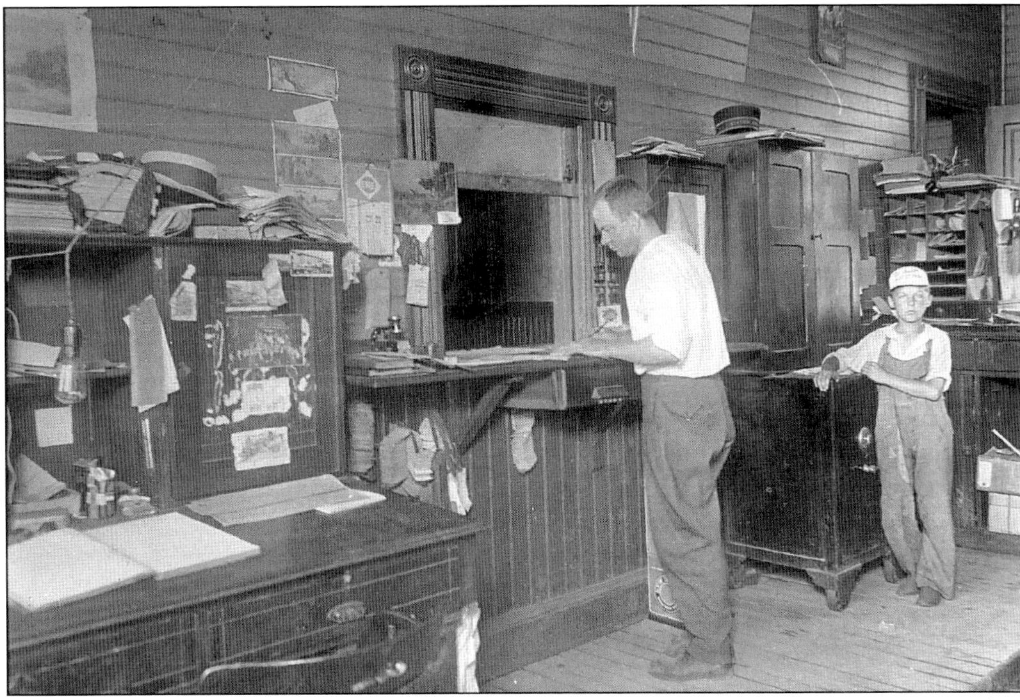

Hartwick M. Mathison is shown in the depot agent's office of the Chicago, Milwaukee, and St. Paul Railroad in Alden around 1914. The young boy in the picture is unidentified. *The History of Freeborn County* states that there were five railroad companies operating seven lines in the county, with the C M & St. Paul passing through Moscow, Oakland, Hayward, Albert Lea, Pickerel Lake, Alden, and Carlston Townships.

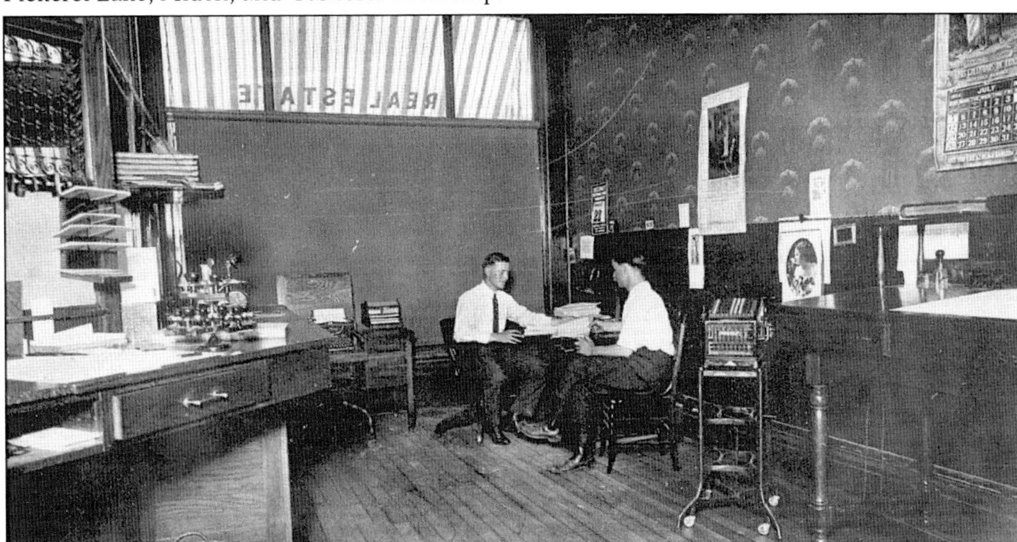

In 1916, the Security State Bank of Alden provided general banking loans, collections, and real estate. E.P. Greeley was president, and Arthur E. Erickson was vice president and cashier. The community also boasted of another bank, four churches, a steam flouring mill, three grain elevators, one creamery, and various other business enterprises. The population in 1916 was 800.

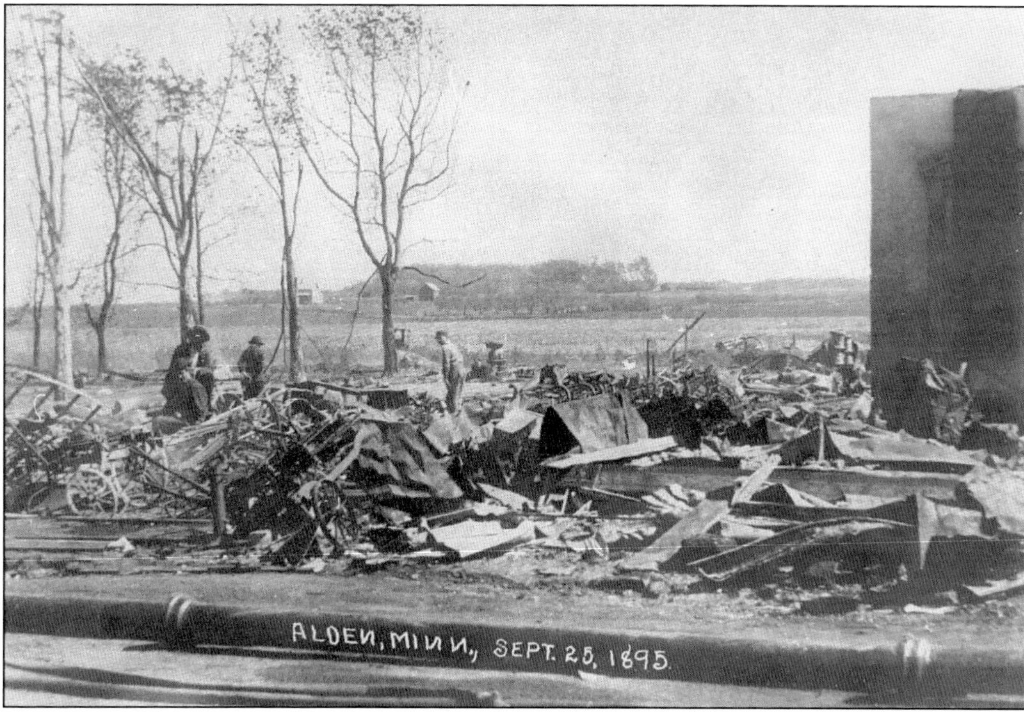

Fourteen Alden businesses burned to the ground on Thursday, September 19, 1895. Supposedly started by tramps in Walker and Valby's barn, the fire destroyed the Methodist Episcopal Church, P. Hemmingson's Store, J. Peterson's Saloon, a meat shop, drug store, furniture store, bakery, the State Bank of Alden, Niebuhr's Hardware and Machinery, Dr. Cowles office, the barber shop, the Chicago Fair Store, the Advance office, and numerous other business and personal properties.

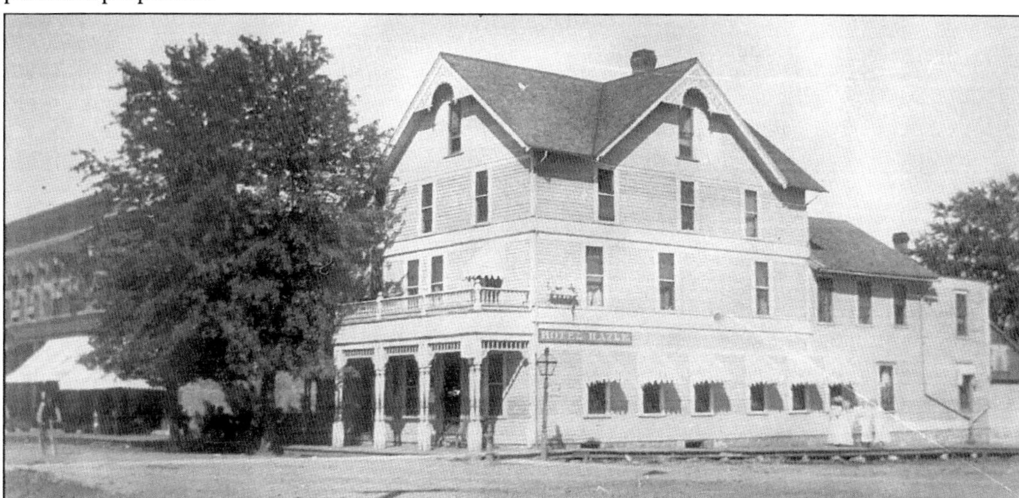

The Hotel Hazle was built around 1872, on the corner of Broadway and Main in Alden. The building was of frame construction, 24 by 40 feet, and its sills were hewn from oak logs cut in the woods just east of the village. The hotel was purchased in 1874 by J.A. Hazle and his wife. They built a 25- by 30-foot addition, which contained a dining room, sample rooms, parlor, kitchen, and several rooms on the second floor.

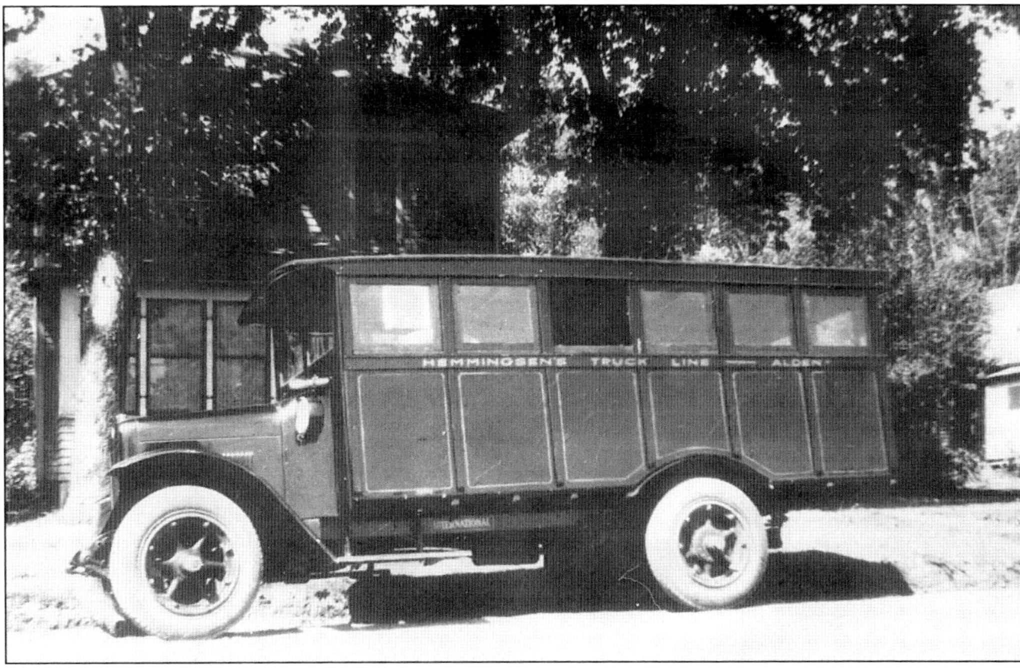

By 1902, Louis Hemmingsen had started a livery service. Traveling salesmen would arrive on the morning train, hire a Hemmingsen rig, transact the day's business, and leave on the evening train. With the advent of motor-driven vehicles, busses and trucks were added to the line. This photograph shows a 1927 school bus. The truck was an International, and the body was made in Albert Lea.

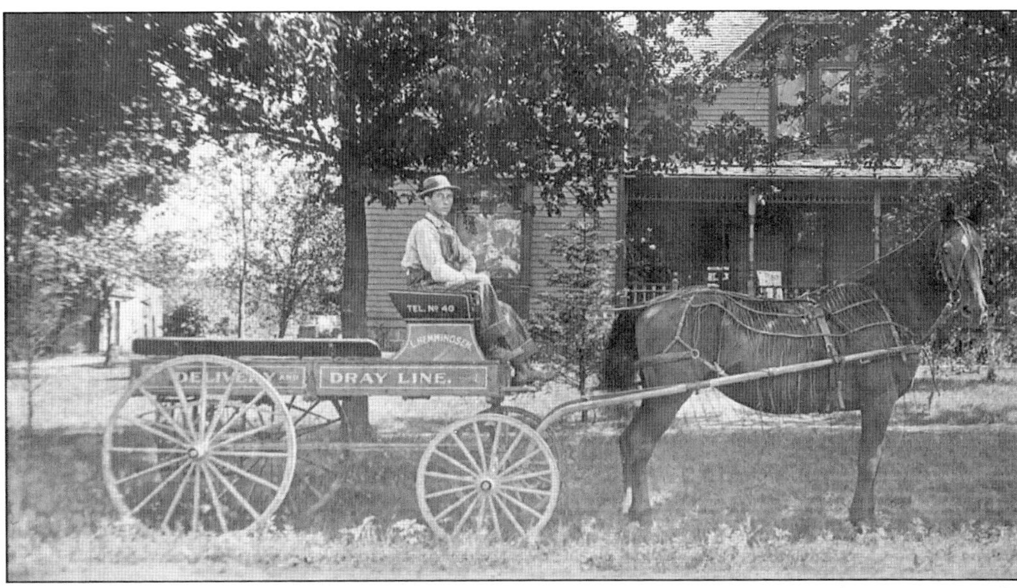

Francis Peter Peterson was born November 21, 1887, in Copenhagen, Denmark. He came to the United States in 1906 and settled at Alden. In 1911, when this picture was taken, Peterson was working for Hemmingsen Dray Line delivering groceries and freight. The horse, Pat, belonged to Peterson. They are shown in front of the Martin Clausen home by Alden Lake.

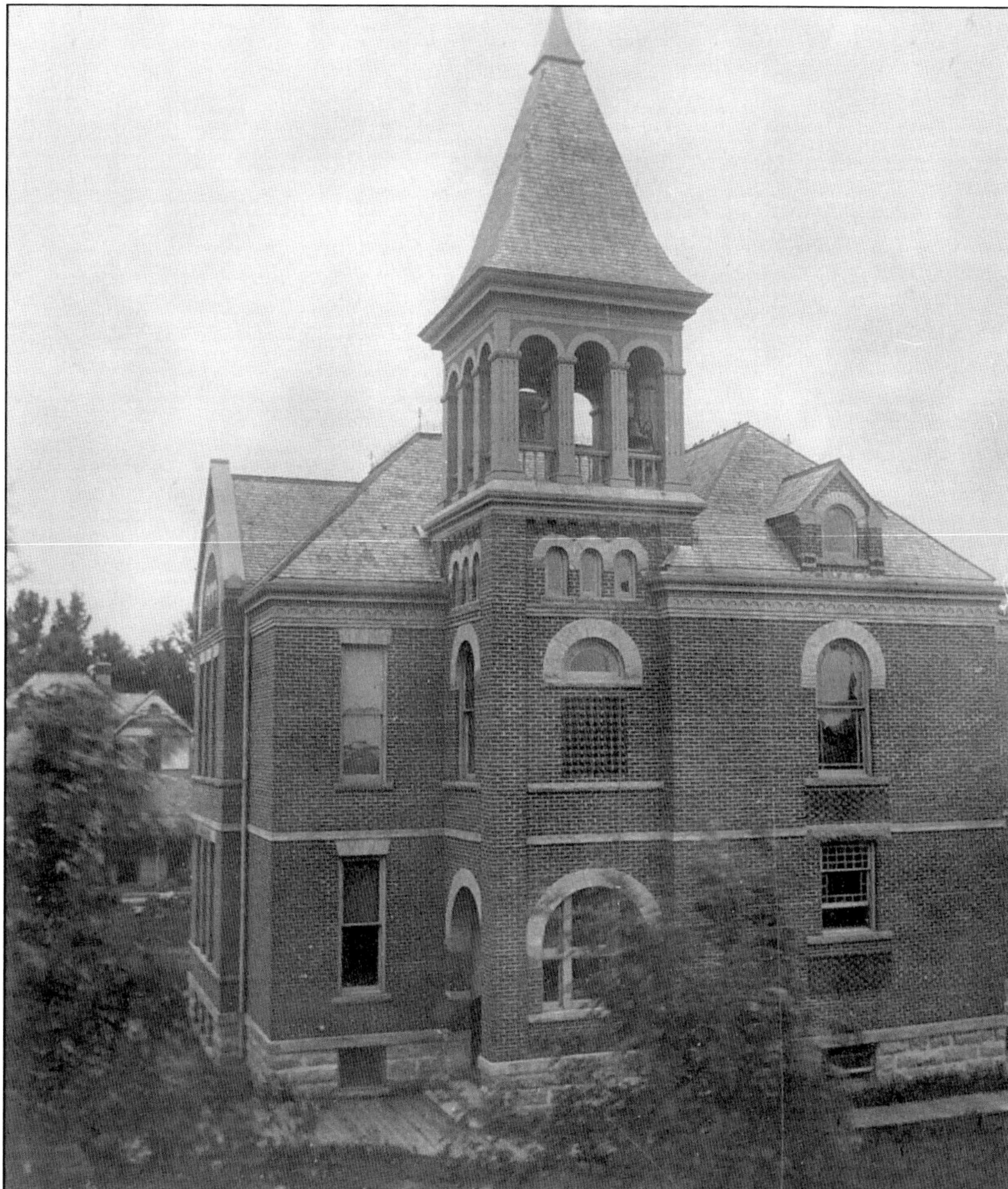

This beautiful brick school was the pride of the community when it was built in 1896. District 93 had several buildings on the same site, but most scholars were still attending country schools. Almost 30 years earlier, District 40 was organized, and Miss Maxson received $15 a month for her services. She had 11 pupils. District 80 was organized in 1866, but it was three years before a school was built at a cost of $600. E.J. Russell taught nine students that first year. In District 70, lessons were given in homes until 1869, when Angela Langdon received $12 per month for teaching 18 scholars; and in Section 27, Olivia Burdick taught for three terms in a sod house, until a schoolhouse was constructed with "patent seats and all necessary apparatus." Throughout the county, one-room schoolhouses were built with no running water or electricity; teachers received very little pay and served several roles, including custodian. The brick school in Alden was a major improvement on the earlier school scenario.

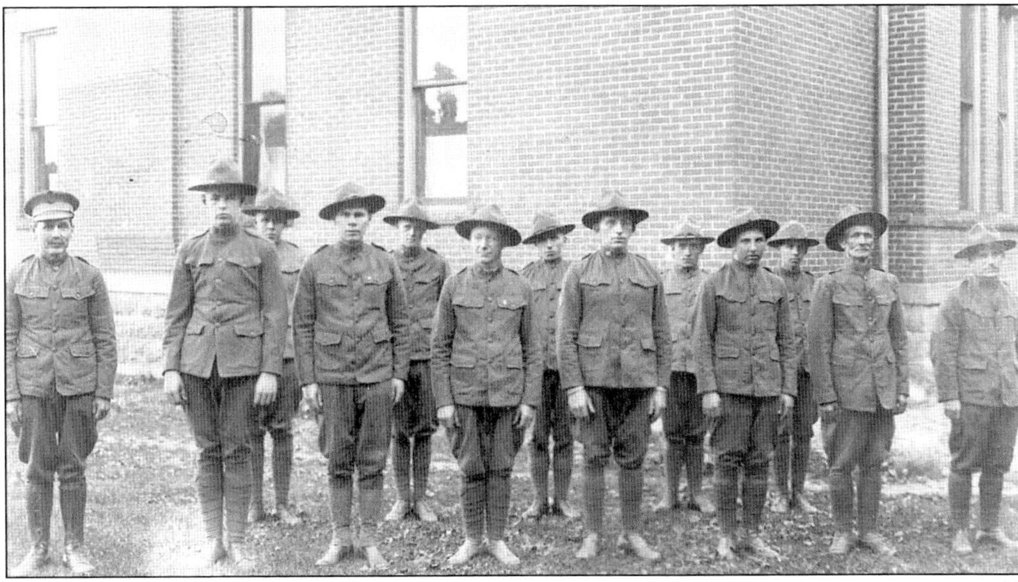

The Alden Company E 17th Battalion Minnesota Home Guard formed in 1918, eventually having 66 members. Pictured here are, from left to right: Captain Fred Holway, Verl Ebert, Harold Hanson, C.W. Nelson, Harold Cooper, Thorwald Svendsen, Wallace Hemmingson, V. Kennison, Fred Schaudt, Bob Sorenson, Burdette Wendt, Cornelius Ostrander, and Bert Hazle. Duties included farewell parades for servicemen, Home Guard Day at the county fair, Red Cross auctions, and helping with War Savings Stamps and Liberty Loan drives.

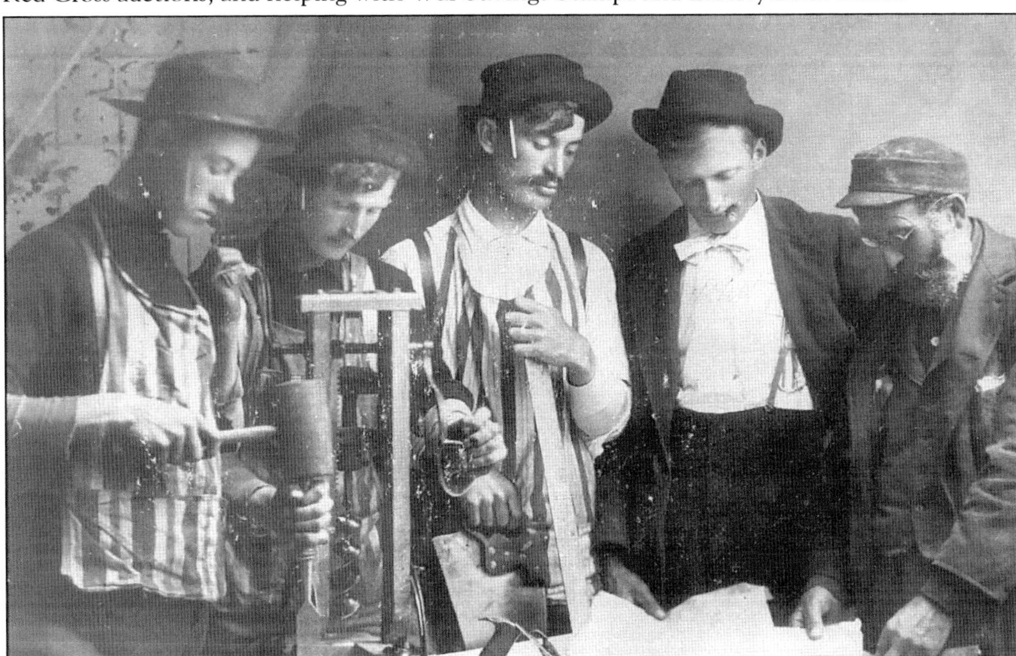

The only description available of this scene is, "photo of Alden men by Jensen Studio at Albert Lea—possibly a master carpenter and his apprentices. Note the striped aprons." What is the real story? Who are these men in this obviously posed photo? What skills and knowledge are being shared by the craftsman on the right, and who is the gentleman in the suit and bow tie?

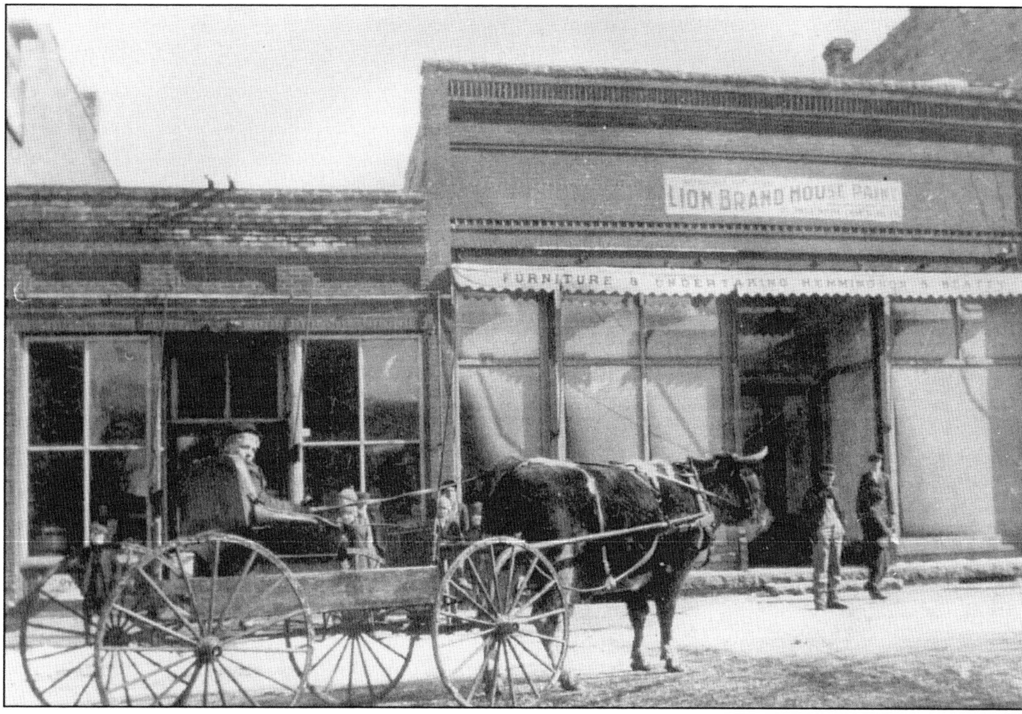

Russell Babbitt and his pet steer bring stares from on-lookers at Alden in 1908. He became a livestock breeder in the Conger area, and also served as Conger's mayor. Babbitt was also on the school board, on the Naeve Hospital board in Albert Lea, and had served as the president of the Minnesota Auction Markets Association. He died at age 64.

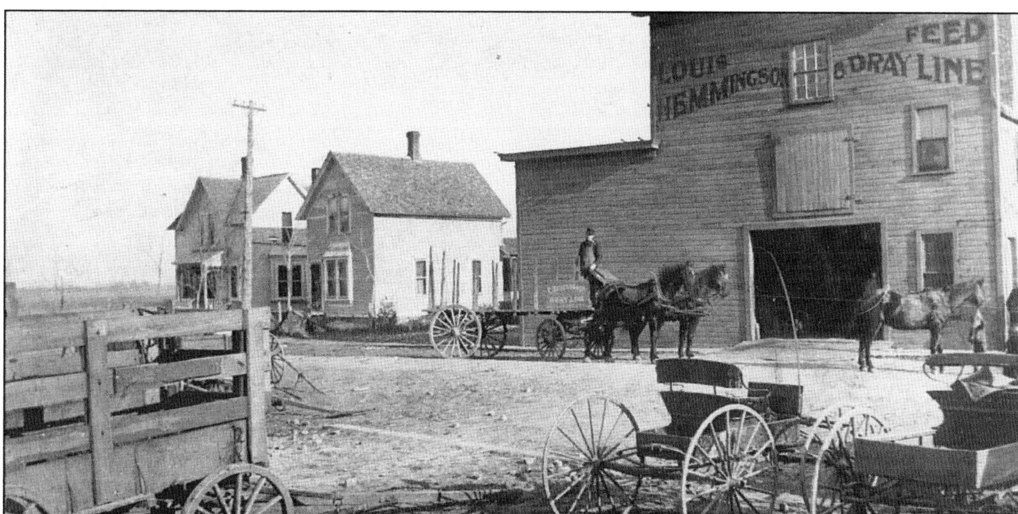

The Hemmingsen Transfer Company is one of the oldest firms in Alden, originating in 1900 with the purchase by Louis Hemmingsen of a feed barn, where farmers and other travelers could leave their horses to be fed and cared for while they were in town. A year later he purchased a draying service, and the horse-drawn wagon was added for the convenience of people who had items needing to be moved.

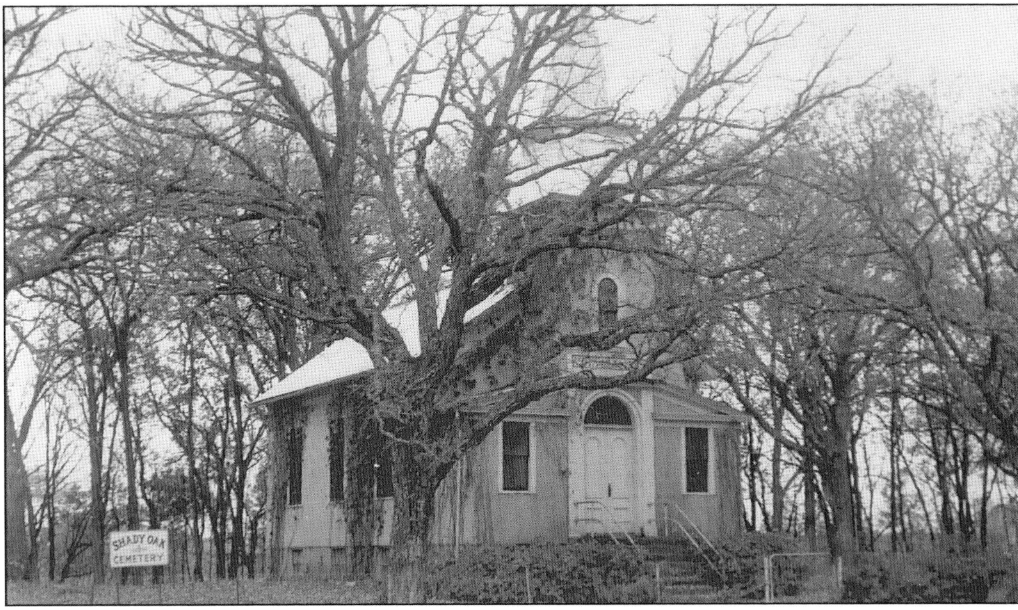

The German Methodist Episcopal Church of Pickerel Lake was built in 1873 on "one of the garden spots of the earth." E.H. Elickson and Besseson were the contractors. They built the church with stone blasters, men with ox and horse teams to dig and haul stones and lime, and stone masons to lay the walls. A year later the church was struck by lightning, but it was soon repaired.

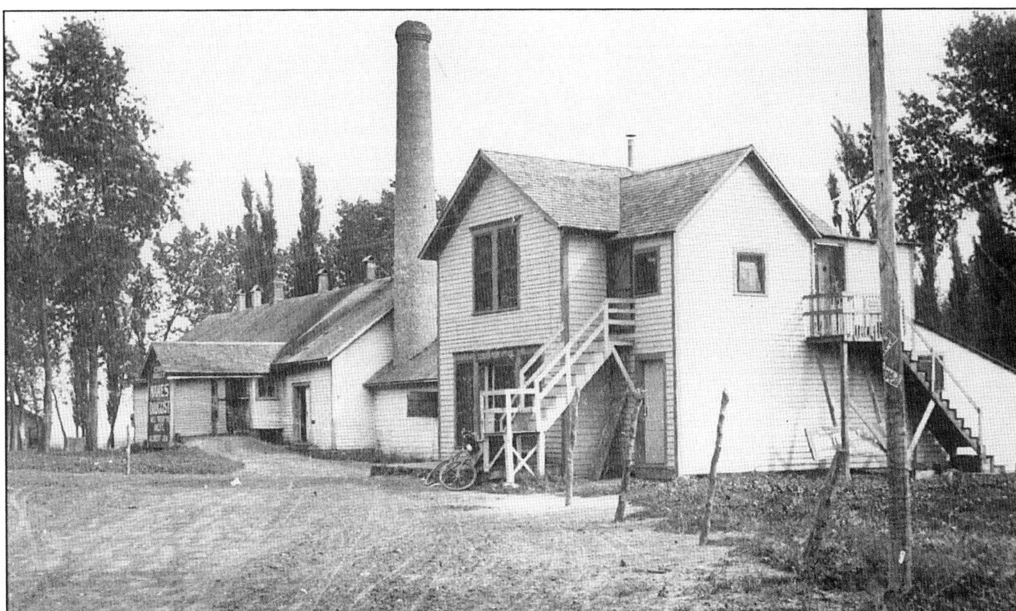

The Village of Clover existed from 1890 to 1915. It consisted of a creamery and a general store/post office, all built on land owned by William P. Pickle. The first directors of the Clover Valley Creamery were Charles Radke, George Hall, William Wohlhuter, Henry Drommerhausen, George Scherb, Fred Fink, and Herman Klukow. Postmasters were William Pickle, William Wohlhuter, Frank Yost, Peter Flesch, and George Enser.

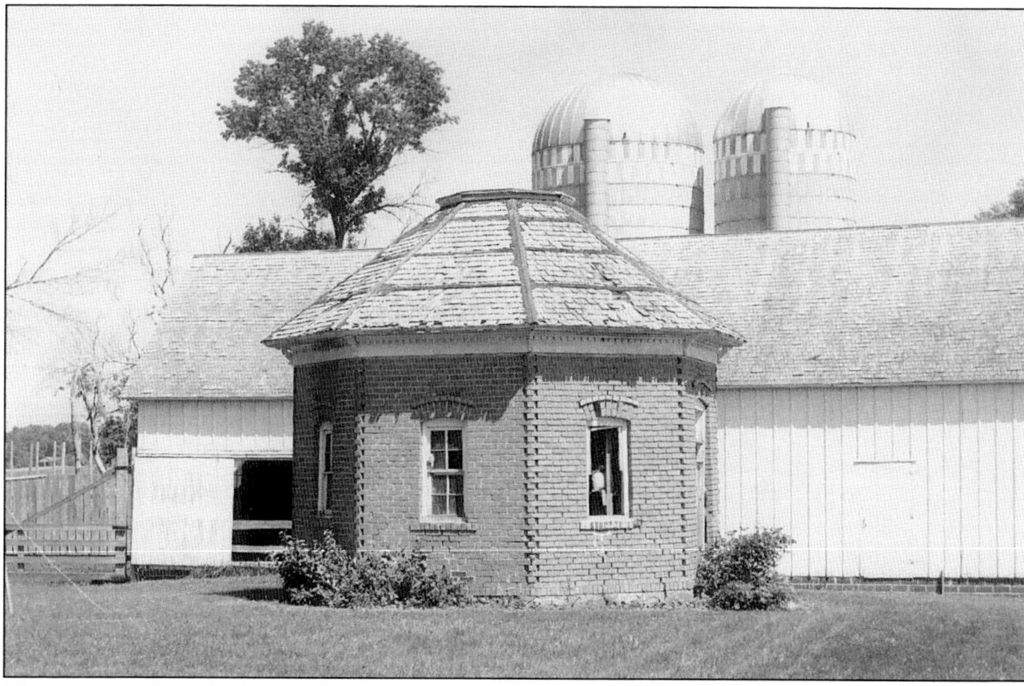

The octagonal brick chicken house was built on the Herman Klukow farm, north of Concordia Lutheran Church on the old Wilson Highway. The 1890 building had a concrete floor, plastered walls, and was of most unusual construction, reminding one of the European dovecote. In most recent years, it was used as a tool house.

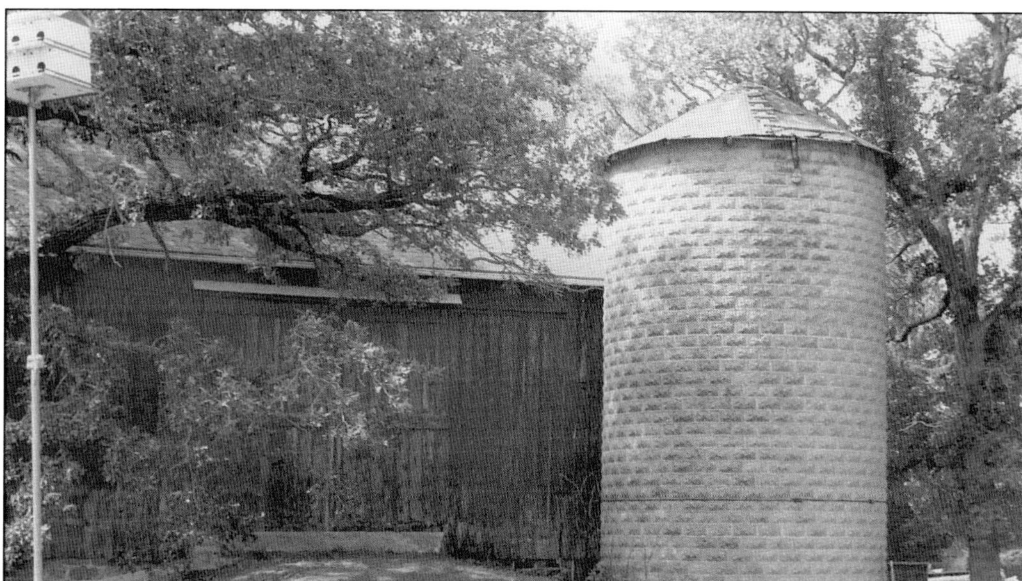

This concrete-block silo was located on a Pickerel Lake Township farm in Section 21. It was built in 1914, with blocks cast and cured on the farm, which is east of the Concordia Lutheran Church. During the 1850s and 1860s, many Lutheran immigrants from Waldeck, Hannover, Pomerania, and other provinces in Northern Germany settled in the areas known as Pickerel Lake, Bear Lake, and Mansfield.

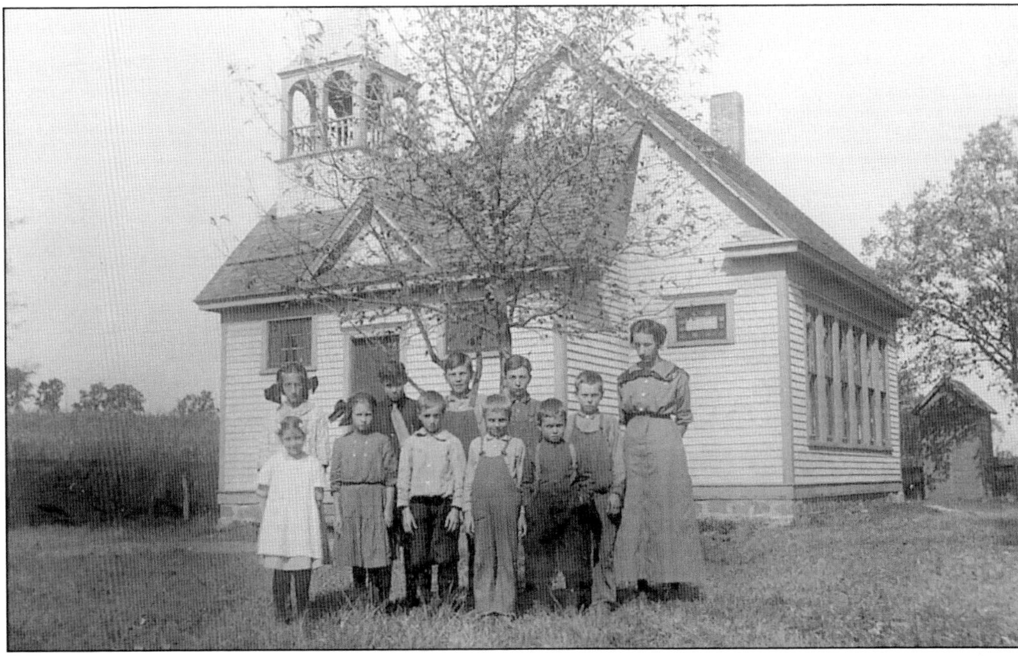

District 102 was first taught in the summer of 1876 in a carpenter shop on Mr. Widman's land. The teacher, Katie Eberhardt, had 18 or 20 scholars. The following year a neat frame building was erected at a cost of $300 in the southwest corner of Section 24. District organizers were George Widman, Mr. Jeklin, and F. Schneider. The photograph was taken in 1913. Elsie V. Lemke is the teacher.

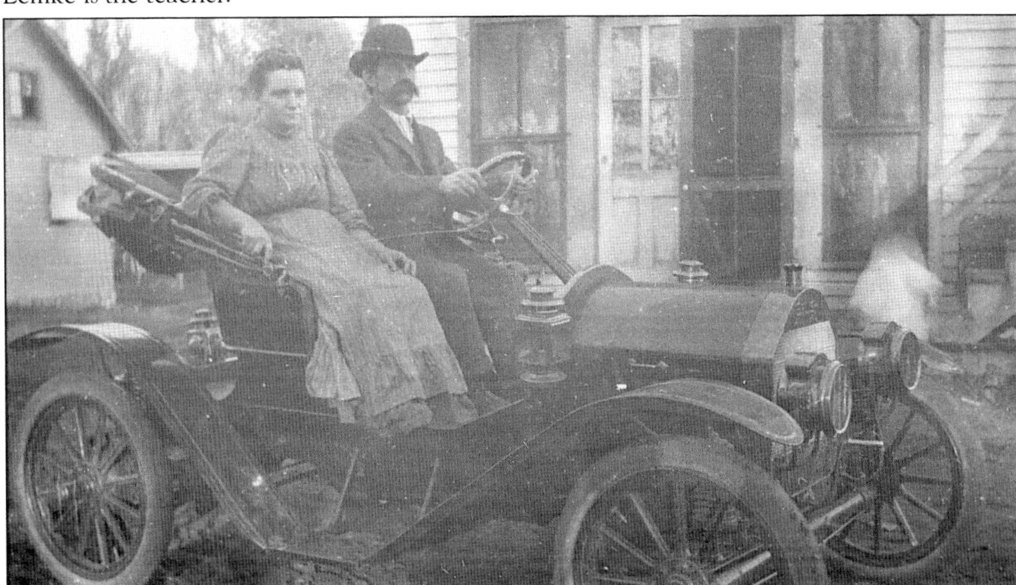

Mr. and Mrs. George Enser are shown seated in their 1910 automobile in front of the Clover General Store that he managed from 1904 to 1916. The Village of Clover was built on land owned by William P. Pickle. He built the general store in 1890, the same year that the post office was established. Originally the office was called Adair but, because of its resemblance to the word Adrian, the name was changed to Clover.

Hi-Lites and Shadows of Yesterday and Today, by Irv Sorenson in 1958, is pictured here.

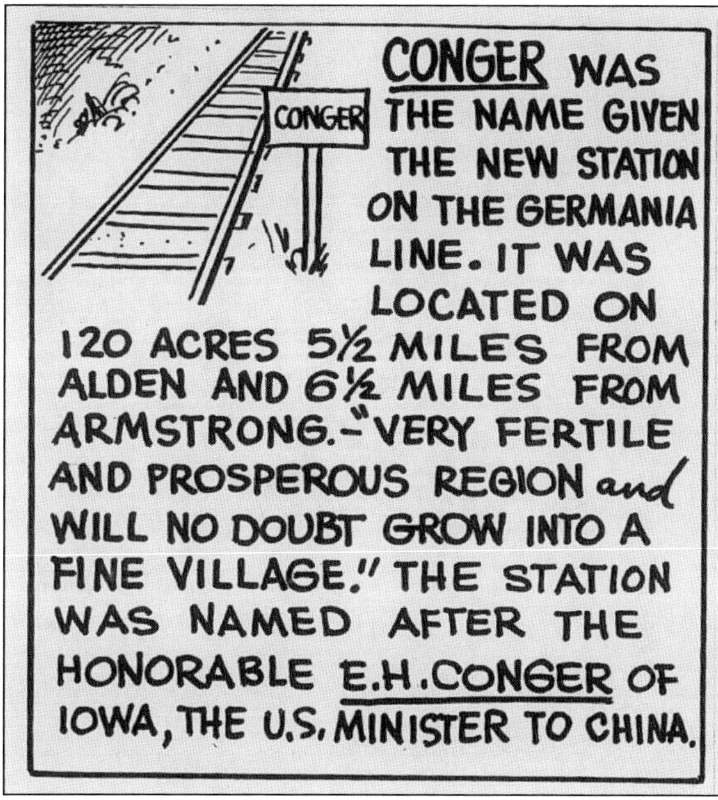

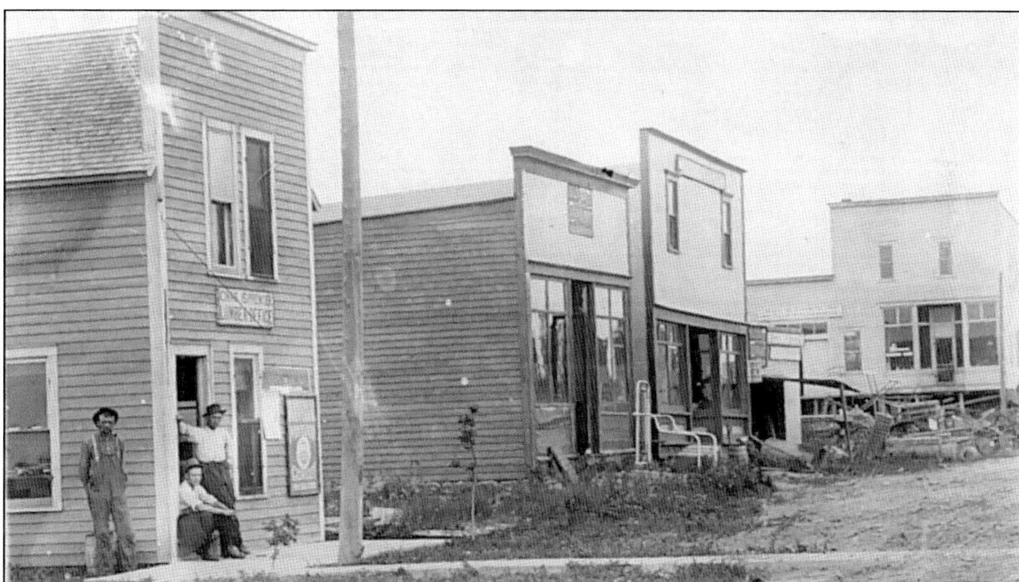

This 1914 view of the east side of Main Street in Conger shows Charles Sprenger standing in the door of his lumber yard and general store. Other businesses in town that year were the Conger Creamery Company, State Bank, blacksmith, hardware store, and the grain and coal company. Conger was located on the Chicago, Rock Island, & Pacific Railroad line 10 miles west of Albert Lea.

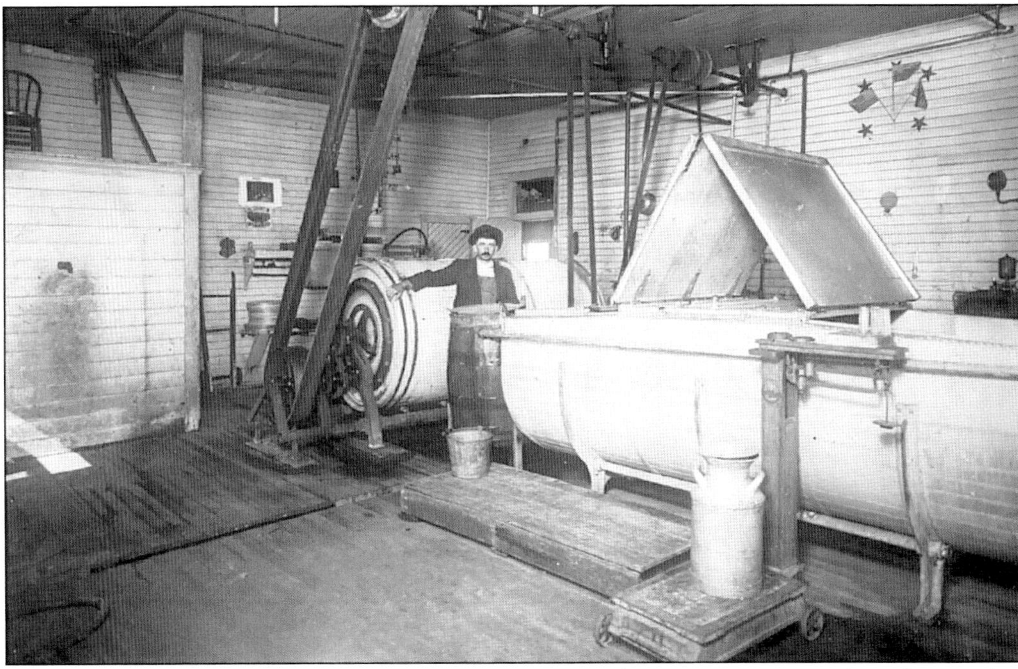

The Clover Valley Creamery Association was organized on June 2, 1890. Area farmers had been patronizing gathered cream wagons sent out from Albert Lea, Alden, and Emmons, and when the meeting was called to establish a modern separator creamery in Clover, there was not one dissenting vote cast. It was in operation until 1915. Note the patriotic flavor of the flags and stars on the interior wall.

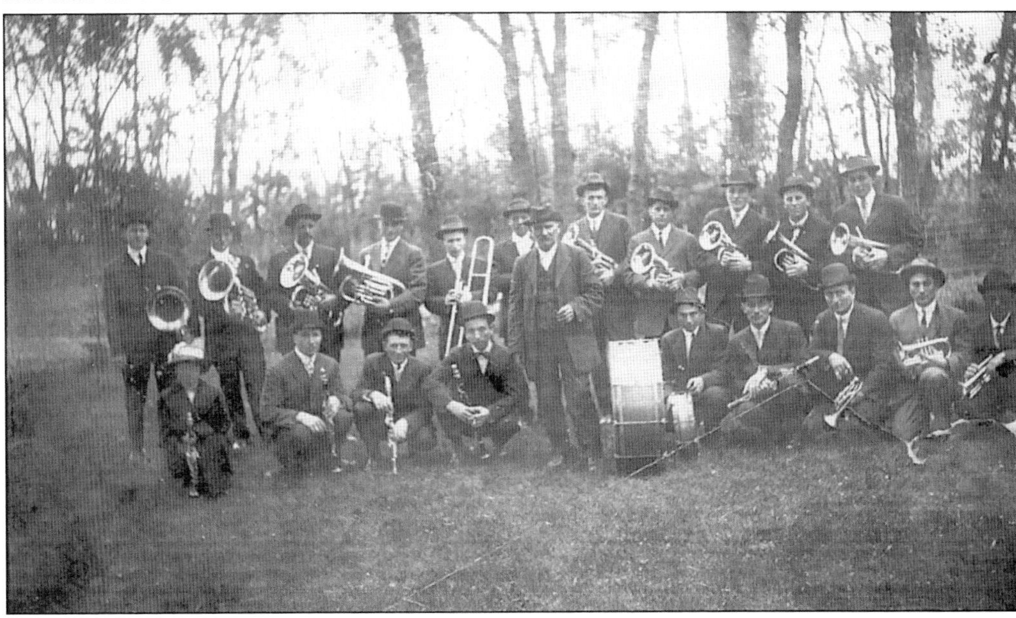

Almost every community, no matter how small, had its own band. Made up of local talent, they played for special events, parades, and Sunday afternoons in the city park. While some bands had their own special uniforms, the Pickerel Lake Band, with Henry Klose as director, posed for this photograph dressed in their Sunday best. Klose was also director of the Lerdal Cornet band.

Three

The Northwest

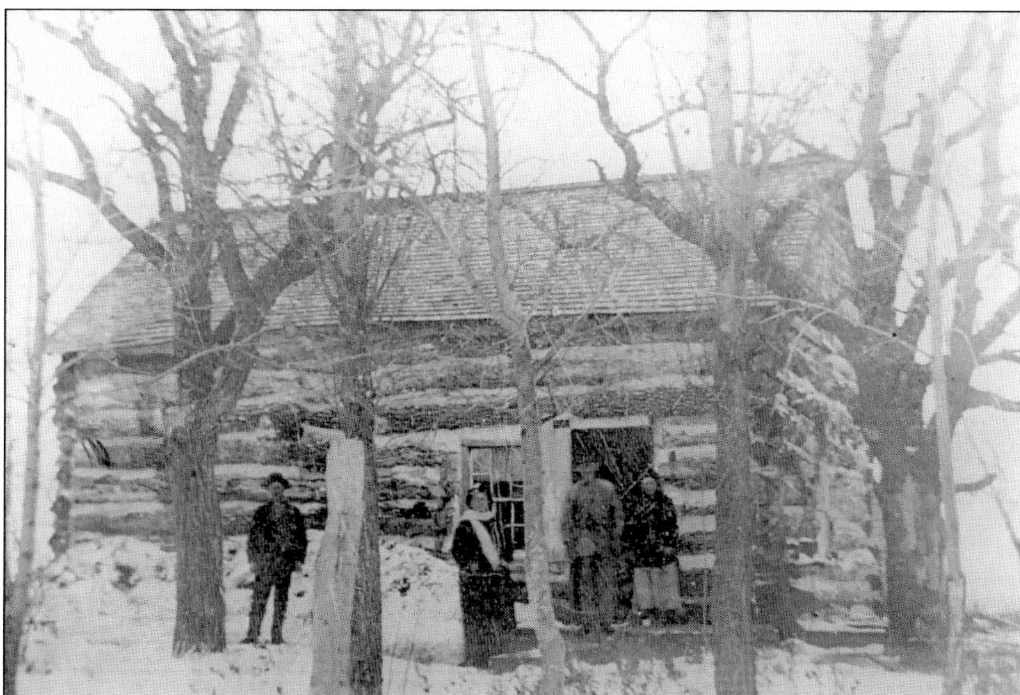

The first log house was built in Manchester Township by Smith Skiff on Section 26. In 1859, their sister Emily, and her husband George B. Chamberlain, arrived from New York, purchased adjoining land, and farmed for the next quarter of a century. The photograph information says, "The Old Homestead in Winter. Father and Eva standing in the door, Mother out in the yard, Karl Kittleson at one side."

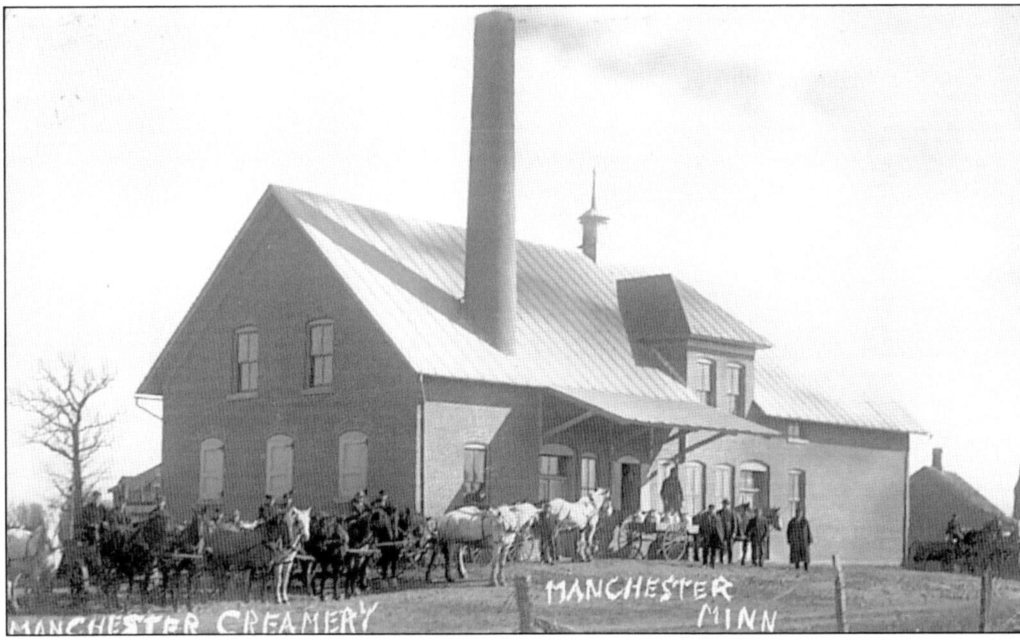

The Manchester Creamery Association was formed in January 1891, with C. Flindt as president and eight other directors chosen. By May the creamery was fully operational, with C.F. Meyer engaged as butter maker. After the original creamery was destroyed by fire, the brick creamery pictured was built in 1910. It was 32 by 84 feet, with 16-foot walls, a concrete ceiling, and a steel roof.

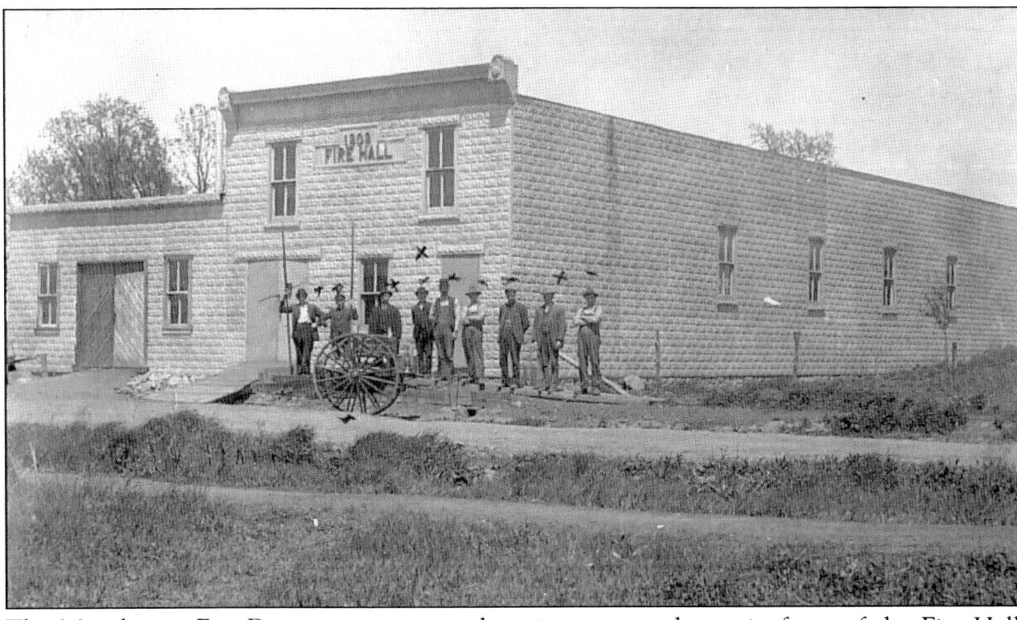

The Manchester Fire Department men and equipment are shown in front of the Fire Hall, which was built in 1909 and used also for theatrical and social purposes. According to the *History of Freeborn County*, another building in Manchester was the blacksmith shop, built by Anton Anderson in 1878, when he "commenced blowing the bellows." He later added a wagon shop and an engine house for his five-horse-power fire engine.

The original West Freeborn Lutheran Church was used by members of the congregation until 1876. It was a sod building with log interior walls and a log roof. In 1876, this frame church was erected at a cost of $5,700. Its imposing steeple contained an 800-pound bell that cost $300. This church was destroyed by fire in 1930.

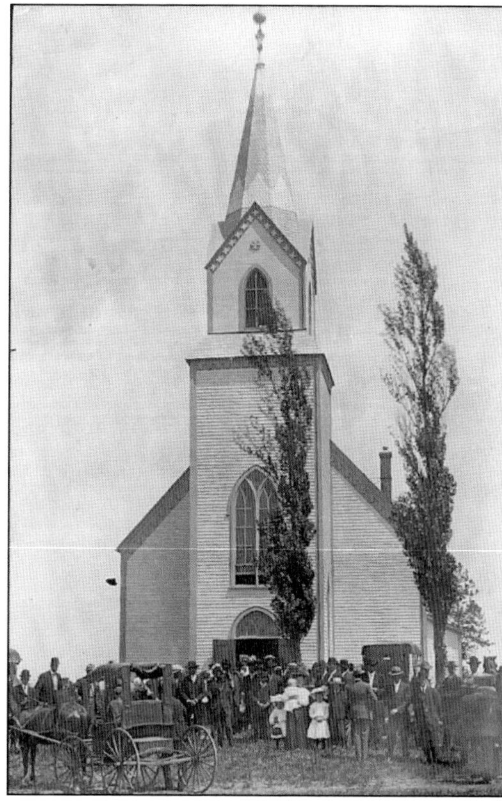

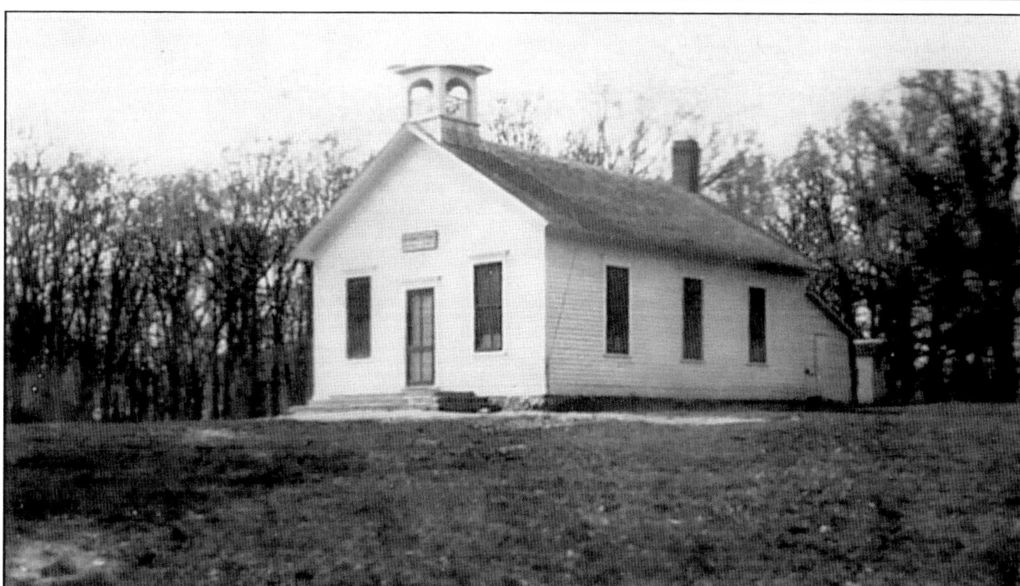

District No. 55 embraced the territory in the southeastern part of Manchester Township. It was organized in the fall of 1864 in the E.D. Hopkins house on Section 34, and the first school was taught by Maggie Colby in a log house belonging to A.M. Johnson. The following year a log house, 18 by 16 feet, was purchased for $100. District 55, or the Hopkins School, is shown as it appeared in 1918.

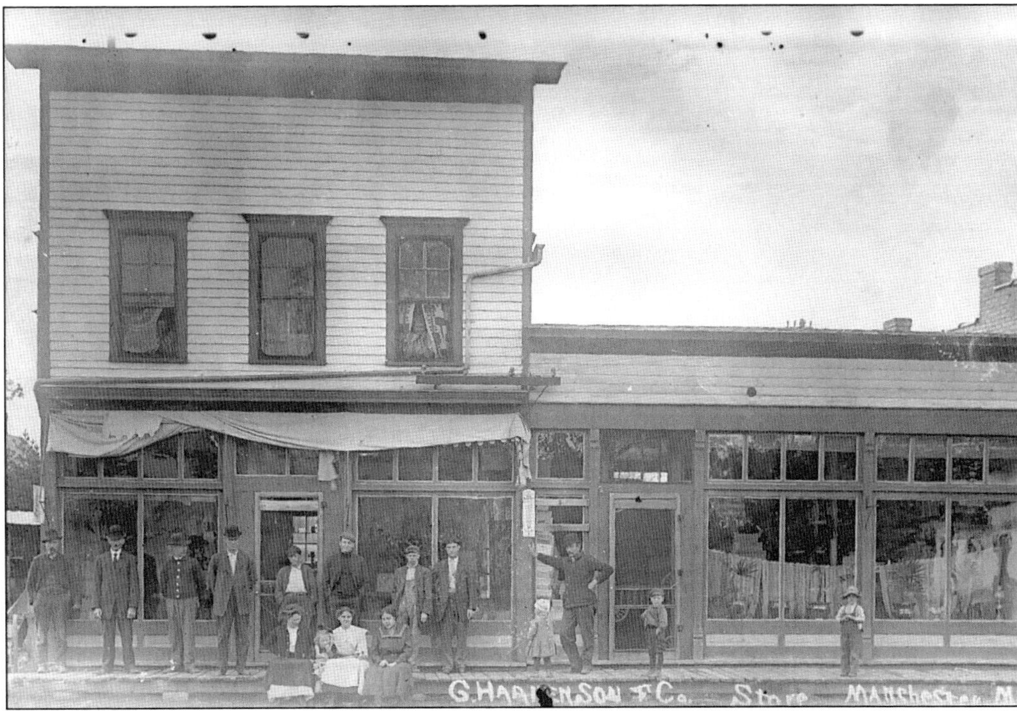

In 1911, the Manchester General Store was owned by Gunder Haakenson, Lyth O. Hartz, and John A. Thykeson. The 1914 city directory lists several names, mostly Haakensons, as employees; and it looks like they all gathered in front of the store for this photograph. The village of Manchester was platted in 1882, and was then re-platted and surveyed in 1898, although by that time there were several businesses in the community.

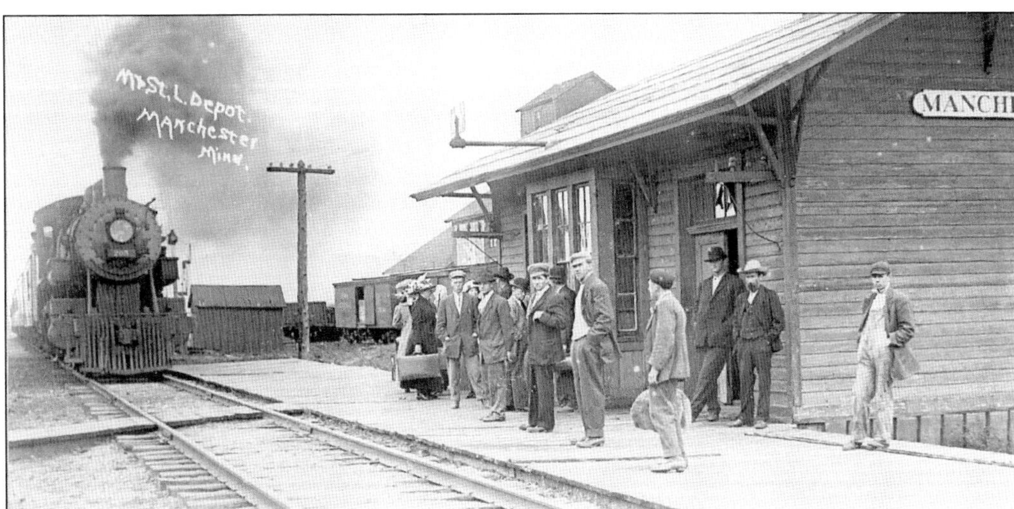

Passengers at the Manchester station await the arrival of the Minneapolis & St. Louis train in 1913. A year later the building burned to the ground. The body of depot agent, Mrs. Irene Coleman, was found in the ruins. She was one of the few women who attended Barry's Telegraph School in Minneapolis, and she had accepted the Manchester position three months earlier. Her husband had arrived only three weeks before the fire.

Hi-Lites and Shadows Yesterday and Today, was drawn by Irv Sorenson, 1956.

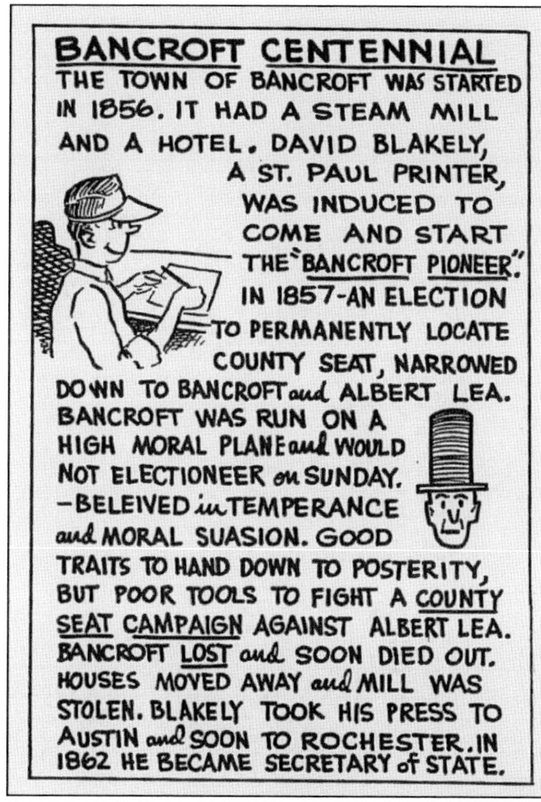

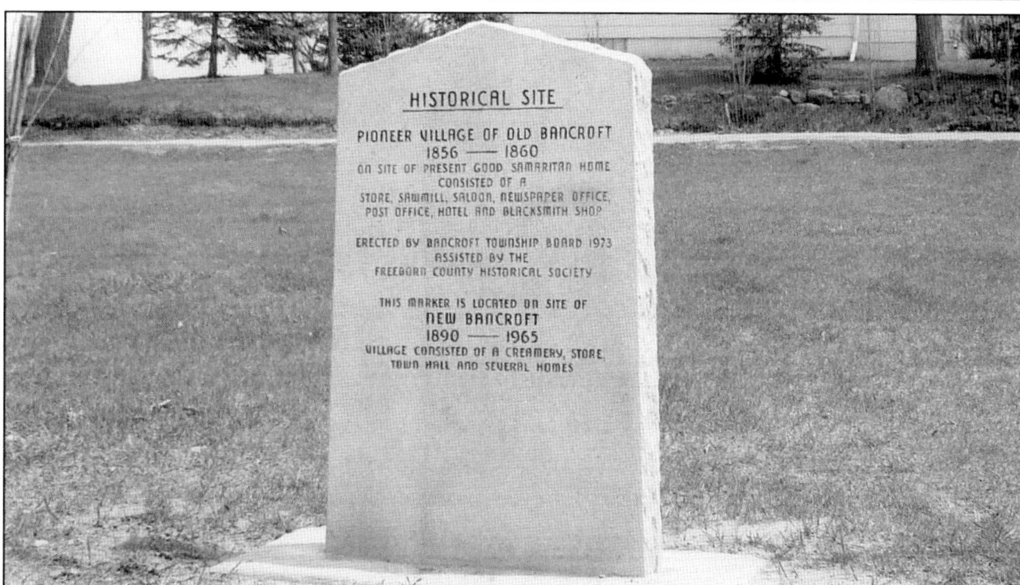

The original village of Bancroft was platted by Morton S. Wilkinson in 1856. The legislative bill enacting this process included a county seat clause, but this was repealed. An early account of the original buildings stated, "The store was removed. . . . Oleson first lived in a dugout. . . . Porter opened a blacksmith shop. . . . Perry started a law practice . . . a sawmill was set up—sold for taxes . . . hotel and saloon had brief existence."

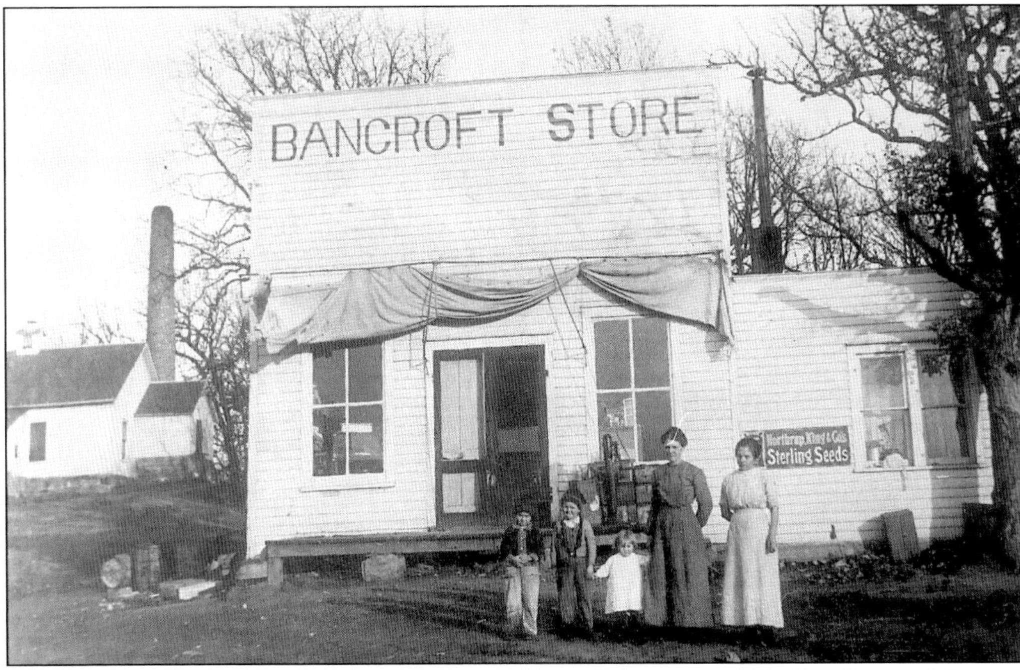

According to the *History of Freeborn County*, "Thomas Edgar erected the first Bancroft Store in the spring of 1857 and put in a stock of goods." The same source states, "A store (in 1857) was also erected, Charles Etheridge being the master builder." This photograph shows the store as it looked in 1912, when it was operated by the Torgeson family. Shown here, from left to right, are: Arnold Hendrix; Arnold, Cora, and Carolina Torgeson; and Gustina Larson.

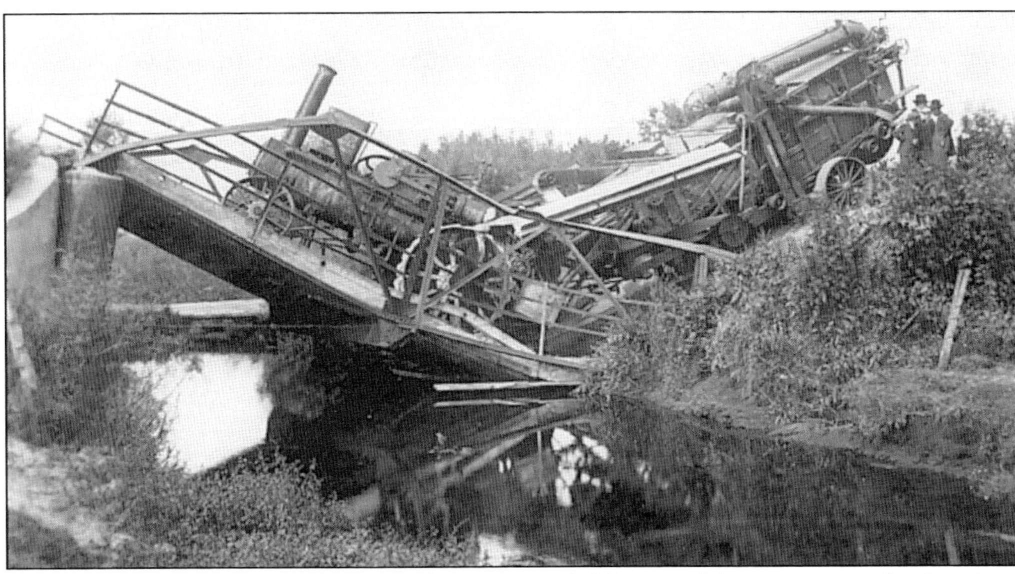

This steam engine and threshing machine was probably owned by one man, who hired out and worked for the neighboring farmers with a threshing crew. The schedule of this "threshing circle" was certainly disrupted when the weight of the equipment caused the Bancroft Creek Bridge to collapse. In 1920, these machines were the heaviest and most powerful equipment for miles around. How did they move them from the bridge?

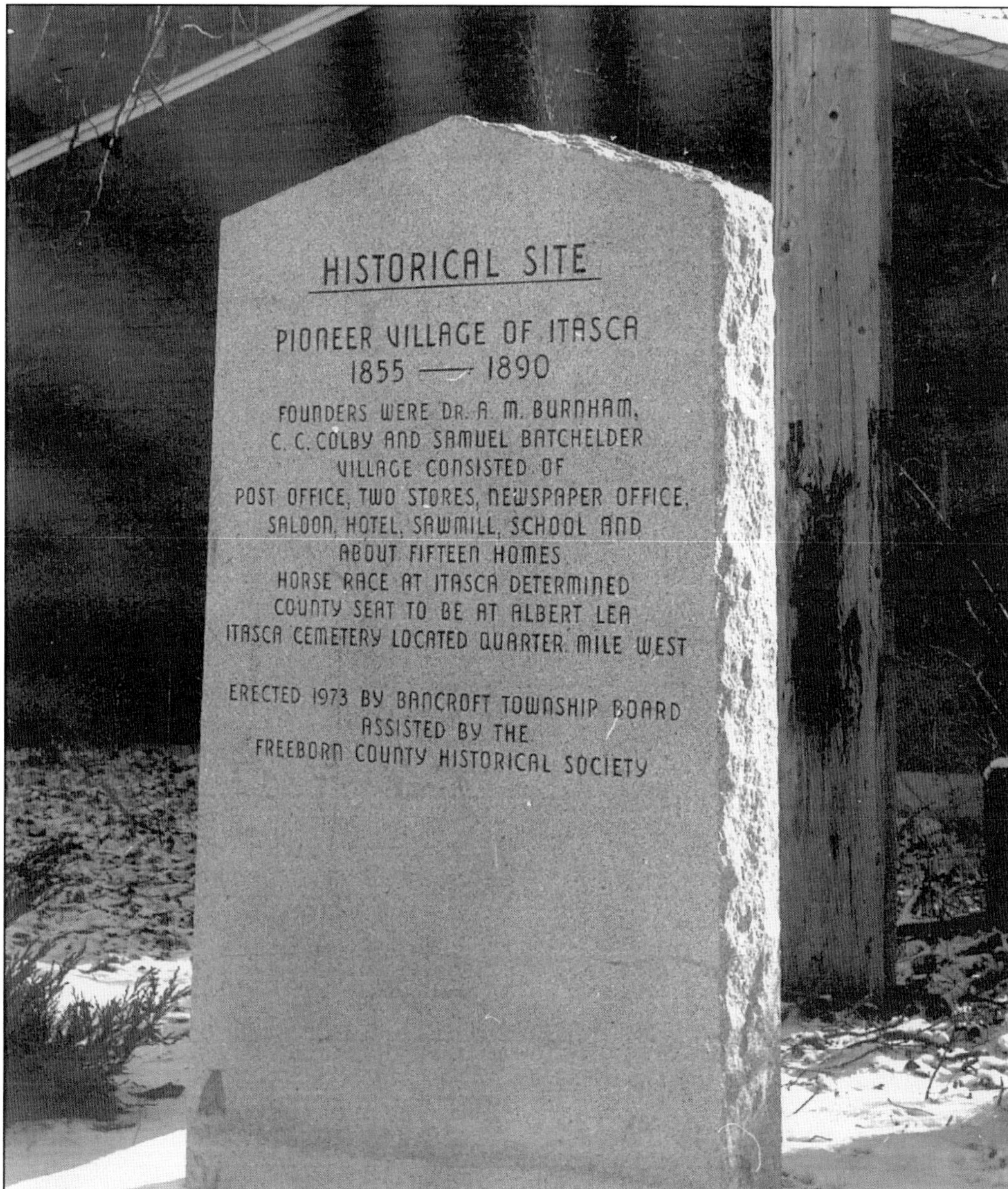

In 1855, Charles C. Colby settled in section 6, Albert Lea Township, and took land in Section 31, Bancroft Township, in which the village of Itasca was platted. Samuel Batchelder and A. M. Burnham arrived, and a post office and newspaper were established. Botsford, Hall, Dunbar, Pickett, and Longworth were also names identified with the village that hoped to become the county seat, but by 1911 it was occupied by Wedge Nursery. The following is from Ida Pickett Bell's 1930 letter, describing her trip to Itasca in the 1850s: "After we crossed the Mississippi River at McGregor (Iowa), our trials began. Roads were mostly cross country trails. Many times a wagon mired and father had to unload everything and sometimes go a long distance for a piece of timber strong enough to pry out the wheels. We had campfires and mother cooked. Sometimes it rained so we had nothing hot. We walked up the big hills, and as we met teams, the constant salutation was 'Hurrah for Lincoln'."

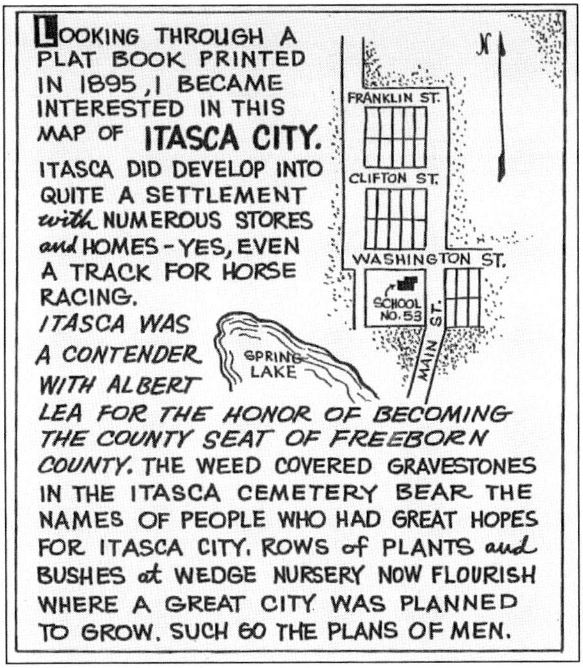

Hi-Lites and Shadows of Yesterday and Today was drawn by Irv Sorenson in 1963.

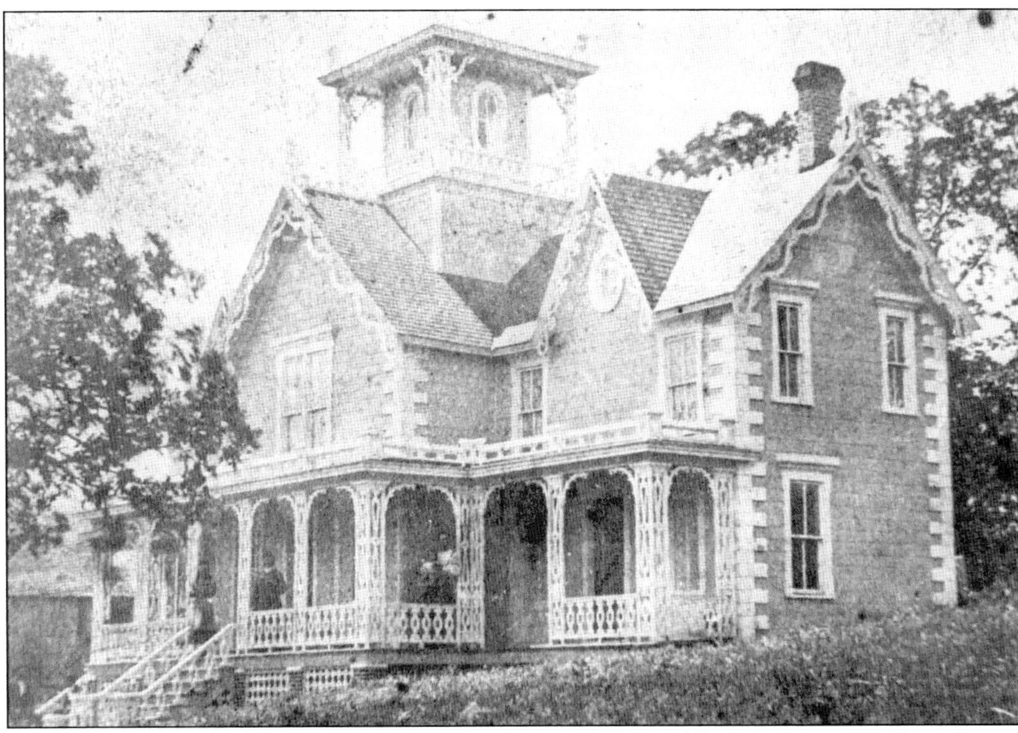

Dr. A. M. Burnham moved from Shell Rock in 1857 and started the "booming" in the village of Itasca (sometimes spelled Itaska, also known as Freeborn Springs). He built this beautiful home, painted pink and white, on the land that Lieutenant Albert M. Lea had called Paradise Prairie, one of the most beautiful spots he had ever seen. Burnham was prominent in the affairs of the community and an important voice in the county seat controversy.

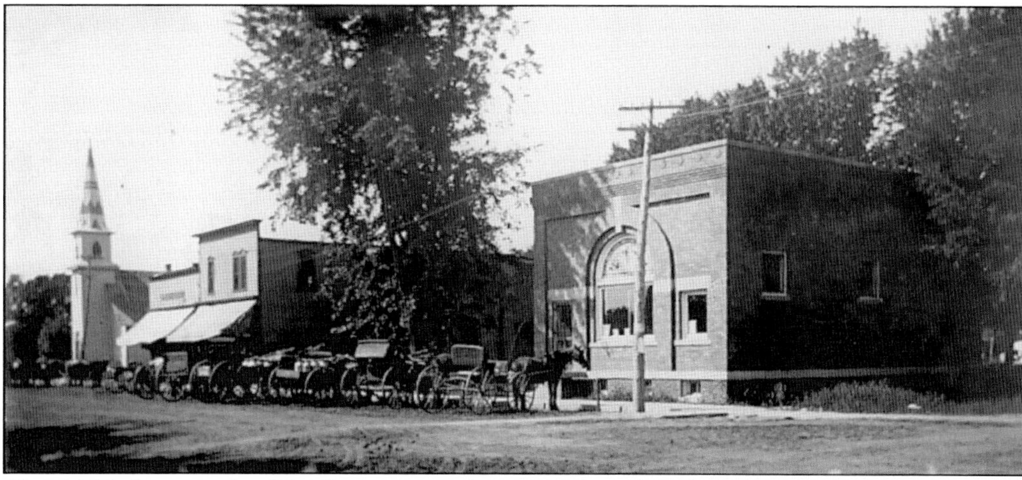

This 1906 photograph of Freeborn shows the Methodist Church, Gilmore & Purdie Store, and the First State Bank. "In 1857, L.T. Scott erected a hotel on the lakeshore. . . . The first religious services in the village were held at this hotel by an itinerant preacher who chanced to stop . . . and was offered free accommodations if he would stay over Sunday and preach." (*History of Freeborn County* [1911].)

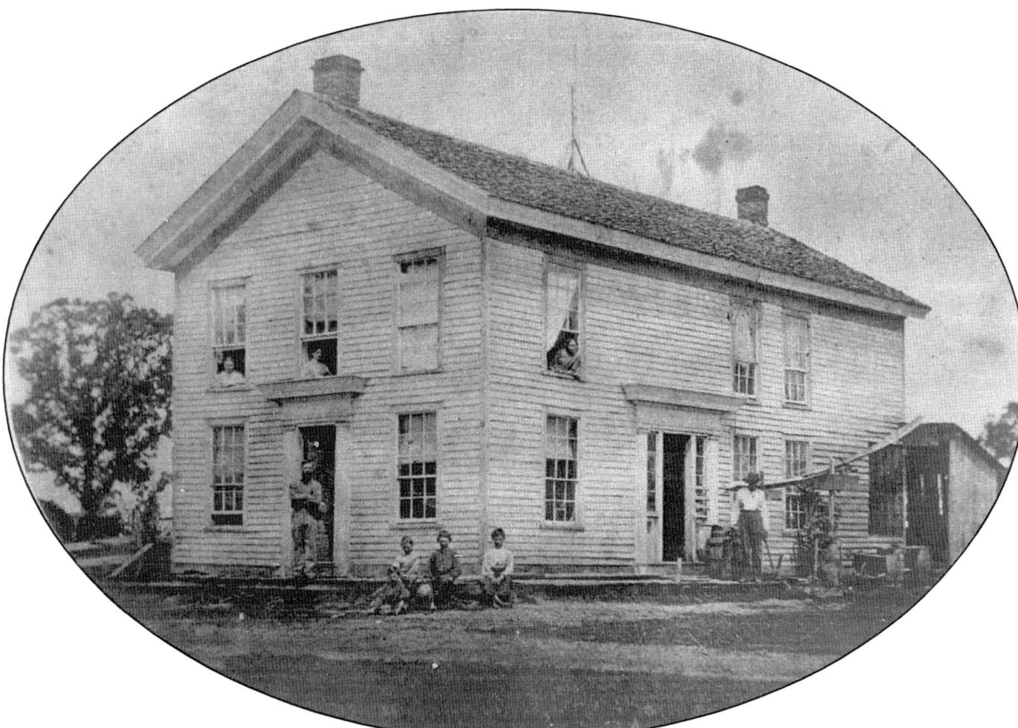

FCHS archives identify this building as the Chase Hotel, 1859–1899, located west of the Freeborn business area. L.T. Scott is said to have built Freeborn's first hotel, which also housed the first general store. Scott was prominent in community affairs and farmed, hauling his grain to Hastings, a six-day trip by ox team. At times he received only 35¢ a bushel for his grain.

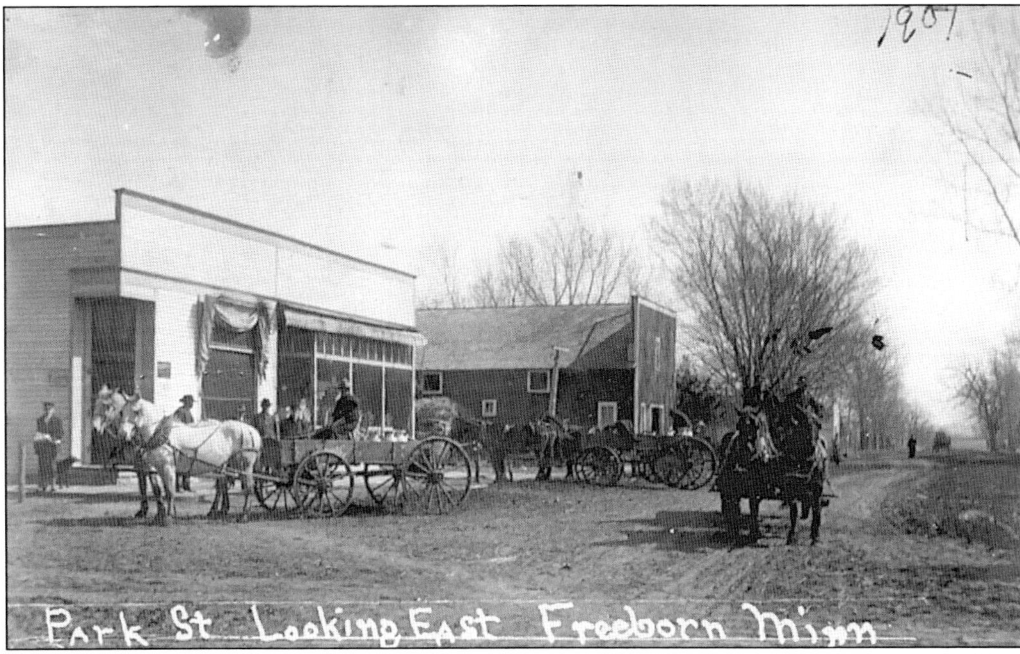

Dr. C.R. Butturff came to Freeborn in 1912 and opened his office and a drugstore in the building on the left side of this photograph. The livery stable is next to it. Other Freeborn businesses listed in the *History of Freeborn County* are: a bank, a creamery, two general stores, a blacksmith shop, an elevator, a hotel, a barber shop, and a meat market.

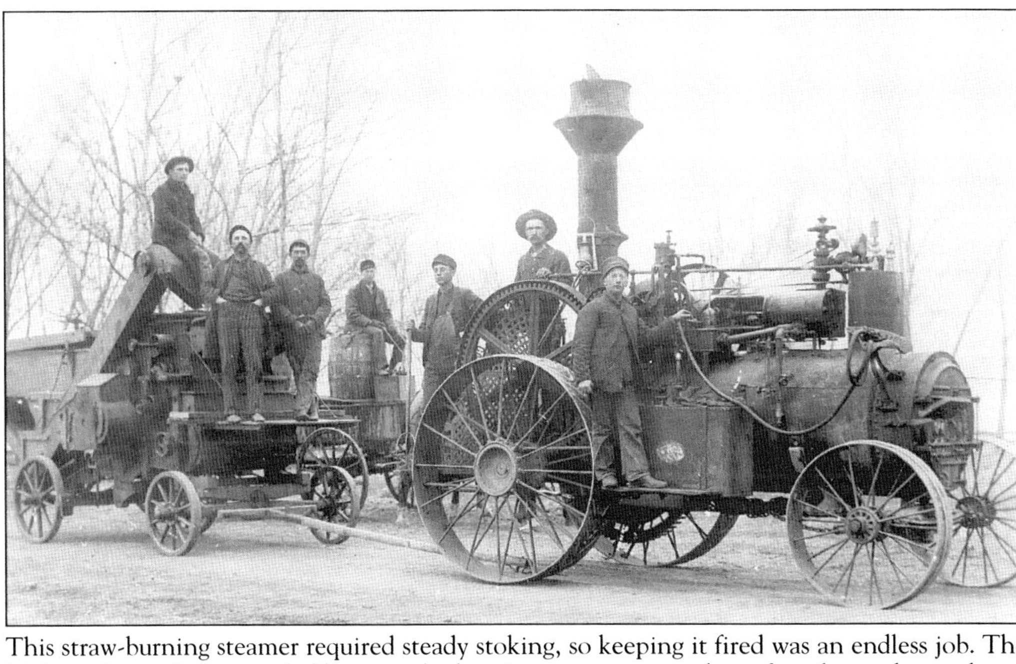

This straw-burning steamer required steady stoking, so keeping it fired was an endless job. The high smoke stack was needed because the burning straw sent out lots of sparks, so the stack was hinged for low clearances. The clover huller is similar to an early threshing machine. It would separate the seed from mature clover to be used for the next season's planting.

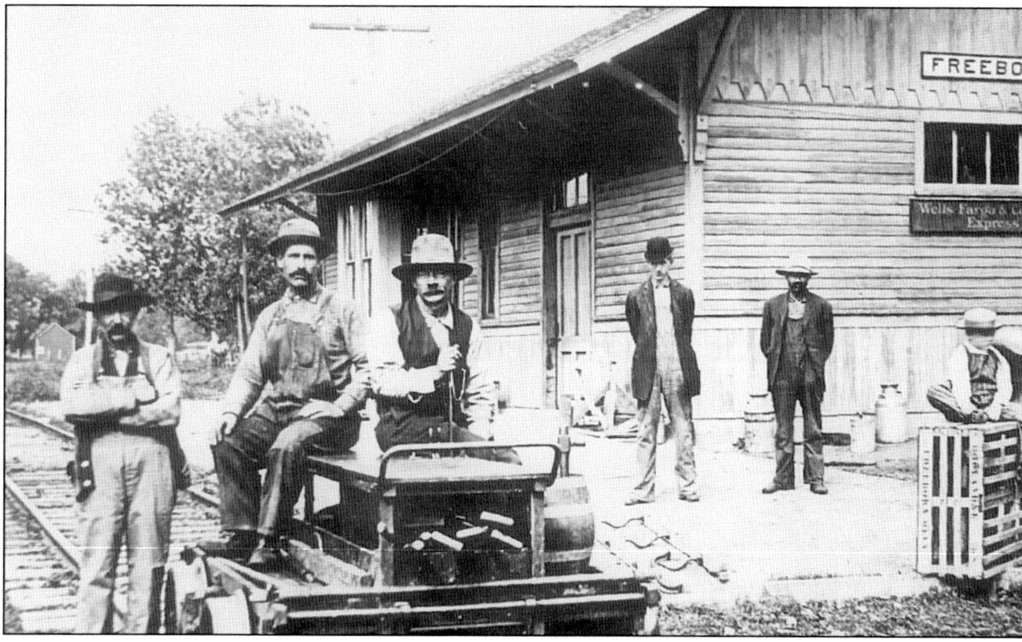

In March 1907, a line called the Duluth, St. Cloud, Glencoe, and Mankato Railroad was completed from Albert Lea, northwesterly through Freeborn, and on to St. Clair. In 1911, the line was sold to the Chicago and Milwaukee Company. It was known locally as "The Alphabet Line," and also "The Bug line." The Freeborn depot also housed the Wells Fargo Agency.

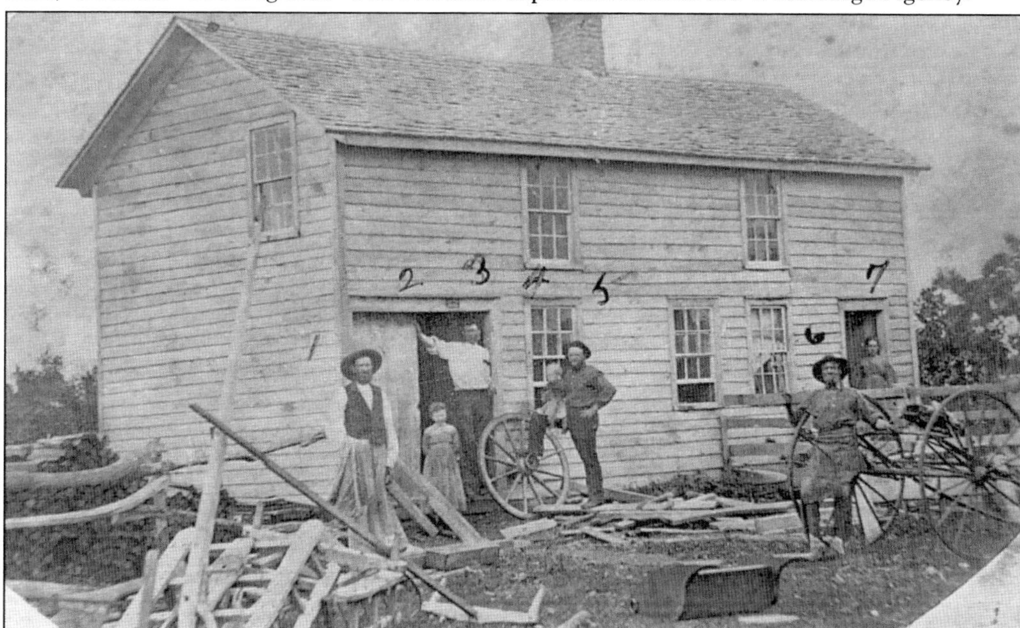

Blacksmith and wagon maker David Scoville (shown #5 holding his son Al) arrived from New York around 1865. He had the ability to cut rock, ash, and hickory trees from the shores of Freeborn Lake to make hubs and spokes of wheels. When moving west, he had shipped four wagons to Chicago by train. There he was offered a quarter of section of land, where Chicago now stands, in exchange for the wagons, but he chose to move on to Minnesota.

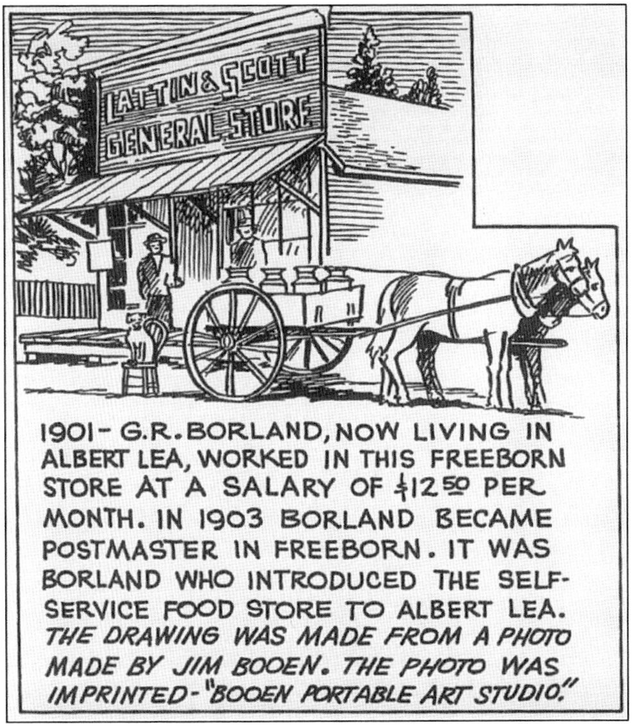

Hi-Lites and Shadows of Yesterday and Today drawn by Irv Sorenson in 1963.

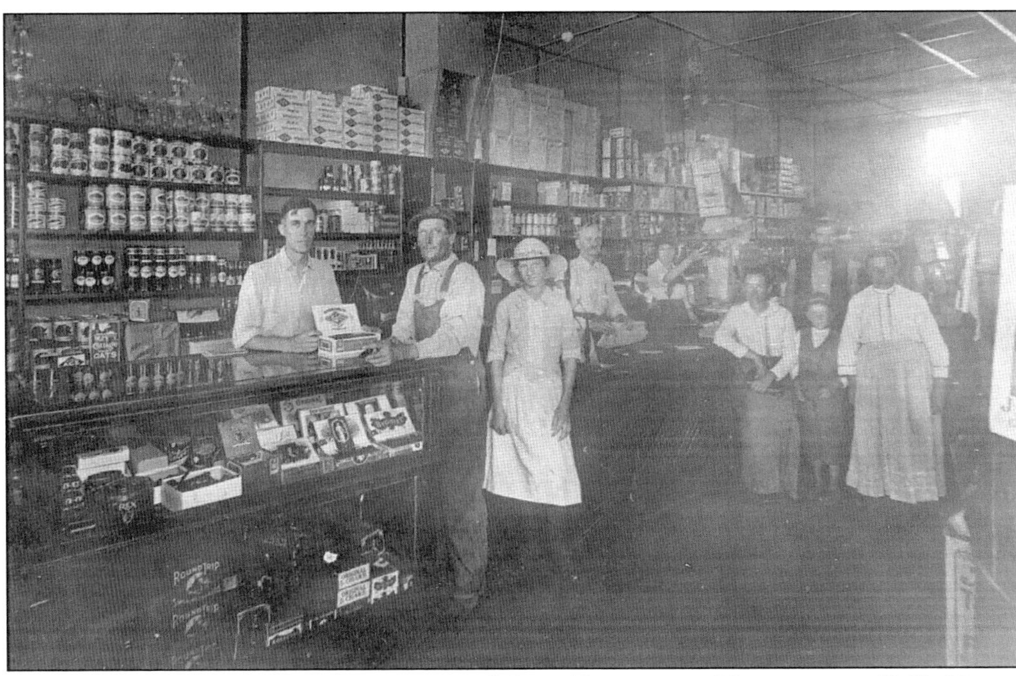

O.S. Gilmore, a Civil War Veteran, moved from Vermont to Minnesota in 1865. He was employed for two years in T.A. Southwick's store before opening his own general mercantile business. It eventually became known as O.S. Gilmore & Son and was operated in Freeborn for almost 30 years. Shown behind the counter are: Ansel S. Gilmore on the left, and John W. Bates and Mrs. Clara Hinkley, clerks, on the right.

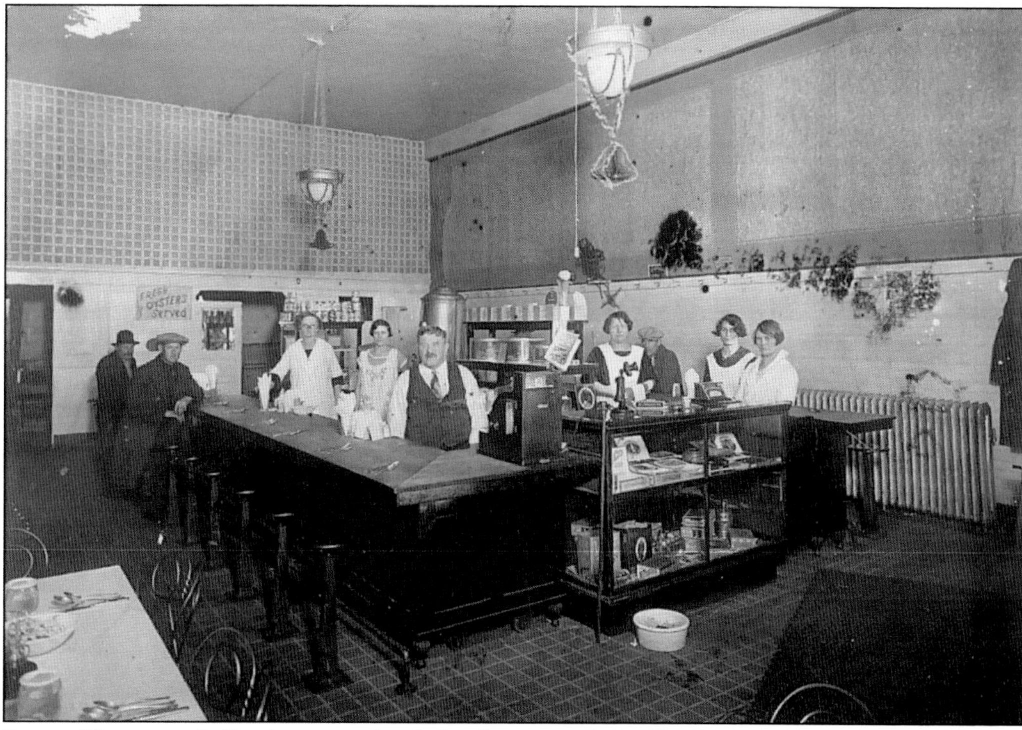

Paper Christmas bells decorate the light fixtures of the Freeborn Café, c. 1920. Caroline Rasmussen is the waitress shown directly behind the telephone. Notice the wooden counter tops and stool setting, the spittoon, the pegs for hanging coats on the far wall, the "fresh oysters served" sign near the kitchen door, and the bentwood chairs at the table.

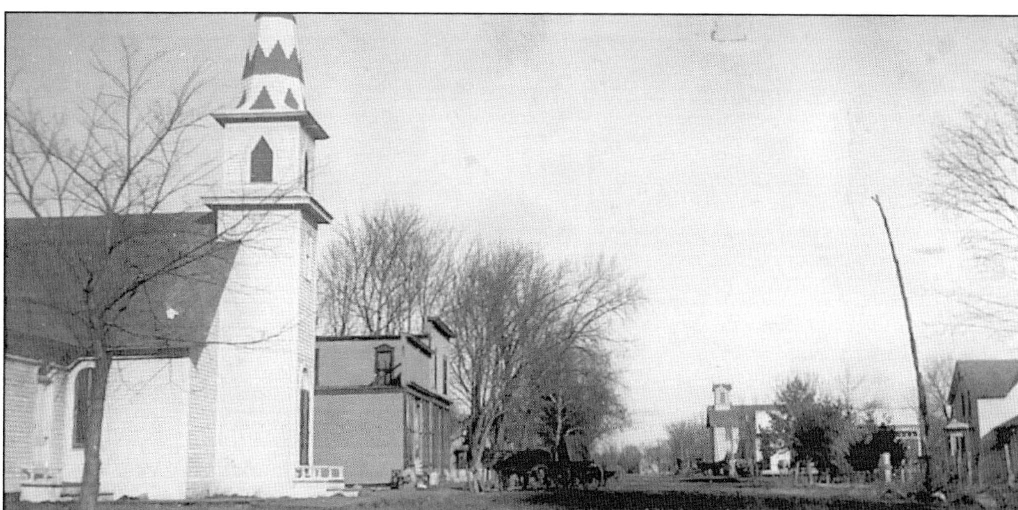

The religious service in Freeborn was held in the L.T. Scott Hotel in 1858. For several years the Baptists, Congregationalists, and Methodists shared the same church buildings, ministers, and church services. In 1919, the Ladies Aids merged, forming the Community Church Society. In 1932, the Methodist Church was struck by lightning and burned, and by 1936, 102 members of the Methodist Church joined the Congregational Church.

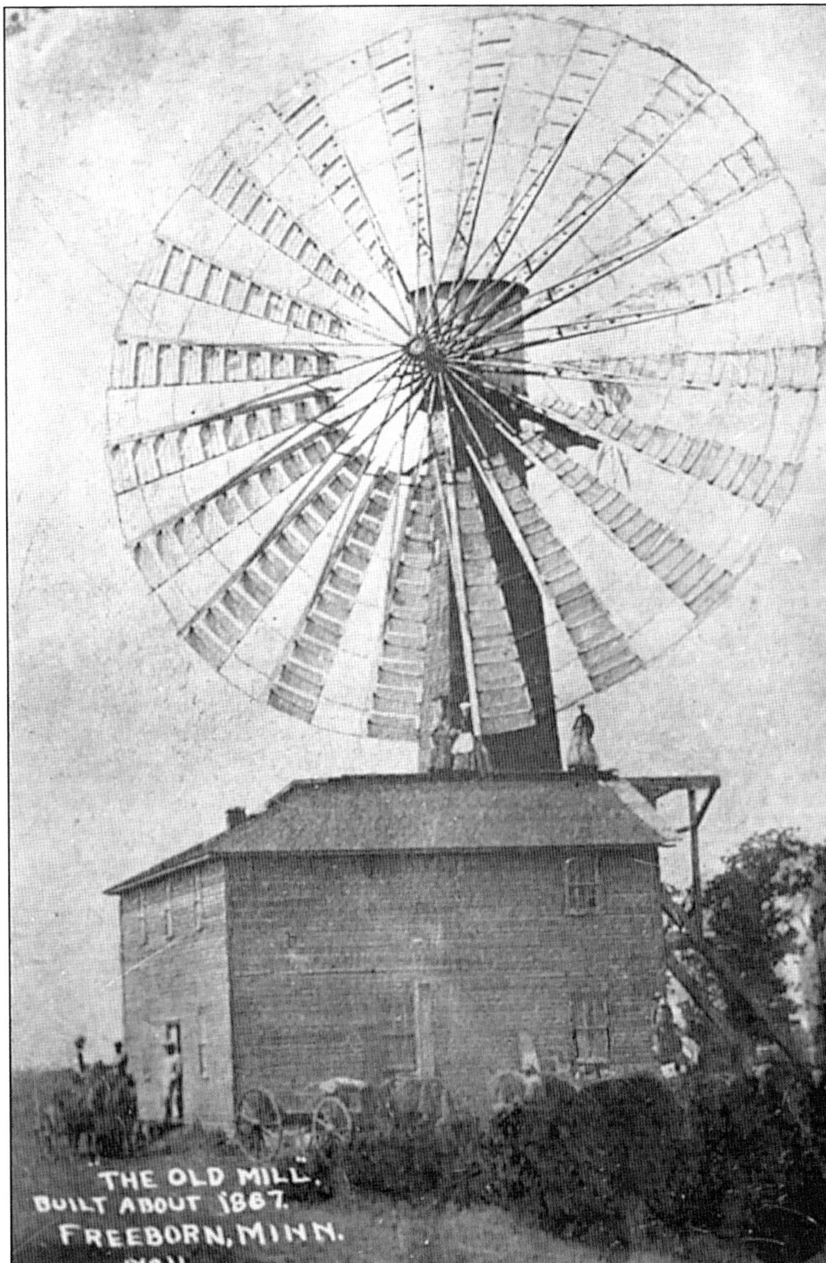

"The Old Mill" in Freeborn ground feed and flour. It was built in 1867 in the western part of town and operated until June 27, 1874, when the 50-foot windmill blew off. One of two such mills in Minnesota, it remained a county landmark for many years, but was finally torn down in 1898. In 1881, *The Graphic*, a London, England newspaper, printed a full page of drawings portraying the English perception of life on a prairie farm in Minnesota. Like this Freeborn windmill, the drawings had a definite European influence. The sketches show a turf house, hay stable, interior fireplace, farmer carrying an umbrella, and fine riding horses pulling farm equipment—all misconceptions of what pioneer life was really like. Immigrants brought these ideas to America and applied them. Some were very successful, and others were not.

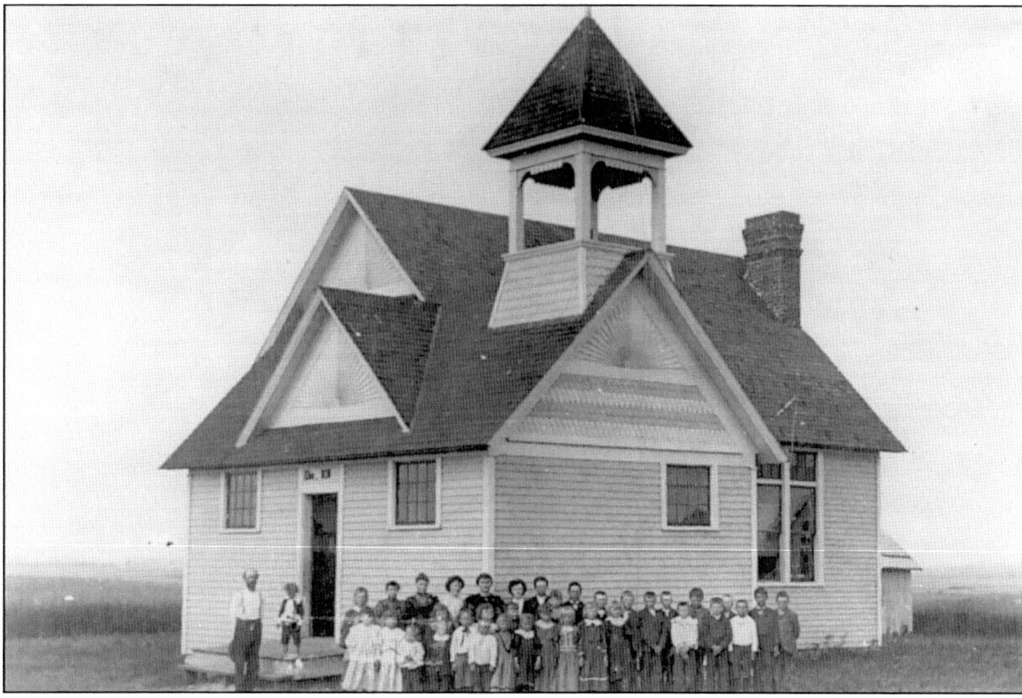

District No. 101 was organized in the spring of 1876, and a schoolhouse was erected in Section 28, at a size of 18 by 22 feet, and a cost of $450. The first teacher was Miss Emily Blighton, with ten scholars in attendance. District 101 joined with Districts 12 and 13 on December 18, 1919, when the first consolidation of country schools in Freeborn County took place.

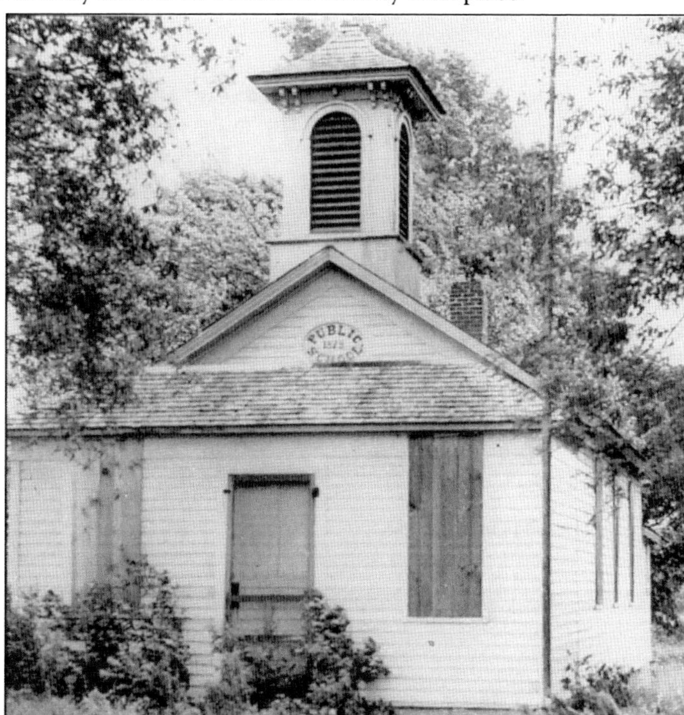

District 15, Carlston Township, was organized in 1859, and in 1860 the first school was taught by Martha Stane in a log house. She had nine scholars and received $18 per month as compensation. A new schoolhouse was built in 1877. At a cost of $640, it was equipped with patent seats for 40 scholars. It was called the Melander School, after John L. Melander, one of the earliest residents of the township.

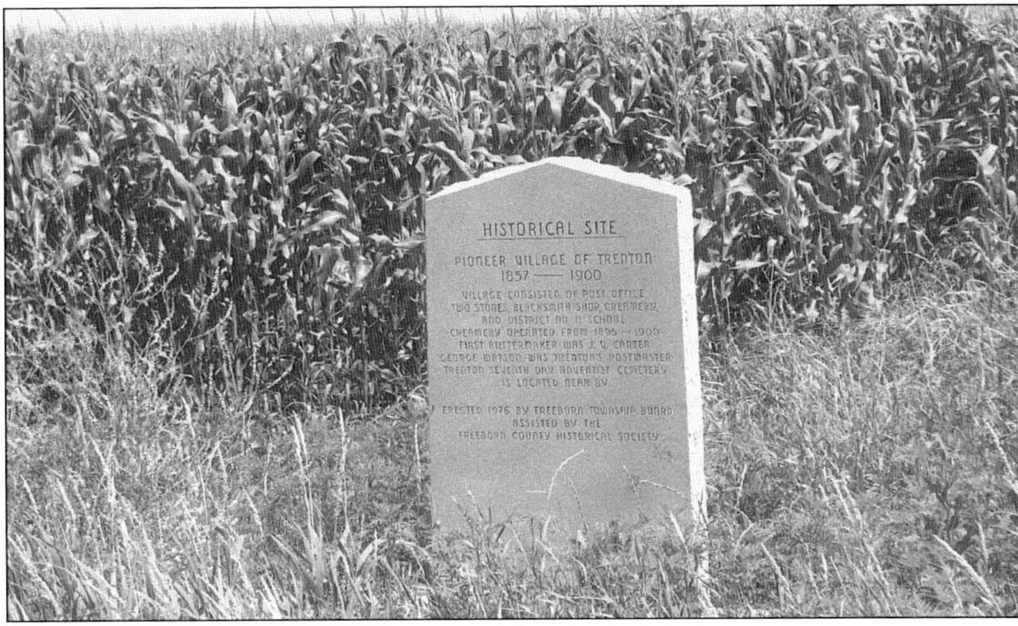

According to the *Freeborn County Heritage*, "On March 4, 1856, an advertisement appeared in a New Jersey newspaper. Written by John W. Ayers, it stated that he had visited Freeborn County, Minnesota and found an ideal spot [in Trenton] to make his home in the northwest corner of the township. . . . Several families were planning to start for Minnesota about the 10th of May, to choose their locations, and make their claims. . . ."

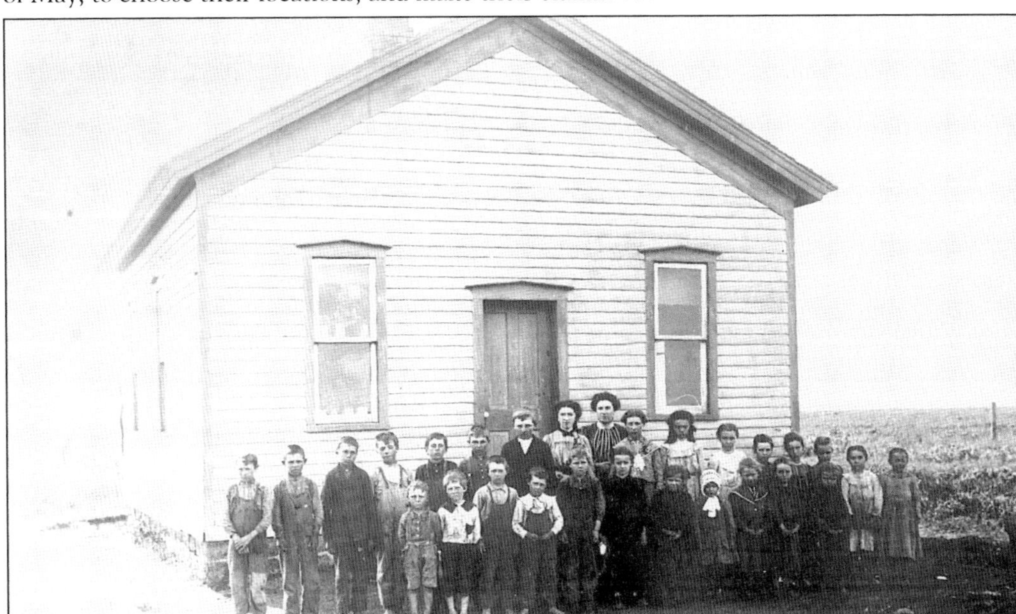

The Ayers party arrived in Freeborn Township in 1857. They immediately established a school (District 11, shown here) and a Seventh Day Baptist Church. John Ayers was an early Indian agent opening his home for the protection of settlers in 1862. He also served as postmaster with the office in his home near Trenton Lake. The mail arrived weekly for Alden by way of Freeborn.

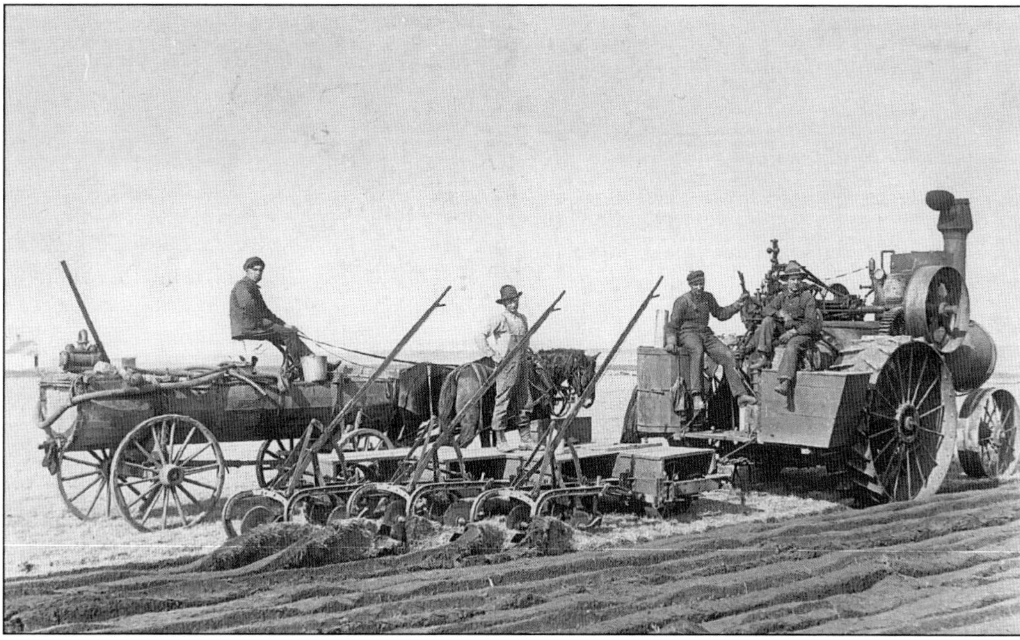

There had to be an air of excitement when prairie sod was turned for the first time—hard work for both man and machine. The steam engine, a brute for strength, moved about 1.5 miles per hour and was refilled from the hand-pumped water wagon. The six-bottom plow was controlled by three handles, requiring less manpower.

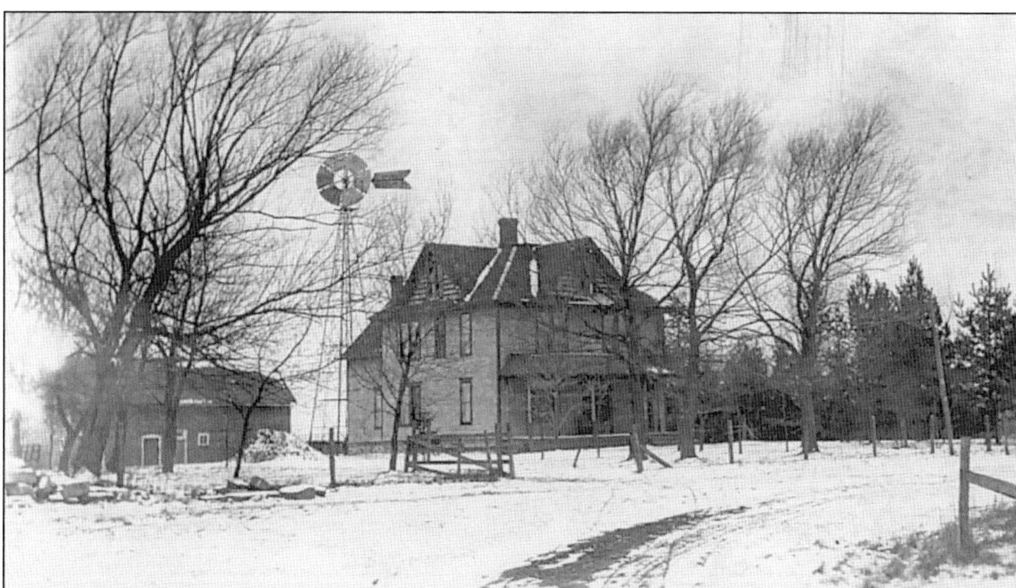

This peaceful, rural, winter scene is only identified in the FCHS archives as a parsonage near Hartland in 1914. The Midwest square architectural style of home building became popular after 1900 because it adapted well to the new plumbing and heating systems. The improvements were known only in the cities, as the windmill by the out building testifies to more traditional water access.

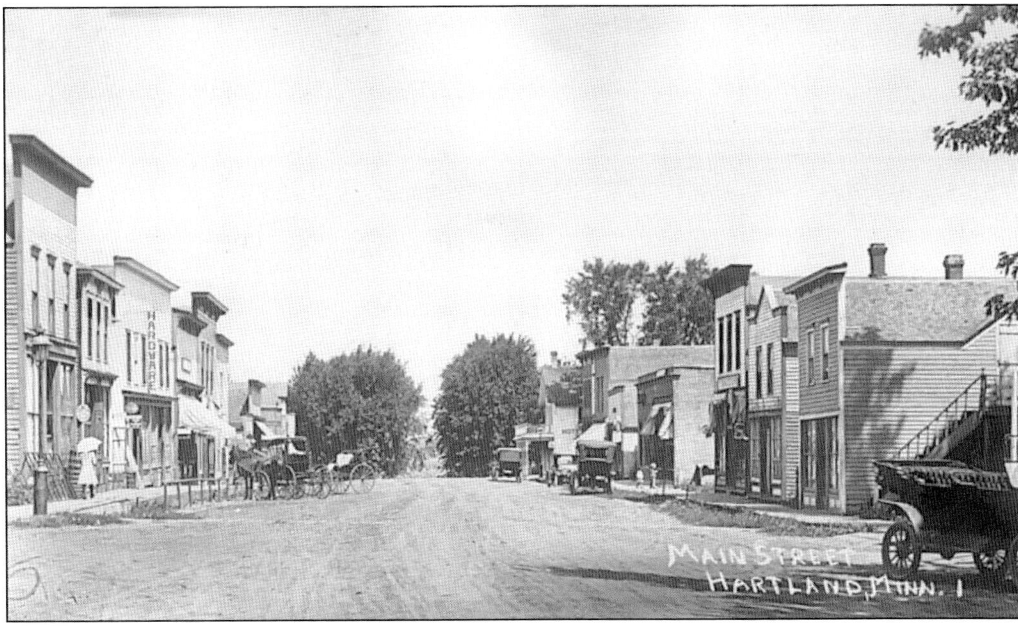

Hartland got its start in 1877. In its first three months $15,825 was spent for new buildings. This amount built 23 business places (many with living quarters on the second floor) and two dwellings. The most expensive building was the dry goods store at $1,500. Included were five saloons, ranging in cost from $400 to $1,000. The barber shop was $50. The dwellings cost $300 and $350. (*Hi-Lites and Shadows*, by Irv Sorenson, 1952.)

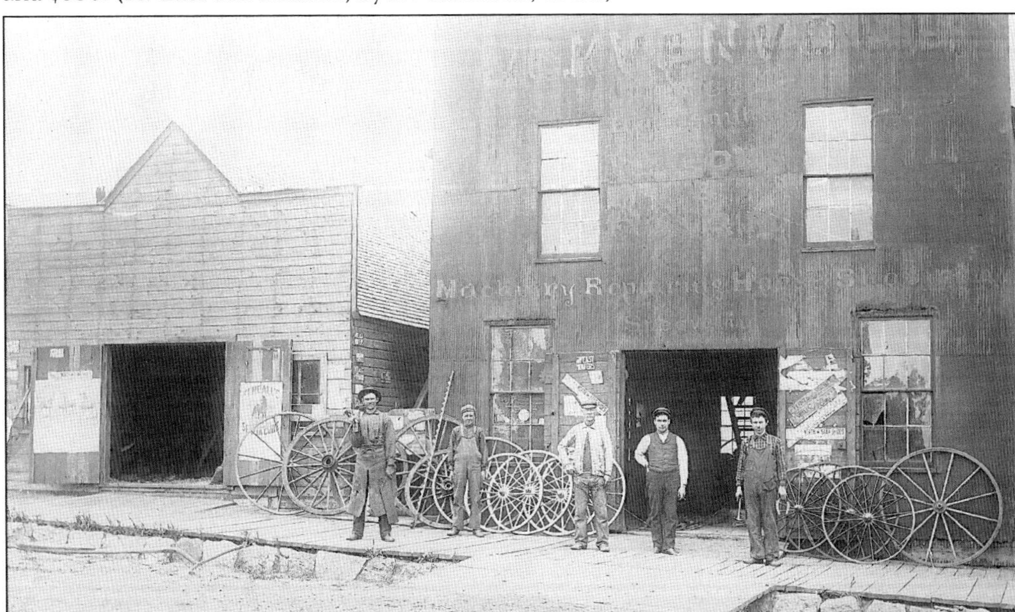

J.O. Kvenvold is shown near his blacksmith and wagon shop in Hartland (1889–1914), with three unidentified men and his helper on the far right. In 1901, the citizens of Hartland voted 39 to 33 to install a water system consisting of a 1,500-barrel tank—100-feet high and on iron supports—an eight-horse-power gasoline engine and engine house, 2,000 feet of water mains, and nine fire hydrants.

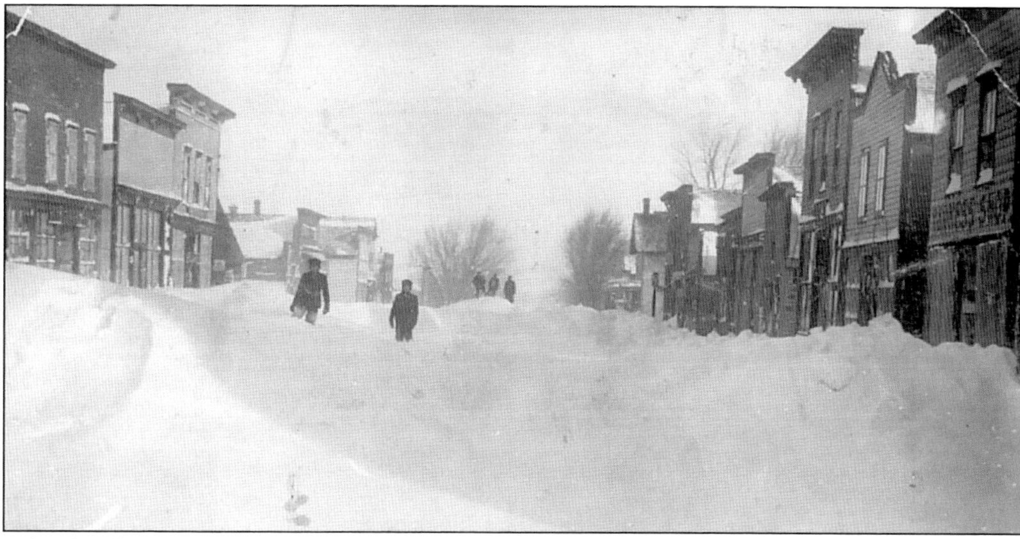

What kind of snow removal equipment did the village of Hartland have in 1909? One can only imagine the muscle power required to clear the streets so that the stores could open for business. Twenty years earlier, Hartland businesses were listed as: general store (3), saloon, temperance saloon and restaurant, carpenters (4), restaurant and hotel, blacksmith, shoemaker, hardware store, lumber yard, coal dealer, cattle buyer, hay barn, and wheat buyer.

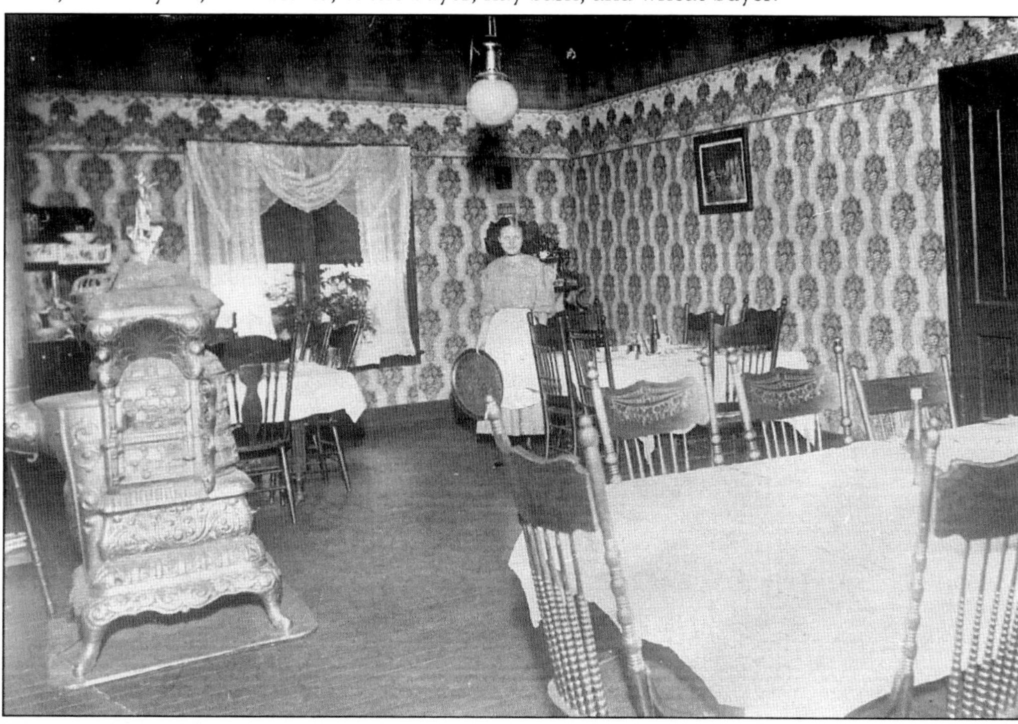

Waitress Alma Olson pauses with her serving tray in the dining room of the American House Hotel in Hartland around 1908. Notice the beautiful, hard-coal heater at the left. The 1899 city directory advertises, "American Hotel with modern improvements, rates $1.50 per day, long distance telephone office, under entire new management. Stop with us and we will try and please you. Thofson & Ackland Proprietors."

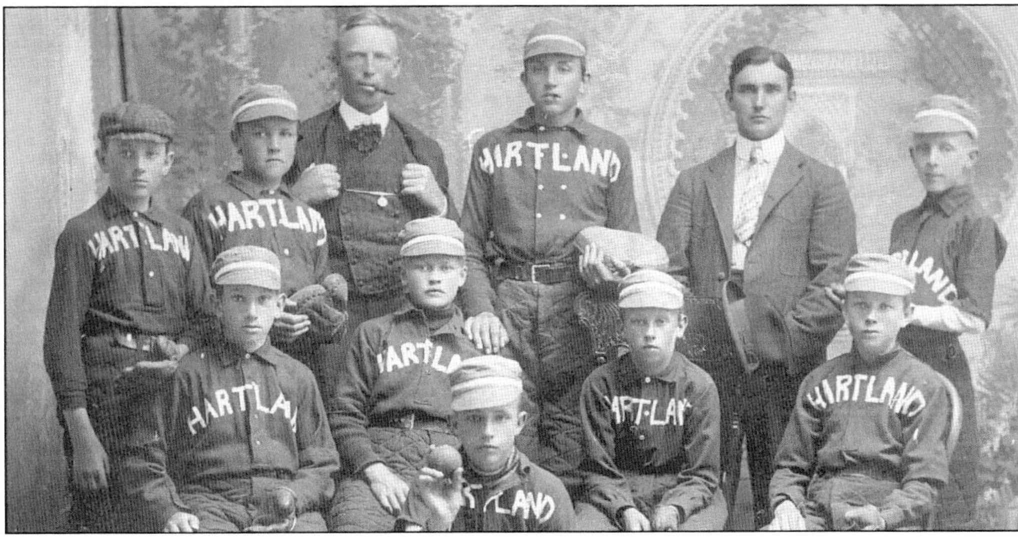

The Hartland boys baseball team members are pictured here from left to right: (in front) unidentified; (first row) Will Harris, Harry Borgen, and two unidentified boys; (second row) Jake Sorlie, Albert Gomsrud, Constable John Hooser, Theodore Gomsrud, John Laudert, and Edwin Stensrud. The names Gomsrud and Laudert surface in a *Hartland Herald* article dated October 13, 1910, which states, "The playing record is of such quality that we are not stretching it any when we claim the amateur championship of southern Minnesota."

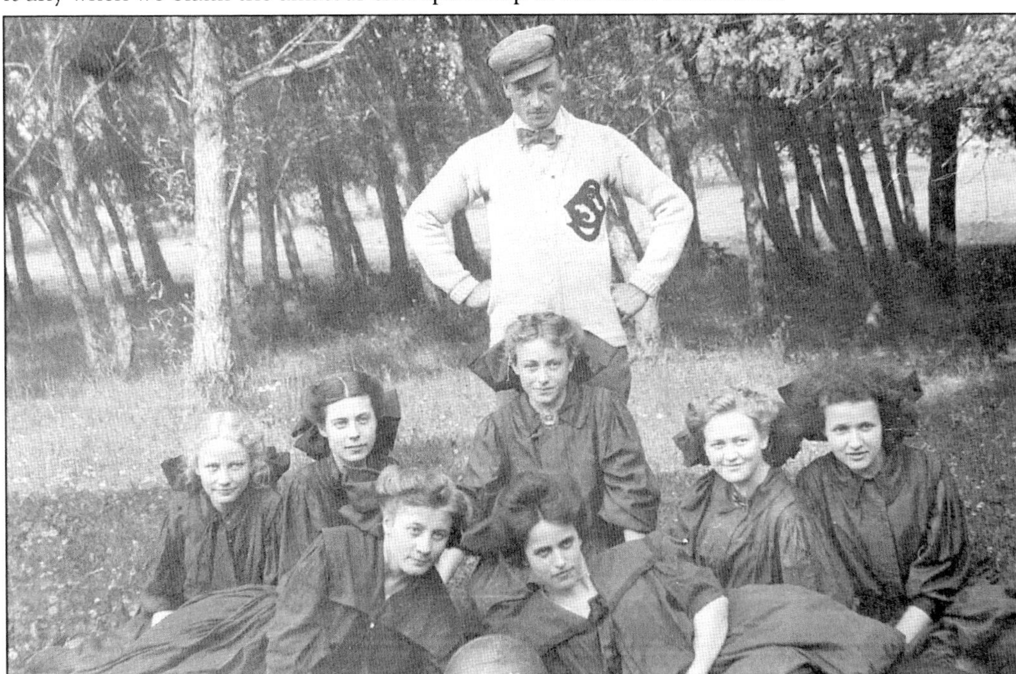

The hands-on-hips stance and the attempted serious look on the face of Coach Art Gaarder are reflected in the expressions on the faces of this 1909–1910 Hartland girls basketball team. When they posed for the camera man, each seemed to be interpreting their season in a different manner. Note their bloomer-skirt uniforms and big bows in their hair. Gaarder taught at both Hartland and Albert Lea Schools.

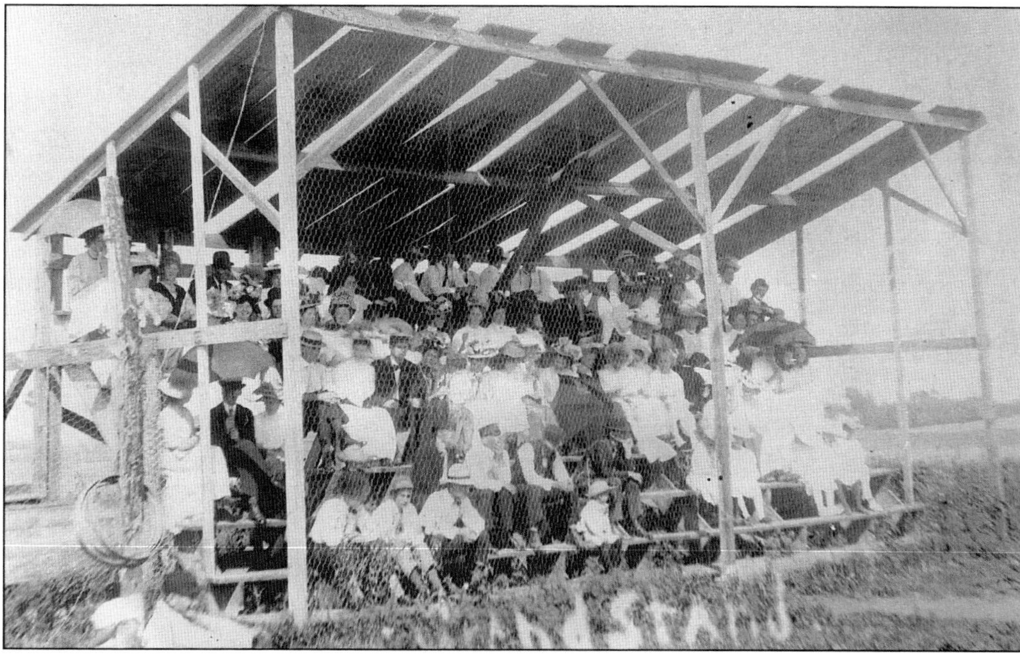

The Hartland bleachers are filled to capacity at this August 1910 ball game with Manchester. In September another game took place between the single and married men of Hartland. A *Hartland Herald* article states, ". . . the hen-pecks challenged the heart-frees to a duel to death . . . in the last death grapple a benedict (confirmed bachelor—newly married) busted the beak off the ball and dusted the doormat of victory. The count stood 10 to 9."

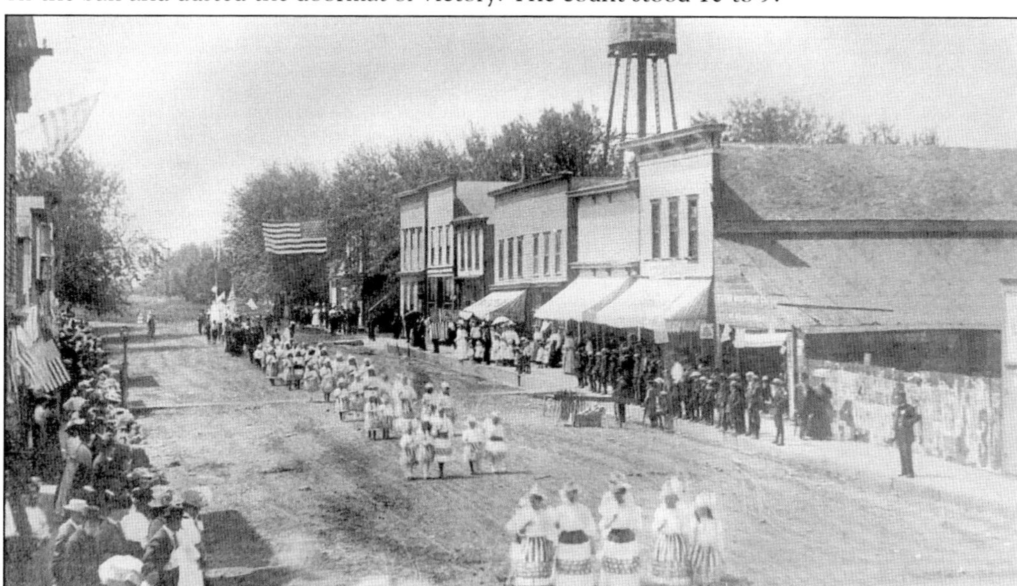

By the time of this patriotic parade in Hartland in 1910, early competitiveness had long been forgotten. In 1877, A.E. Johnson owned land on the west side of the railroad, and William Morin on the east. Both platted their land, beginning "a merry townsite fight" (*History of Freeborn County*). Buildings sprang up on both sides and, finally, Morin purchased land to the west of Johnson's, allowing business to center on the west side.

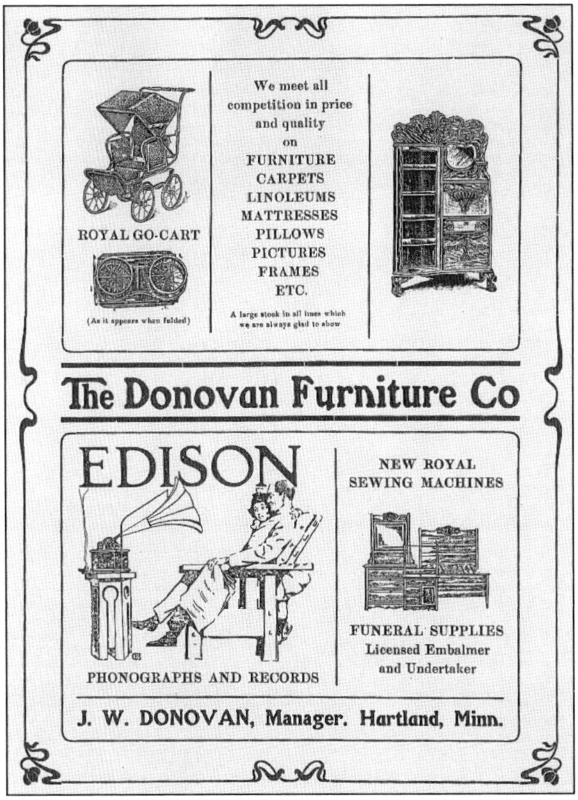

This Donovan Furniture Company advertisement is from the 1909 *Hartland Herald*.

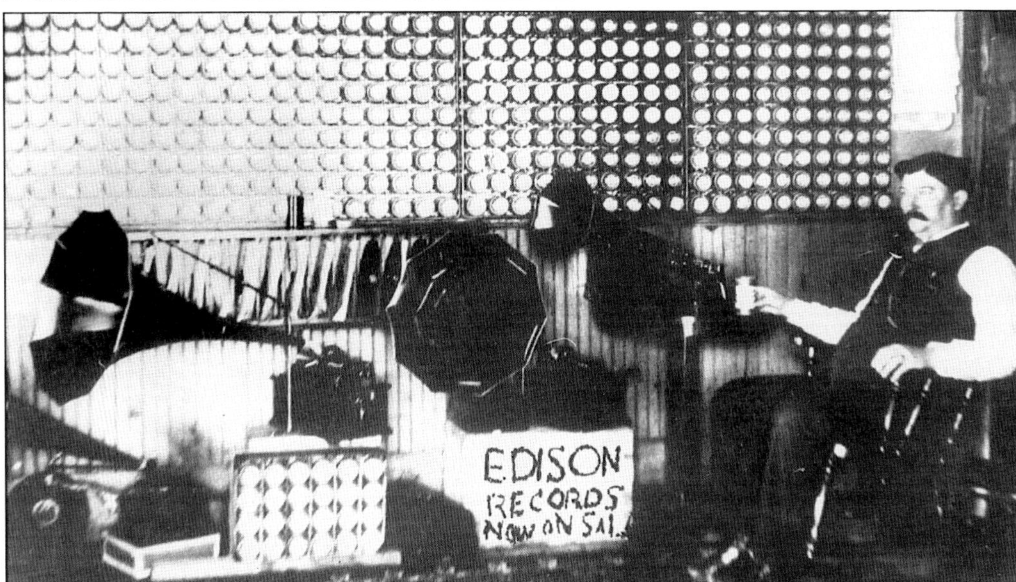

J.W. Donovan is shown with his large stock of Edison cylinder records displayed on a unique wall rack in his Hartland furniture store. He also sold phonographs, furniture, sewing machines, go-carts, mattresses, pictures, carpets, and linoleums. This multi-faceted business also offered funeral supplies and the services of a licensed embalmer and undertaker. His advertising stated, "A large stock in all lines which we are always glad to show." (*Hartland Herald*, 1909.)

Dr. Morton L. Head and R.H. Gardner opened this Hartland Drug Store in 1898, and in 1905 Dr. Head bought out his partner. In 1909 he advertised drugs, medicines, druggist supplies, and prescriptions accurately compounded. He also sold wallpapers, "the finest of this year's styles and designs," and, "paints for everything—interior decorating, house, barn, or buggy." Standing in front of the store, from left to right, are: Polly Sybilrud, Peter Sybilrud, unidentified, Helma Wulf, and Art Gaarder.

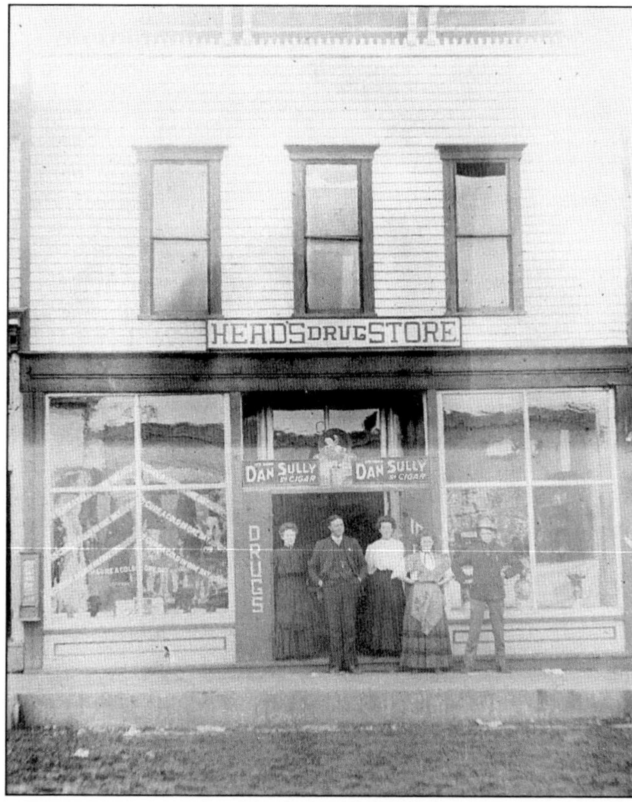

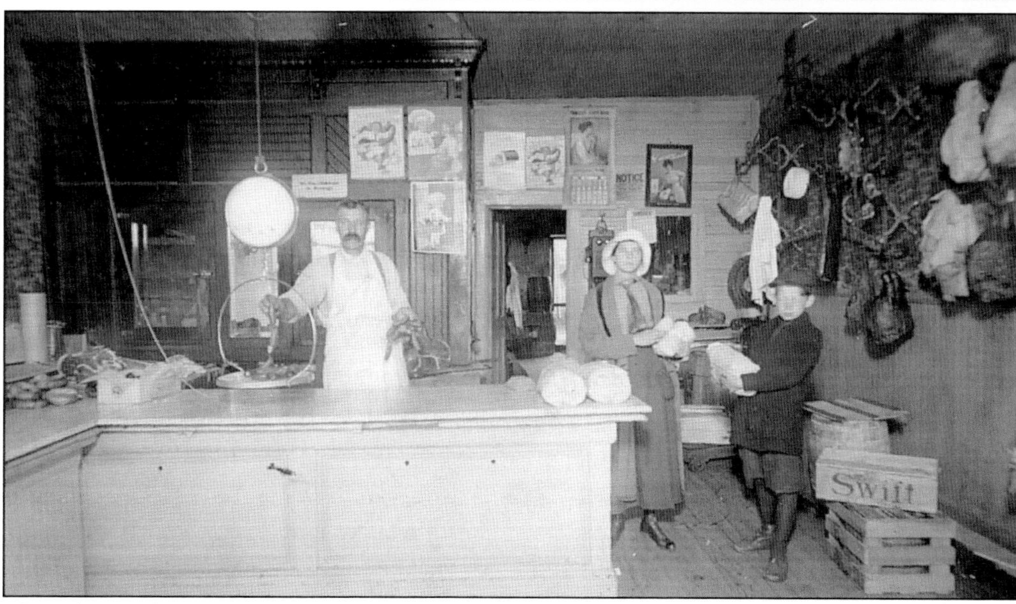

The Christopherson Brothers Meat Market was in operation in Hartland from approximately 1896 to 1915. The business was owned by brothers Carl, who in 1918 purchased Brundin Meat Market in Albert Lea, and Hans M., who was a stock buyer, one-time mayor of Hartland, and member of the school board. Owner Carl Christopherson and customers Edna Olson and George Brown are shown in the photograph.

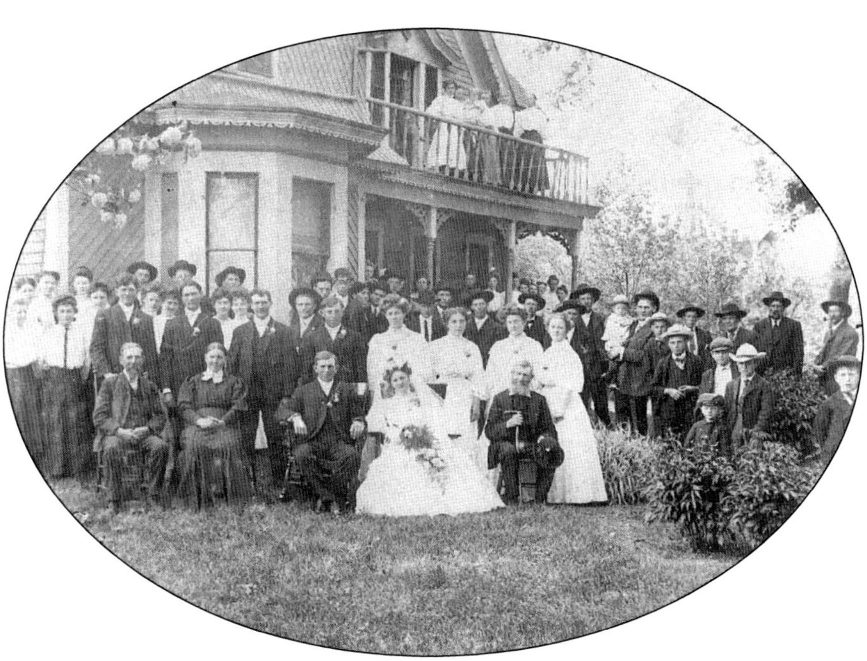

On June 2, 1906, the wedding of Miss Ida Knutson and Albert Miller took place at the synod church, and the reception was held at the home of B.L. Knutson. "The groom is a rising young man of sterling qualities and much ability. . . . That nothing but joy and prosperity may be the lot of this worthy young couple is the sincere wish of their many relatives and friends." (*Times-Enterprise*, June 6, 1906.)

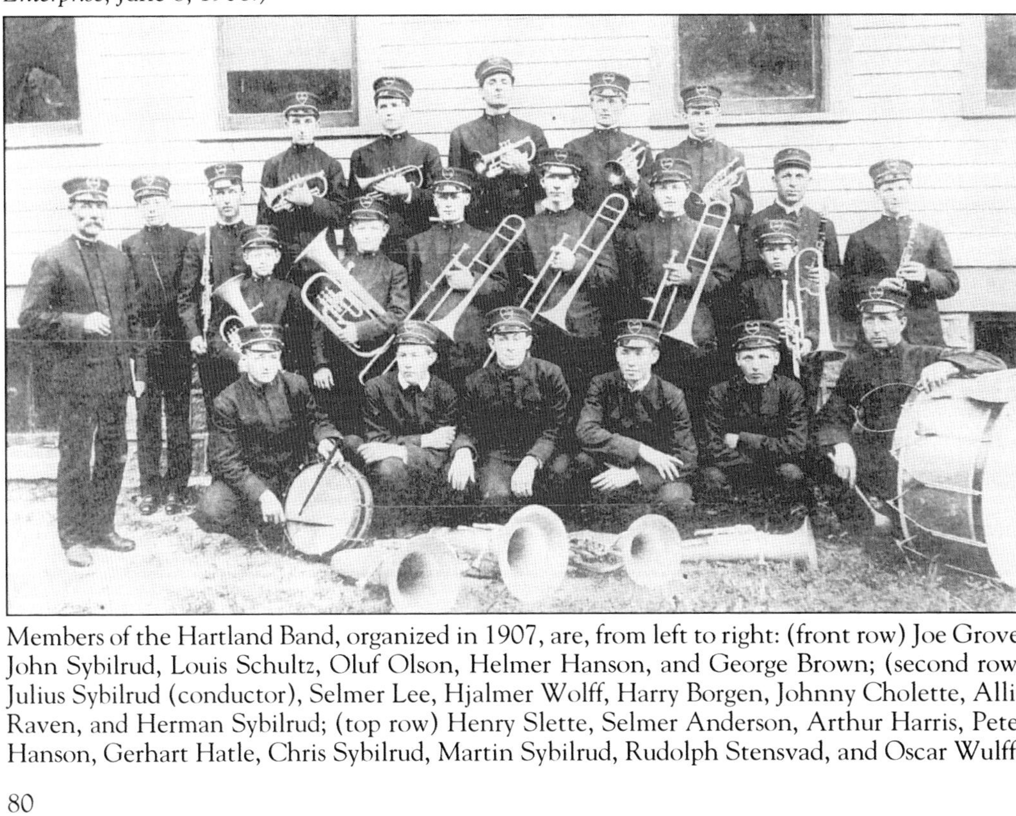

Members of the Hartland Band, organized in 1907, are, from left to right: (front row) Joe Grove, John Sybilrud, Louis Schultz, Oluf Olson, Helmer Hanson, and George Brown; (second row) Julius Sybilrud (conductor), Selmer Lee, Hjalmer Wolff, Harry Borgen, Johnny Cholette, Allie Raven, and Herman Sybilrud; (top row) Henry Slette, Selmer Anderson, Arthur Harris, Peter Hanson, Gerhart Hatle, Chris Sybilrud, Martin Sybilrud, Rudolph Stensvad, and Oscar Wulff.

Four

The Northeast

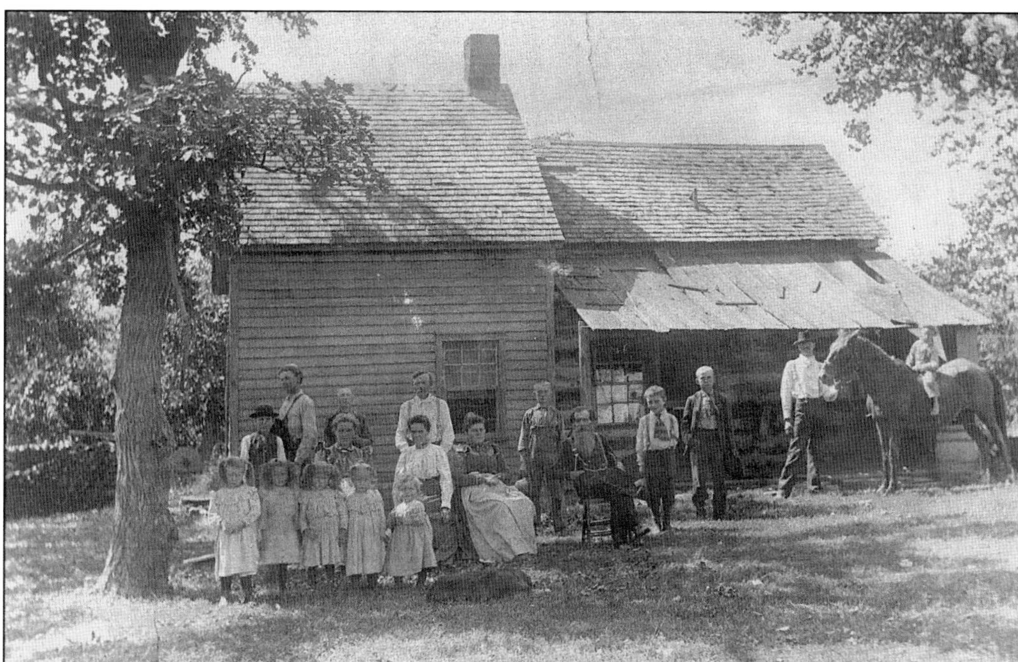

This undated photograph shows the Dearmin homestead near Moscow. The residence shows the original log house and an addition with wooden lap siding. Three Dearmin brothers and their mother and sister settled in Moscow Township in 1856. All three brothers, George, Robert, and Matthew, served in the Civil War. George and Robert were honorably discharged, and Matthew died in 1863 at Fort Abercrombie, Dakota Territory.

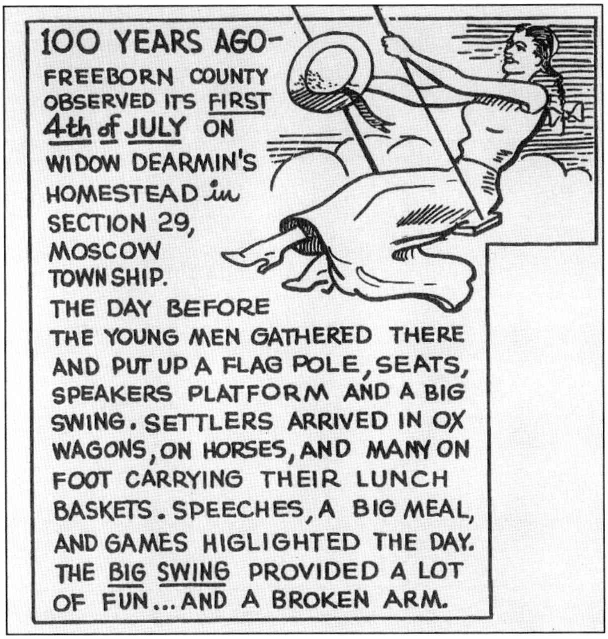

Hi-Lites and Shadows of Yesterday and Today drawn by Irv Sorenson - 1957.

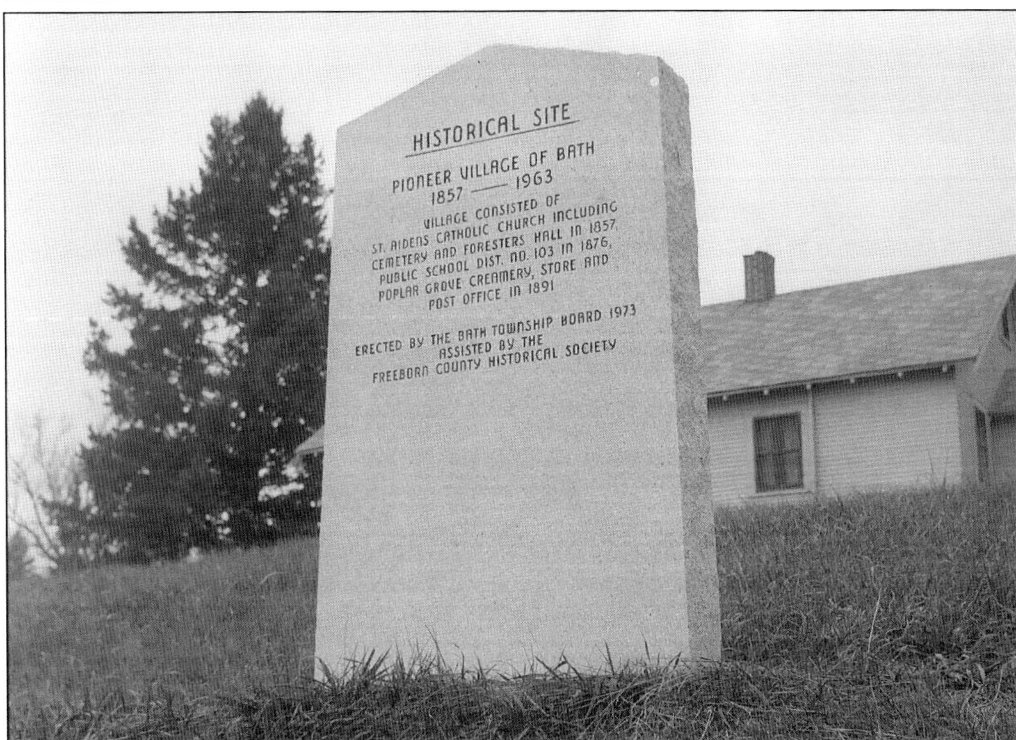

Bath Village was a small settlement located on the line between Sections 7 and 8 in Bath Township. It consisted of a store, post office, St. Aidens Catholic Church and cemetery, Foresters Hall, Public School District #103, and the Poplar Grove Creamery, which was originally called the North Star Creamery. Organized at an earlier date, the creamery began operations on May 20, 1892.

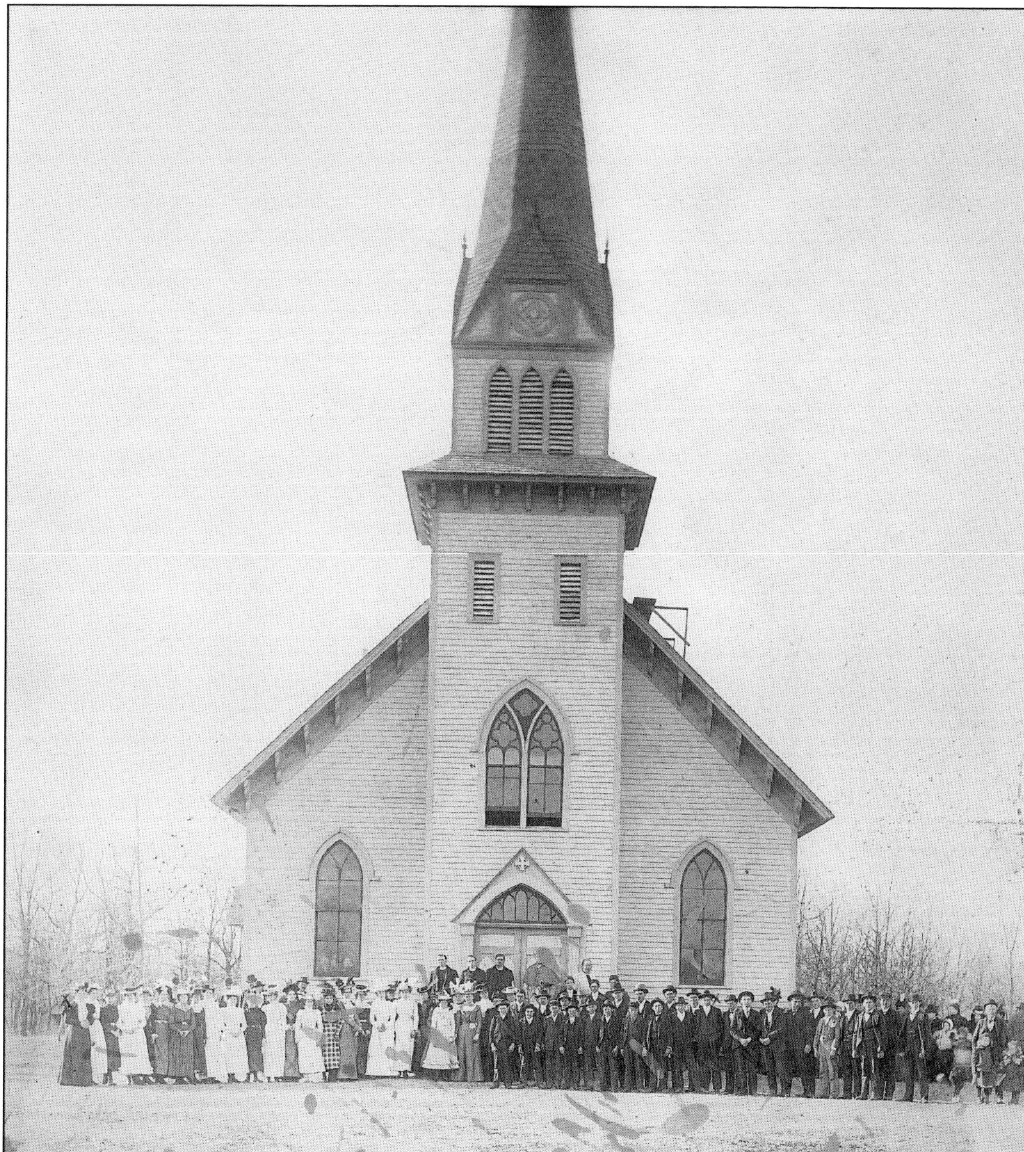

The congregation and confirmation class are shown here in 1899, in front of St. Aidens Catholic Church in Bath. The first St. Aidens was a log church built in 1857, and the second was a frame structure built in 1865. The third, according to the *Freeborn County Standard*, was built in August of 1882: "The Catholics of Bath, are about to commence the erection of a new church edifice in that town on Section 8, near the site of the old church. The main building will be 39 x 64, with a 16 foot octagon sanctuary in the rear, and a spire 85 feet high in front. The cost of the building will be about $4,000, which amount has been almost wholly raised by the liberality of the people of the neighborhood. The contract has been let to Thomas Walsh of this city, which insures a good job."

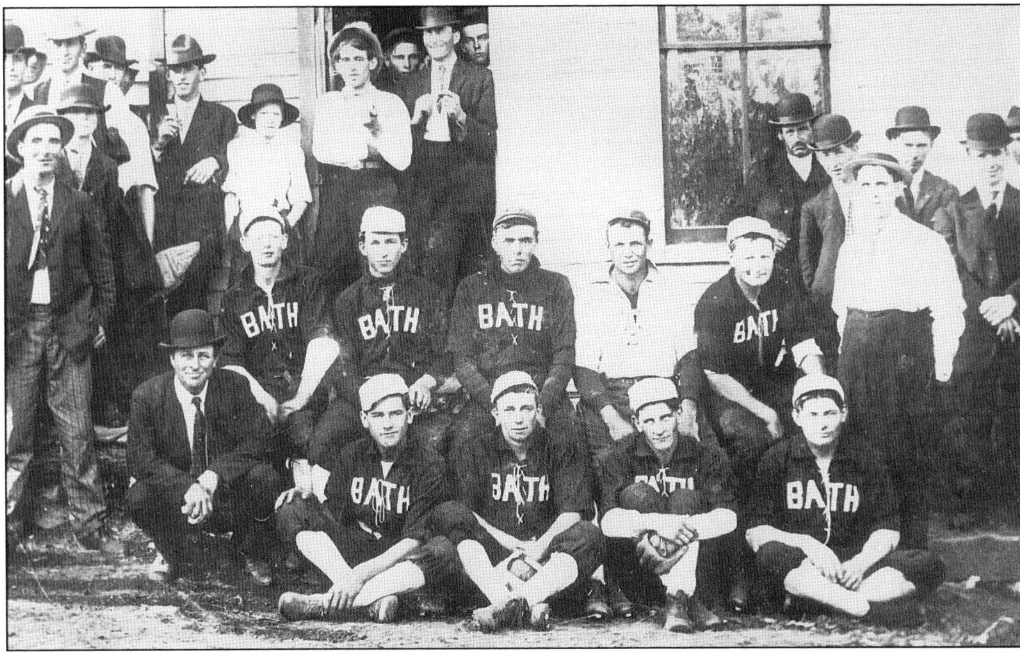

The 1908 Bath baseball team consisted of, from left to right: (front row) Roy Eustrom, unidentified, Frank Harty, and Tom Connor; (back row) Martin Bartness, George Laudert, Olaf Nygaard, Earl Pickering, and Henry Harty (manager). A 1908 *Freeborn County Standard* article describing a 4-to-3 game won by Bath-Hartland states, "the winning score was made through corner cutting, wrangling, and kicking on the umpire, leaving the grounds, returning, and leaving again . . . till Manchester gave in."

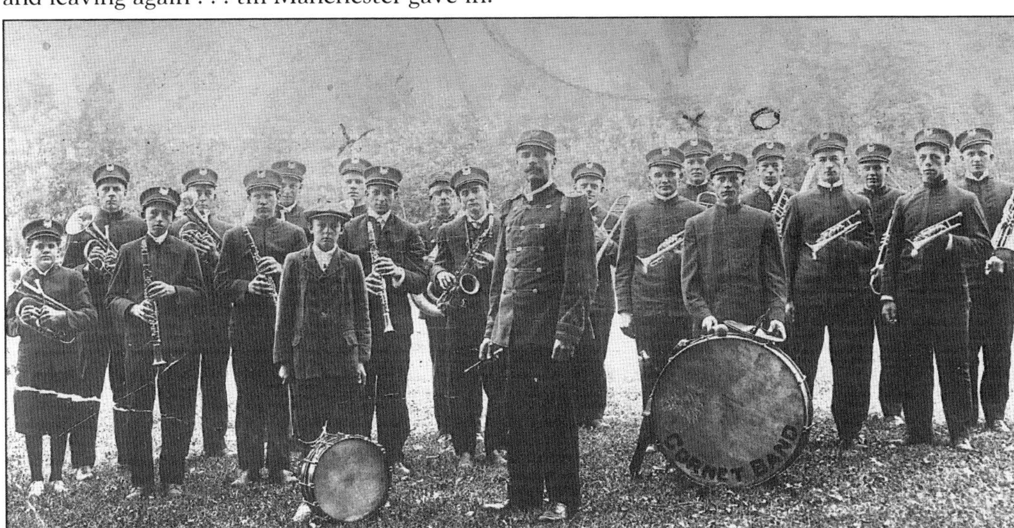

The Geneva Cornet Band was formed in 1916 and entertained the community and surrounding areas with Saturday-night concerts. Members were: Jens Wayne, Earl Jensen, Bill Benson, W.C. Gruetzmacher, Walter Johanson, Chris Wayne, Chris Nelson, Paul Skaug, Arthur Jensen, Carl Knudsen, Russel Rasmussen, George Gay, Henry Murray, Lars Swenson, Arnold Wayne, Irvin Wayne, Clifford Rasmussen, Abel Wayne, John Schad, Harvey Heegard, Olaf Olson, and Ray Rasmussen.

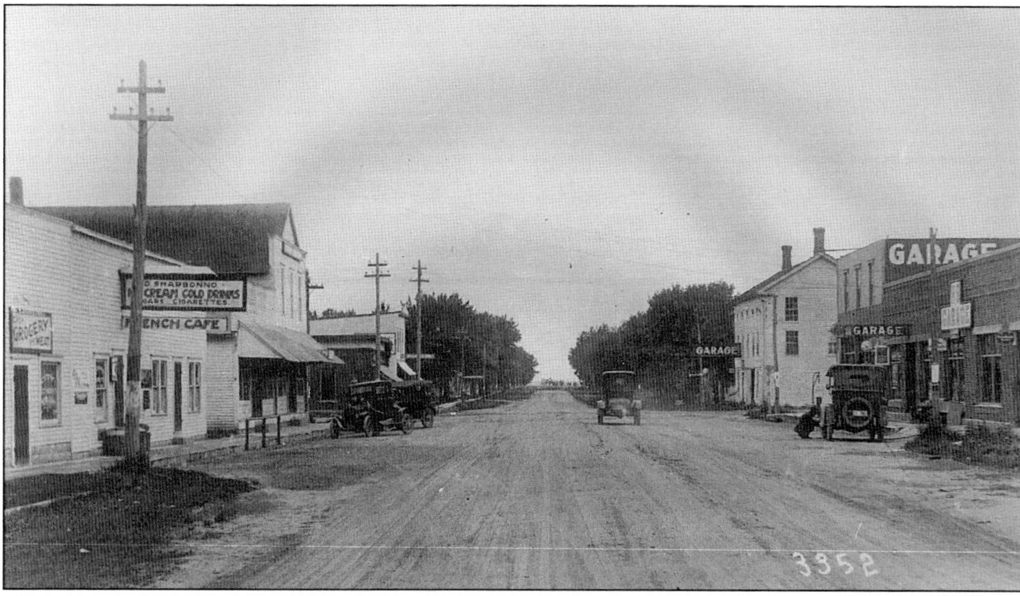

This view of Geneva in 1928 shows an up and coming rural community with a variety of businesses on either side of a graveled Main Street. The 1890 business listing included two general merchandise stores, a druggist and notary public, a physician and surgeon, a contractor and builder, a wagon maker, two blacksmiths, a butcher, two well drillers, a postmistress, and a hotel.

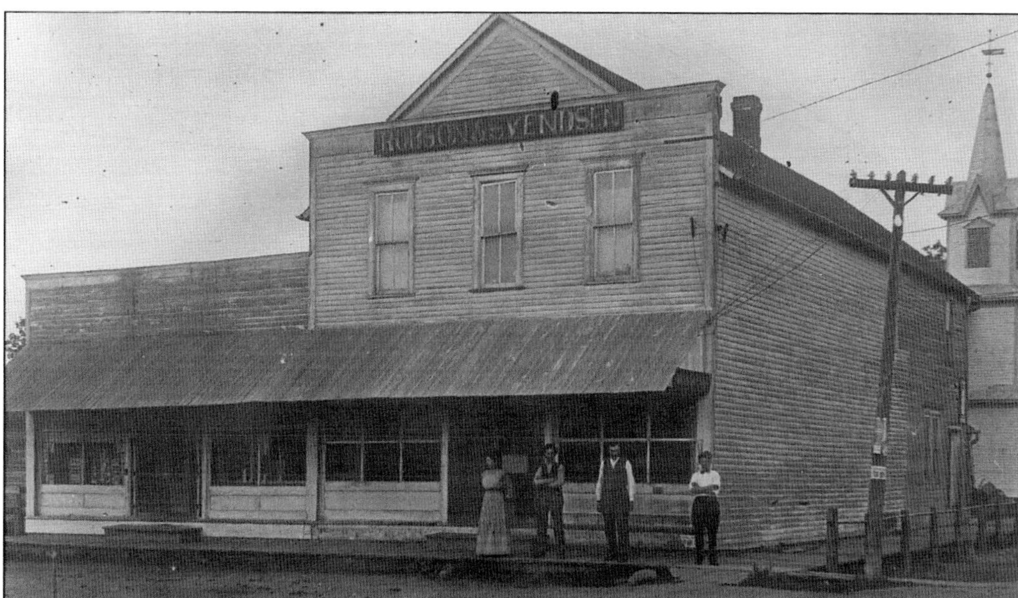

John T. Robson and Svend Svendsen operated the Geneva General Store until 1910, and then Svendsen continued ownership until 1919. It was said that he, a soft-spoken man of large build, once proposed to his childhood sweetheart, Libby Schad, who clerked in the store. She made no reply, and he never asked her again. They are buried side by side in the Geneva cemetery.

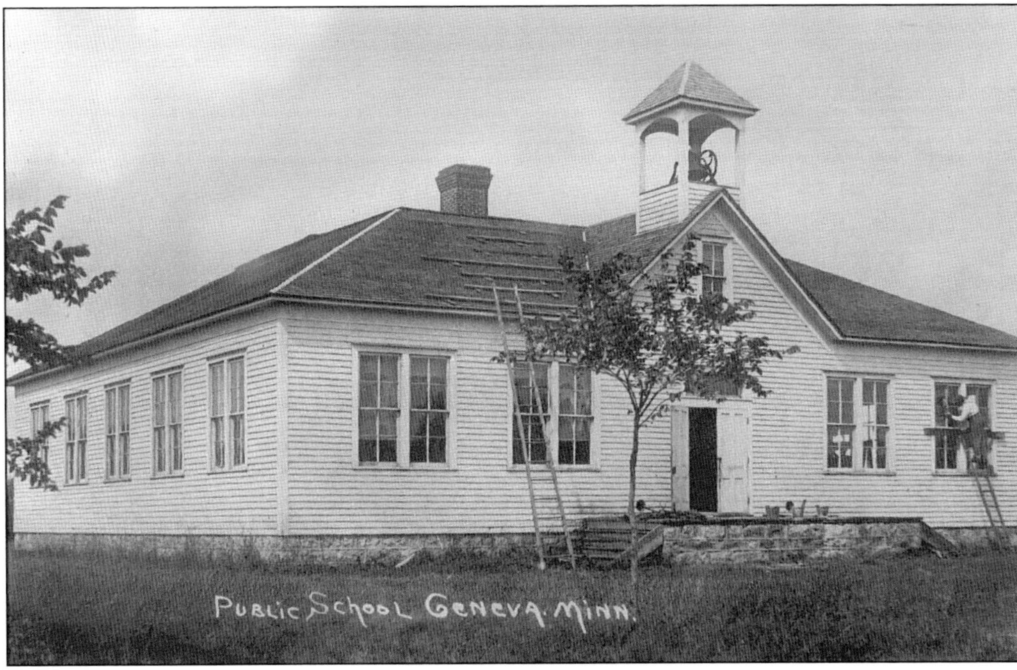

In Geneva, school classes were held first in a log shanty, then in a one-room school built in 1865. A two-story school built in 1888 burned to the ground in 1903, and in 1904 this large four-room school was built for eight grades and two years of high school. The eighth graders were allowed to take one or two subjects to prepare themselves for high school.

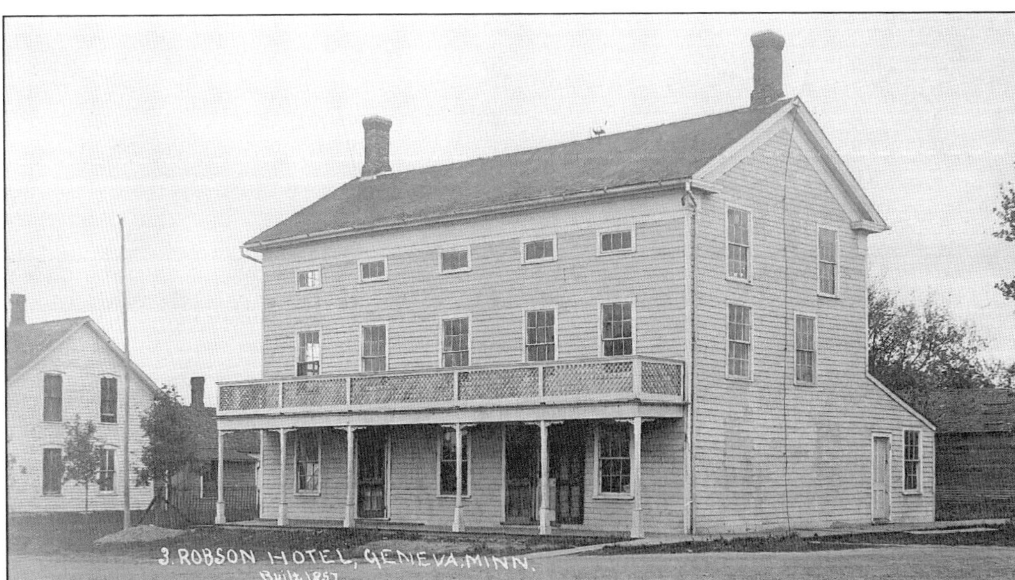

Built in 1857, the Robson Hotel was three stories high, with beautiful, black walnut interior trim. The first floor contained the gentlemen and ladies parlors, office, bar room, dining hall, and kitchen. The second floor was divided into parlors and bedrooms, and the third floor was a spacious hall. One thousand dollars worth of furniture was purchased for the hotel, and the opening included a grand ball.

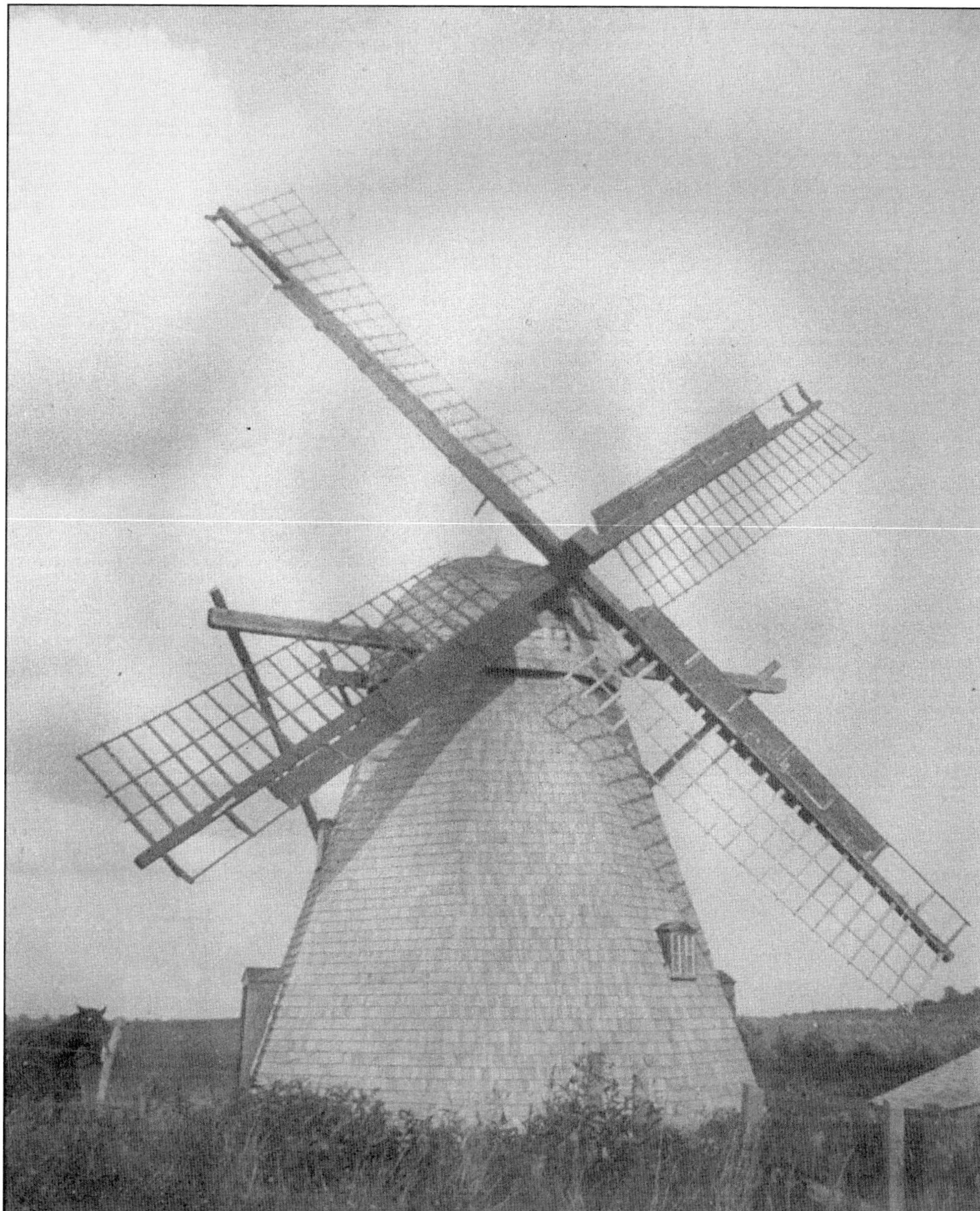

The Clarks Grove windmill, owned by William Frost, operated from 1898 to 1904, grinding rye, white, graham flour, cornmeal, and feed for farmers. The mill, completely dependent on wind power, operated only when the wind was blowing. There were times when Mr. Frost would wake his family in the middle of the night because he needed their help. During the busy times, farmers with horse-drawn wagons would be lined up on Main Street waiting for their turn. The farmers would bring their own sacks for feed, using wire or cord to tie the top of the sack. They came from Bancroft, Lerdal, Geneva, and the Hollandale/Clarks Grove area. Several times throughout the year, a government inspector from the State of Minnesota would pay a visit, checking the corn both before and after grinding.

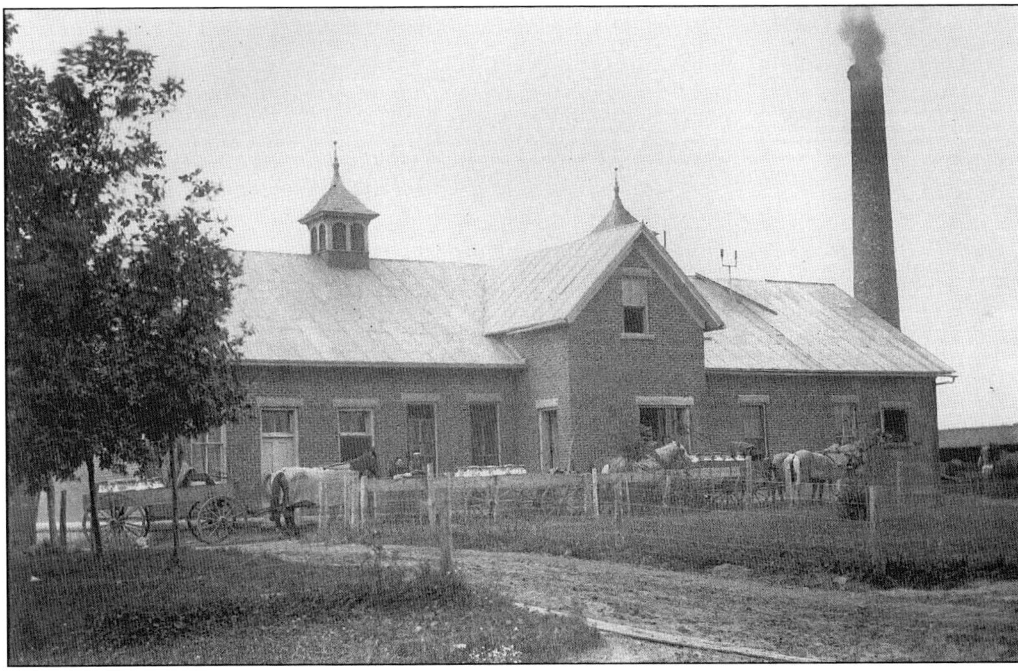

The Clarks Grove Creamery, the first cooperative creamery in Minnesota, opened its doors on May 15, 1890, with 82 area farmers as patrons. That year, 84,097 pounds of butter were manufactured. In 1895, this new, brick creamery was built at a cost of $9,000, which included materials, labor, equipment, well, and sheds. The building burned down in 1927, and a new creamery was built within eight months.

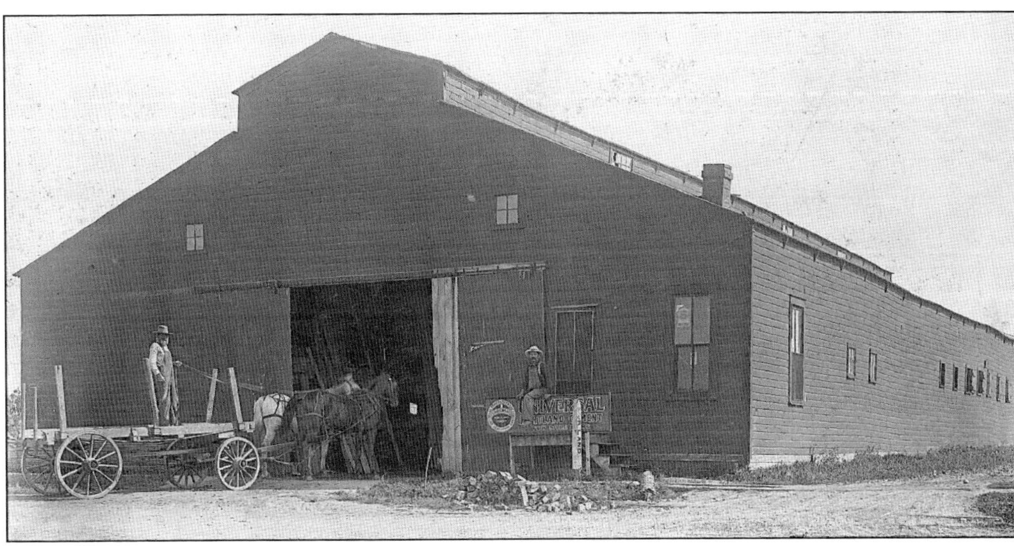

A third cooperative venture in Clarks Grove—the Lumber, Fuel, & Stock Company—was established in 1902. Its main purpose was to buy and sell building supplies, drainage materials, and fuel. Theodore Jorgenson was the company's first manager. In 1903, 26 train-car-loads of lumber, 21 car-loads of coal, and 2 car-loads of salt were sold. Mads Mortenson and "Grandpa" Jorgenson are shown in this 1910 photograph.

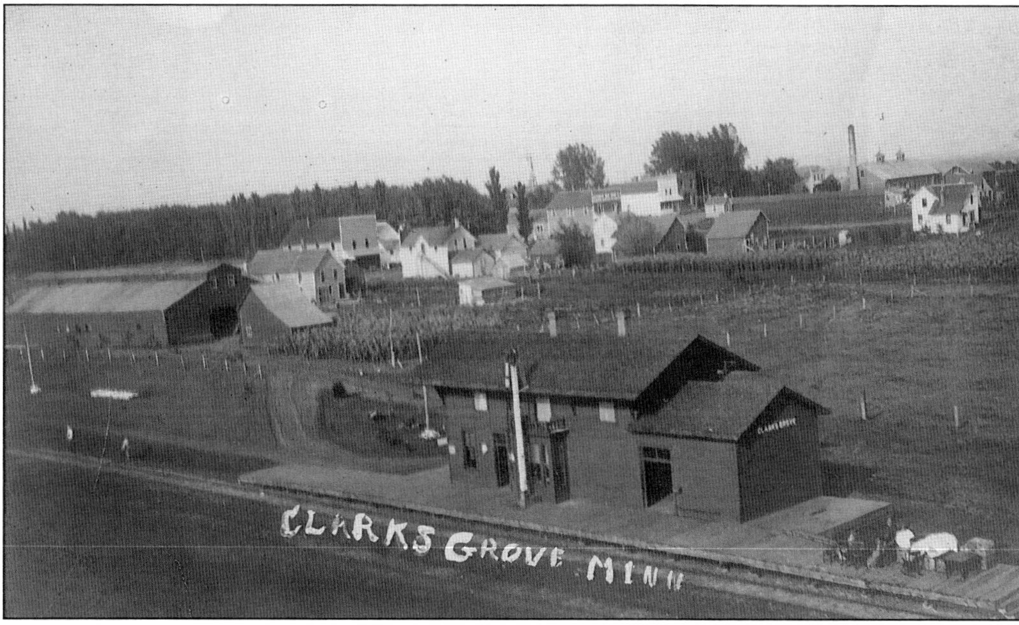

A postcard view of Clarks Grove, c. 1910, taken from the elevator, shows the depot, lumber yard (at the left), and the business district (upper right). The original Burlington, Cedar Rapids, and Northern Railroad depot was built 1 mile south of Clarks Grove at the proposed Village of Dorwart. Community resistance to this site eventually caused the depot to be moved north. In 1903, the B.C.R. & N. was taken over by the Chicago, Rock Island, & Pacific.

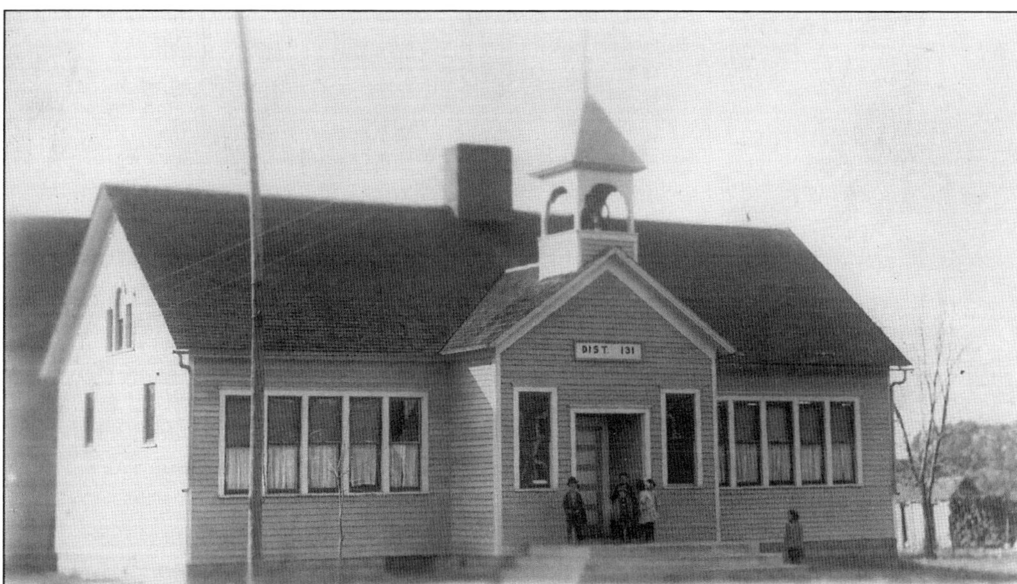

Clark Grove's School District #131 was created, and this building was erected in 1901, when Districts 5, 23, 82, and 7 consolidated. The school doors opened on December 11, 1901, with Olga Peterson as the first teacher. The slate blackboards arrived on February 5, 1902, and a community celebration was held on the schoolhouse lawn on April 2, the close of the first school year.

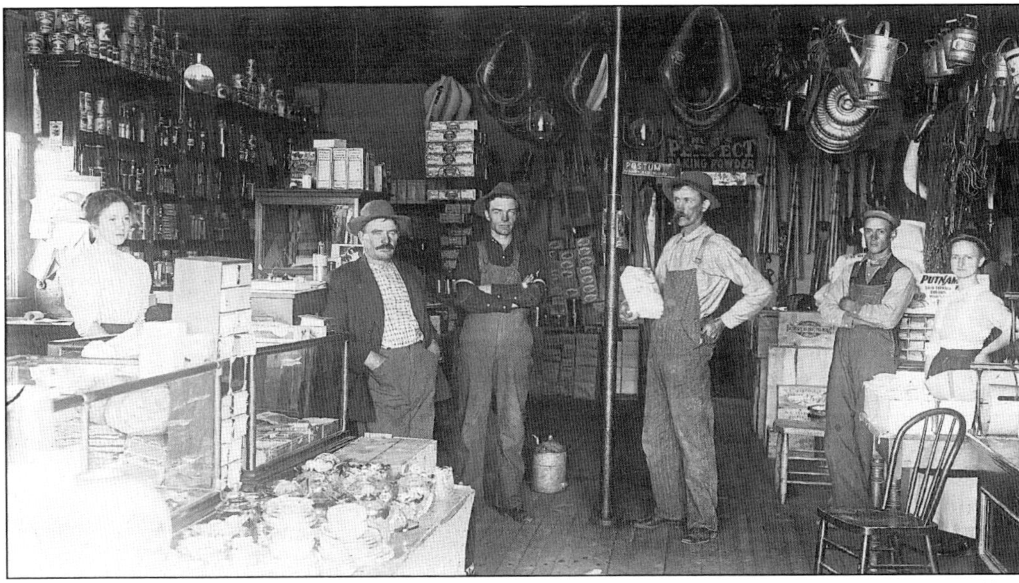

J.W. Peterson operated a general merchandise store in Clarks Grove from 1890 to 1917. Selling his first establishment, he then went into business with his brother, Charles, who also ran the post office. When his brother's health failed, J.W. Peterson continued the business. Merchandise included horse collars, bushel baskets, and kerosene cans. Shown in this photograph are, from left to right: Lola Peterson, Nels M. Jensen, Louis Larson, Chris A. Hanson, Henry Peterson, and Martha Peterson.

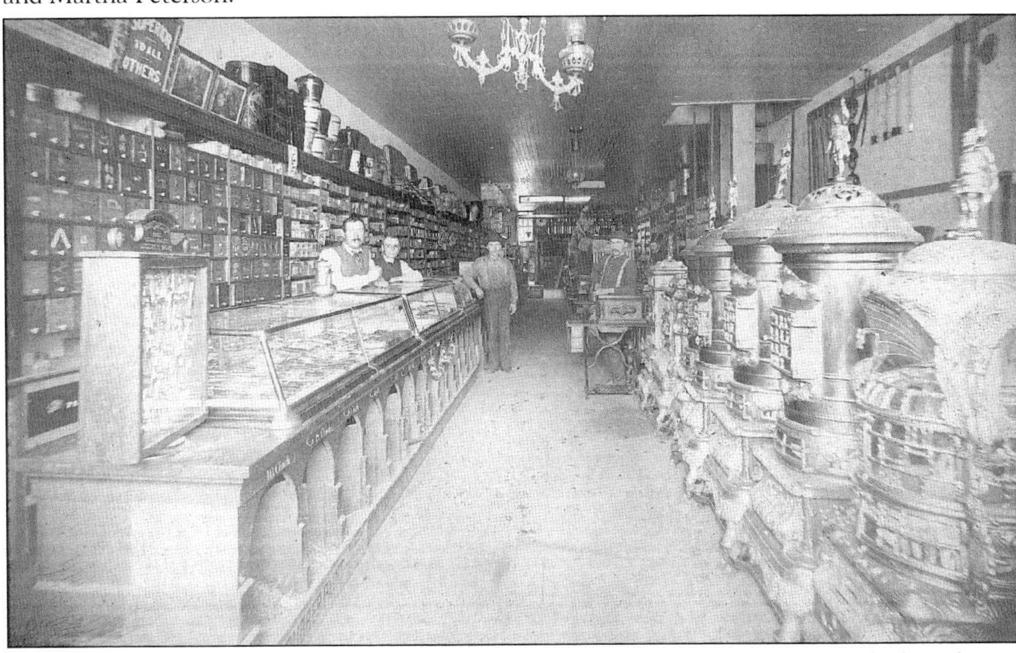

In 1896, J.W. Peterson and his brother opened a hardware store and a blacksmith shop, leasing the smithing business to H. Peterson of Albert Lea. They were known for shoeing as many as 30 horses a day. The Peterson Brothers carried a large inventory of hardware supplies and farm implements, including the Collins Plow and the McCormick Machine 'Extra'. In 1910, the Petersons sold out to a cooperative venture.

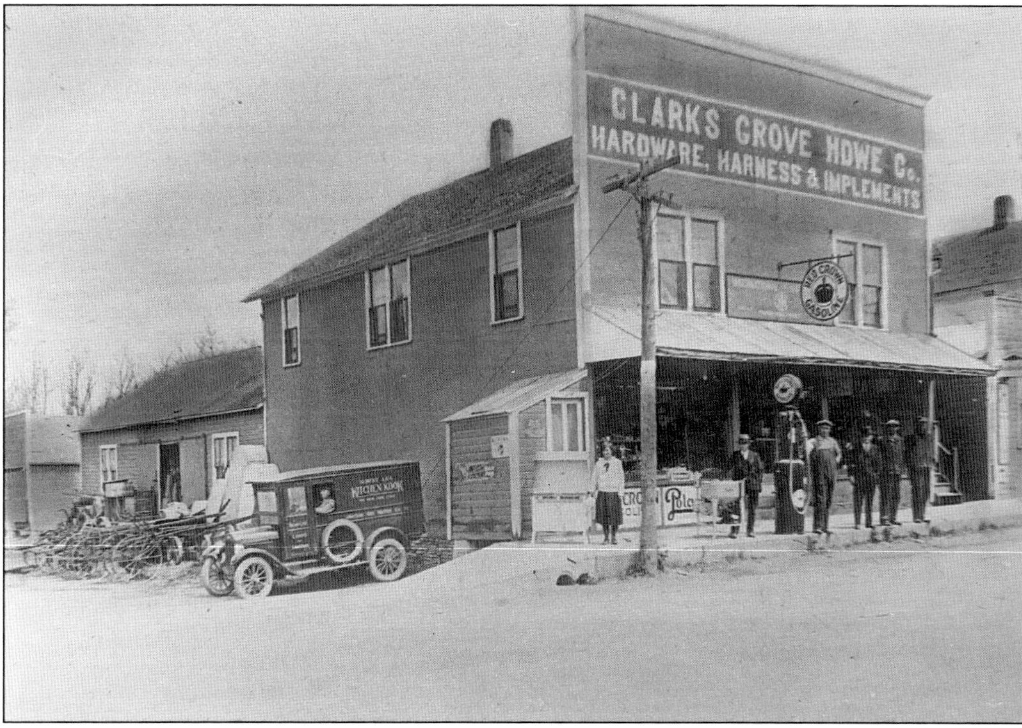

The Clarks Grove Hardware started in 1910 with the purchase of Peterson Brothers. This cooperative venture added several new lines of equipment, including LaCrosse manure spreaders and International F-12, 14, and 20s with steel wheels. They also sold New Idea and Minnesota equipment made by inmates at Stillwater State Prison, as well as Ford cars and Harley-Davidson motorcycles.

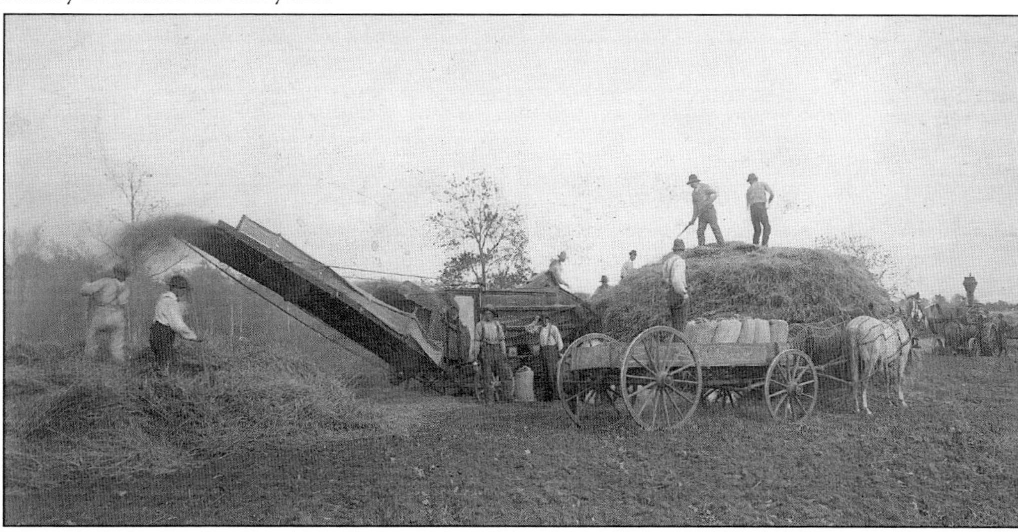

Even though the threshing machine owned by Tom Olson and Elling Hove was powered by a steam engine, several men and a lot of hard work were needed for the threshing process. Notice the men pitching the bundles from a stack into the thresher, and then others bagging the grain while the straw is carried by the elevator to another stack. This is a very early-model threshing machine, c. 1913.

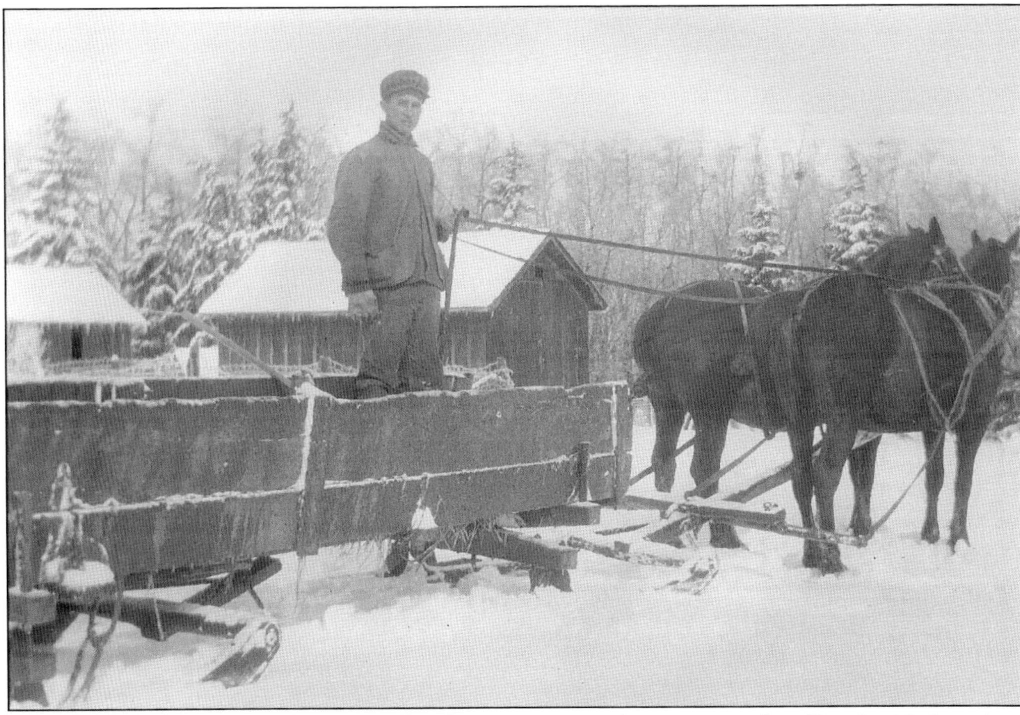

A Moscow Township farmer pauses for the camera on a busy winter day. His double box (two boards high) bob sled is typical of the equipment used for everyday farm chores. The sled was used for feeding livestock, cleaning barns, or hauling straw bedding and corn bundles. Its wide track made it less likely to tip. The well-cared-for, well-matched team of horses indicates a prosperous farm.

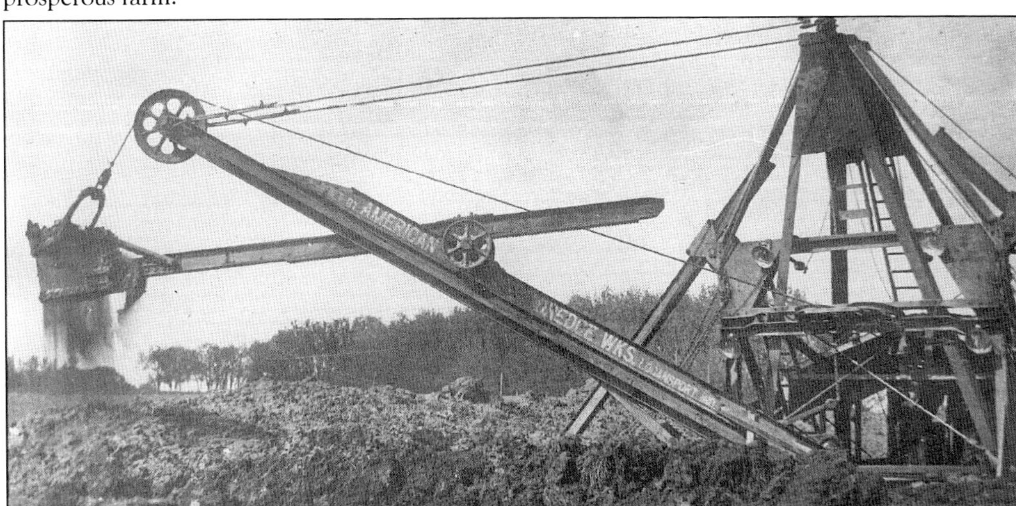

The *History of Freeborn County* states: "Turtle Creek is the principal water course in the town[ship], entering from Riceland by way of Sections 7 and 18, and taking a southeasterly course crosses the town[ship] and leaves Section 36 to enter Mower County. This stream furnishes an excellent waterpower in Section 22, which has been improved to some extent." This ditching machine is being operated on Turtle Creek near the Moscow Creamery in 1903.

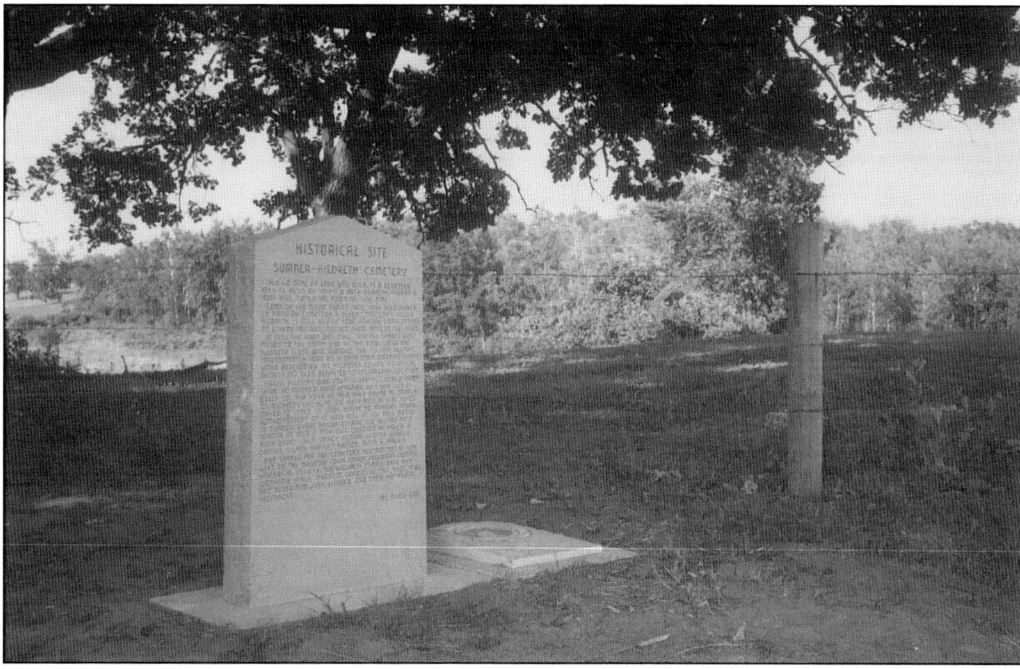

The Village of Sumner in Moscow Township was laid out by Rufus King Crum in 1856, and a post office was established with George Watson as postmaster. In 1858, Mr. Crum erected a log house hoping to entertain prospective community residents, but to no avail. The stagecoach trail is still visible. The original livery barn was built with home-sawed lumber and square pegs, and was destroyed by a storm in 1998.

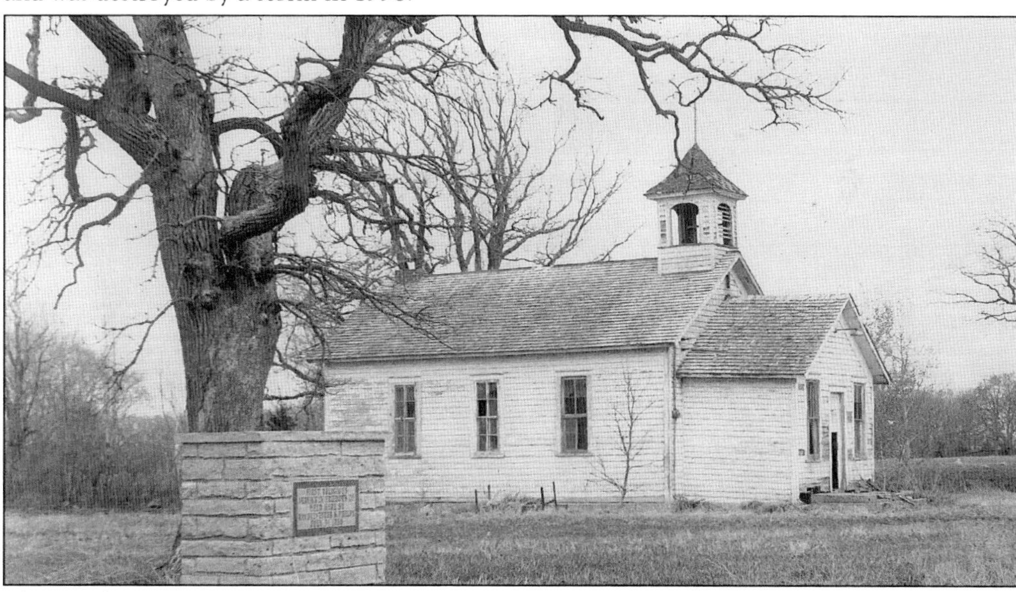

This marker in Moscow Township, Section 28, denotes the site of the first religious service to be held by an ordained minister in Freeborn County. Reverend Sylvester N. Phelps, of the Methodist Episcopal Church, was sent by his church to Austin, Minnesota, and, on August 31, 1856, he preached "the first gospel sermon ever heard within our borders" at the home of Rufus K. Crum. (*History of Freeborn County.*)

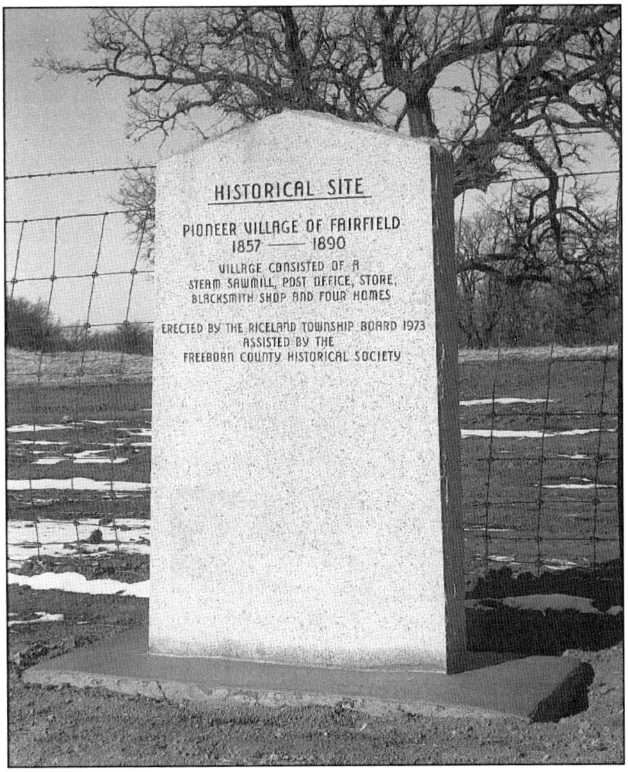

Fairfield was platted by Samuel Beardsley on the south shore of Rice Lake on a proposed road to Shell Rock. A post office was established, and there was a regular mail route; it was on the same section as the saw mill, and everything looked promising for rapid growth. However, the railroad never came, and the village became a thing of the past. (*History of Freeborn County.*)

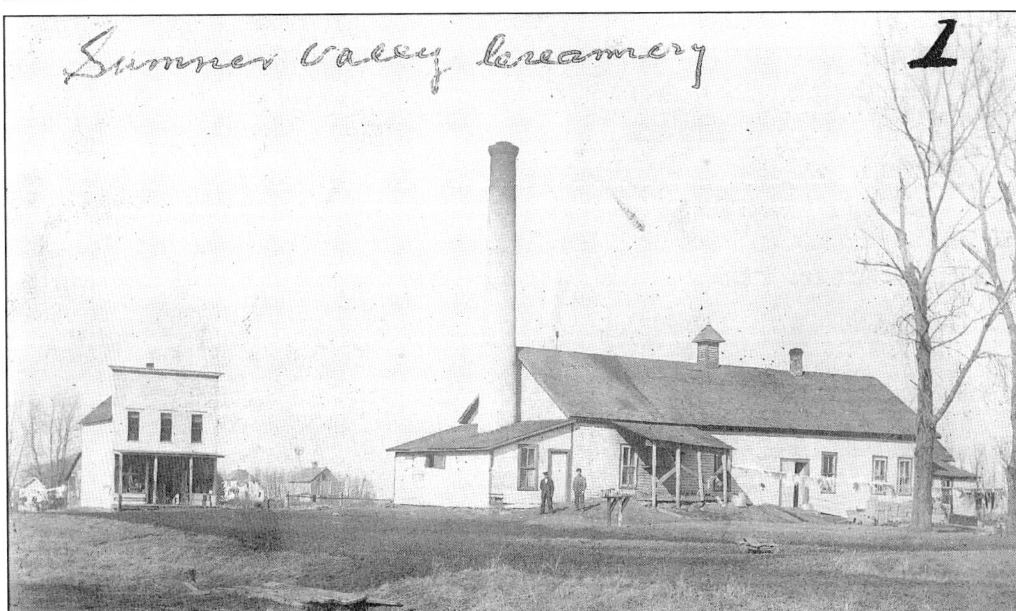

The Sumner Valley Creamery was organized in the summer of 1893 and began operations that fall. An attempt was made to manufacture cheese in addition to butter, but this was later abandoned. The creamery was named after a valley near the Oakland Lutheran Church, and was located on land owned by M.J. Tufte. The Sigsbee General Store is also shown in this photograph.

Charlotte Hanson enjoys an ice cream cone on the front porch of the Sigsbee General Store in 1928. Sigsbee was located in the southwest corner of Section 26, Riceland Township, and included the store owned by Martin Christopherson (and later Irvin Hanson), a post office, and the Sumner Valley Creamery. Sigsbee is another example of a small Freeborn County community that did not survive.

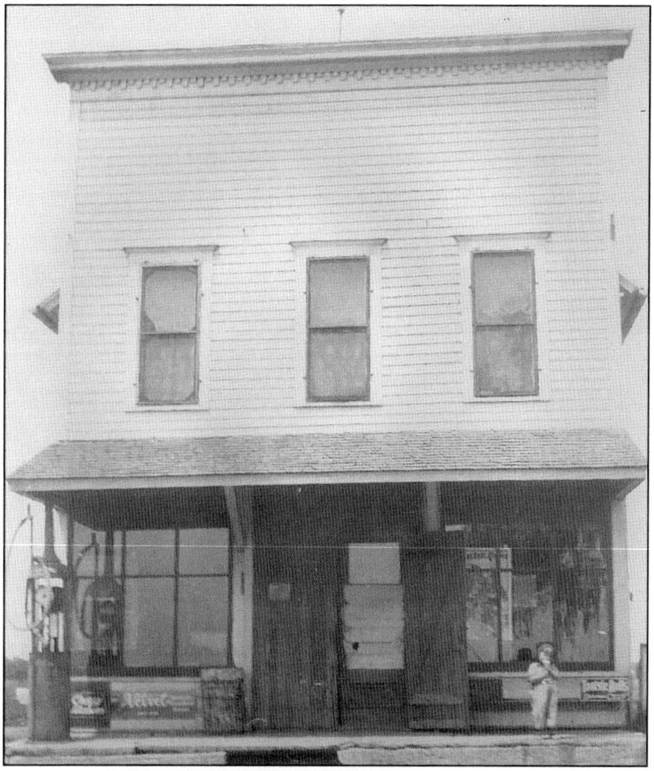

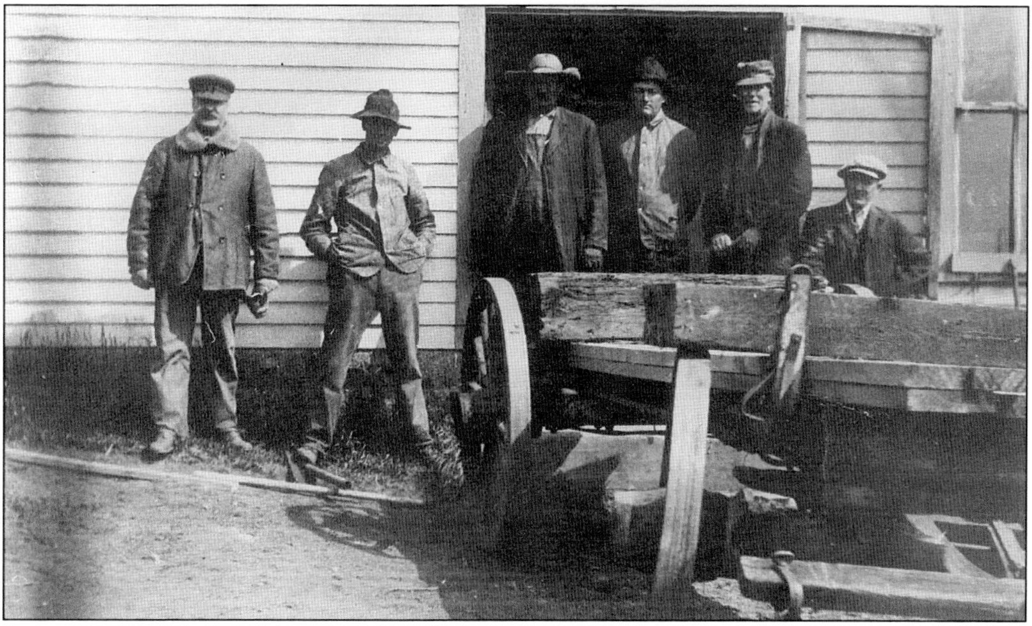

Severt Tufte, Ole Boe, three unidentified men, and Iver Tufte are shown here, from left to right, after delivering a new churn to the Sumner Valley Creamery at Sigsbee. This photograph, taken before 1920, exemplifies the pride and trust in the future of the dairy industry shown by the rural people in Freeborn County. At the turn of the century, there were 28 creameries and two cheese factories in the county.

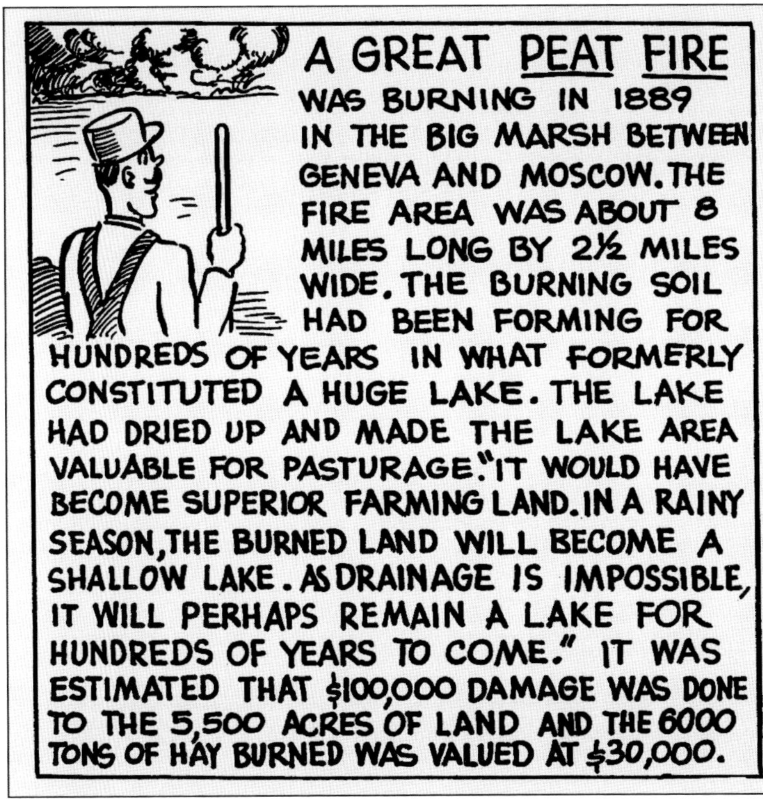

Hi-Lites and Shadows of Yesterday and Today drawn by Irv Sorenson in 1959.

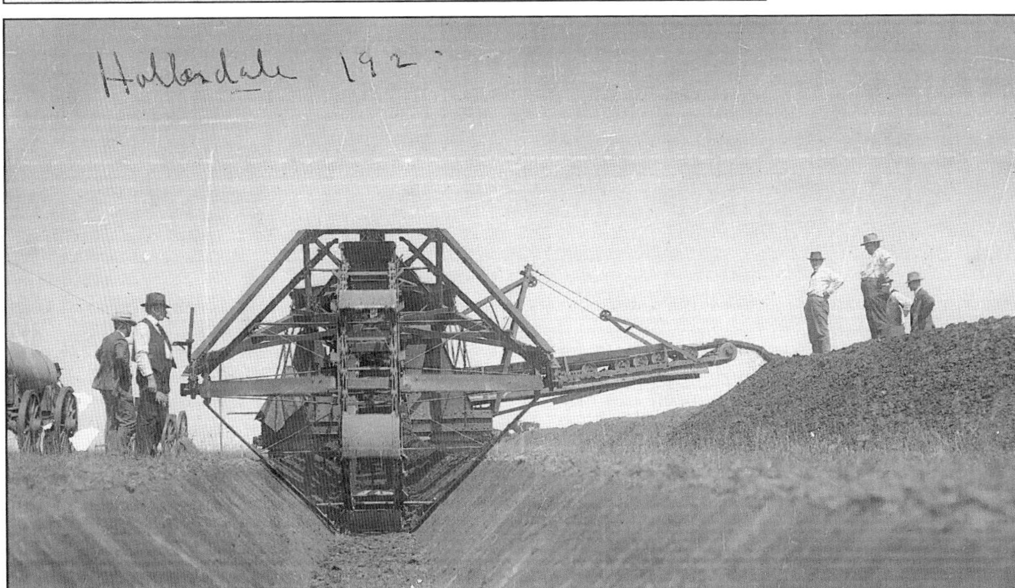

Rice Lake, once 15,000 acres of marsh, became 15,000 acres of fertile farmland thanks to the dream of George Payne, the Albert Lea Farms Investment Company, and the Buckeye ditching machine. With 120 horse power and weighing 76 tons, this machine could dig a ditch 12-feet wide at the top and 7-feet deep. The men who operated the digger lived in the house on top of the machine.

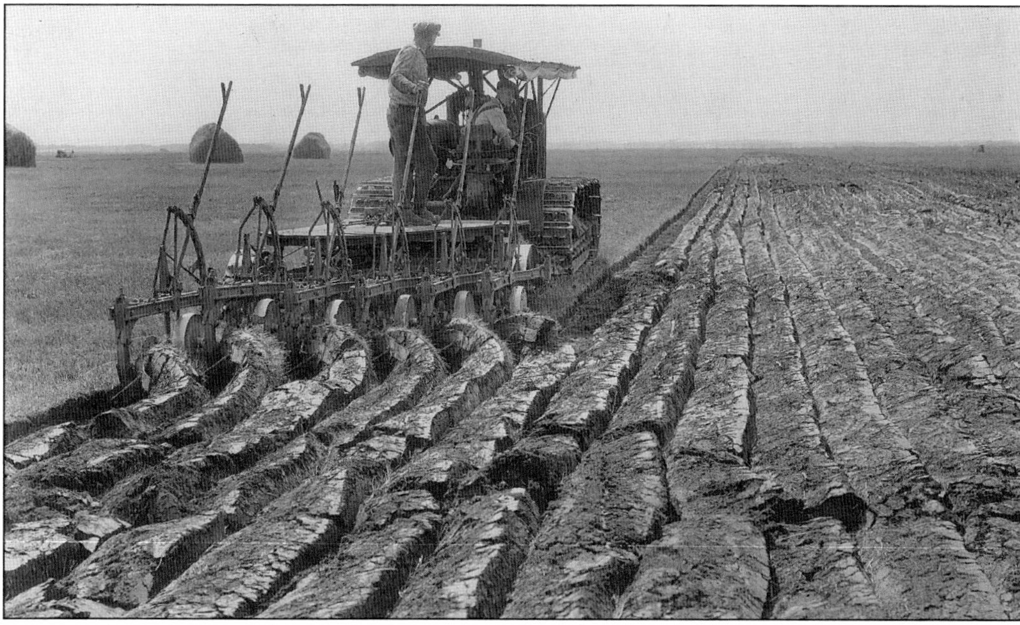

In spite of environmental concerns by citizens of Freeborn County, attempts were made to drain Rice Lake as early as 1907, although the most successful efforts began in 1919. This photograph shows the Bagley Brothers, with their caterpillar tractor, turning ribbons of sod—plowing land that had never grown anything but wild hay, and introducing to the next generations acres of fertile farmland.

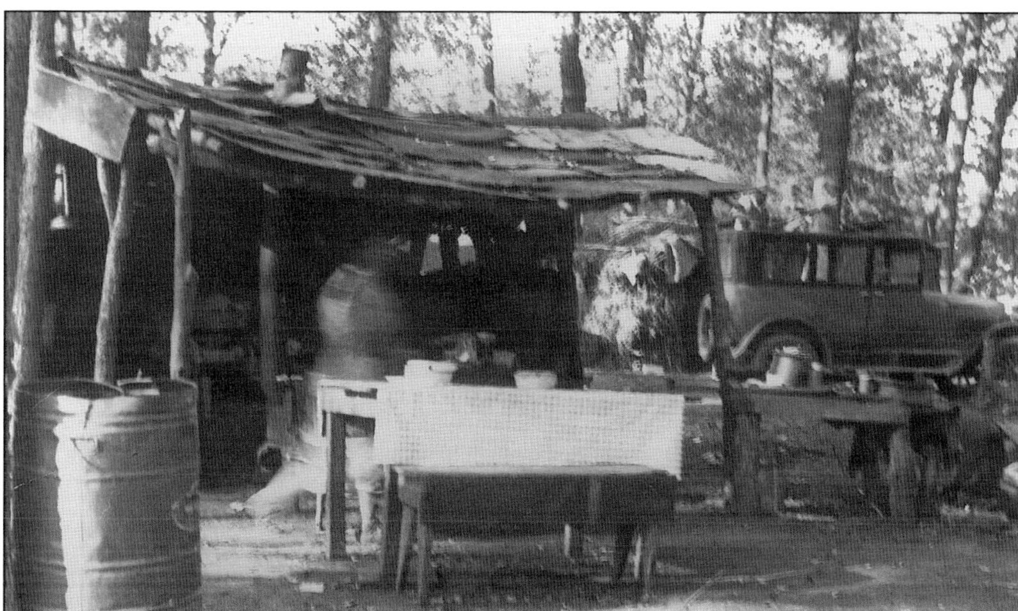

Migrant workers provided much of the labor, and they often worked alongside the farm owner and his family in the Hollandale-area vegetable fields. The migrants, many of whom came from Southern Texas, lived in housing provided by the farmers—some very adequate accommodations, and some very humble. Many chose to stay in Minnesota, to find permanent jobs, and to blend into established communities.

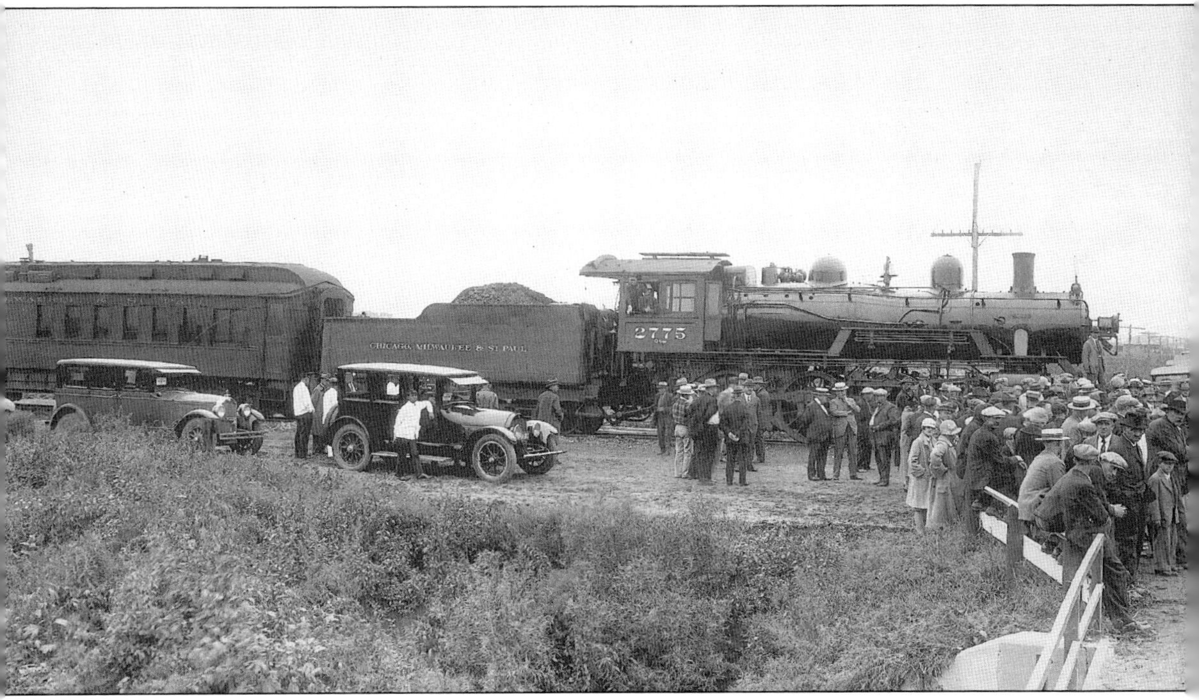

". . . Hollandale is one of the most productive areas for its size in the world. Where thirty years ago there stood a cattail swamp under an average of four inches of water, today grows 80 square miles of the richest, most productive truck garden crops in the rich Midwest of America. From this 'useless swampland' growers this season harvested 15 to 30 tons of cabbage per acre . . . upwards of 750 bushels of onions per acre . . . 2,000 dozen of celery plants per acre . . . 15 to 30 tons of carrots per acre . . . and an average of 200-600 and more bushels of potatoes per acre. These figures are truly the basis for a miracle story, and that is exactly what Hollandale has proved to be. In spite of the bad years, financially and weather-wise, Hollandale has become certainly one of the miracle acreages in the world.

Early in the project, 25 years ago to be exact (1924), the need for marketing procedures was recognized. The Hollandale Marketing Association, a cooperative venture, was established to secure standards of quality which would find favor with buyers all over the nation; and to establish outlets which would buy Hollandale produce to the greatest advantage of the growers.

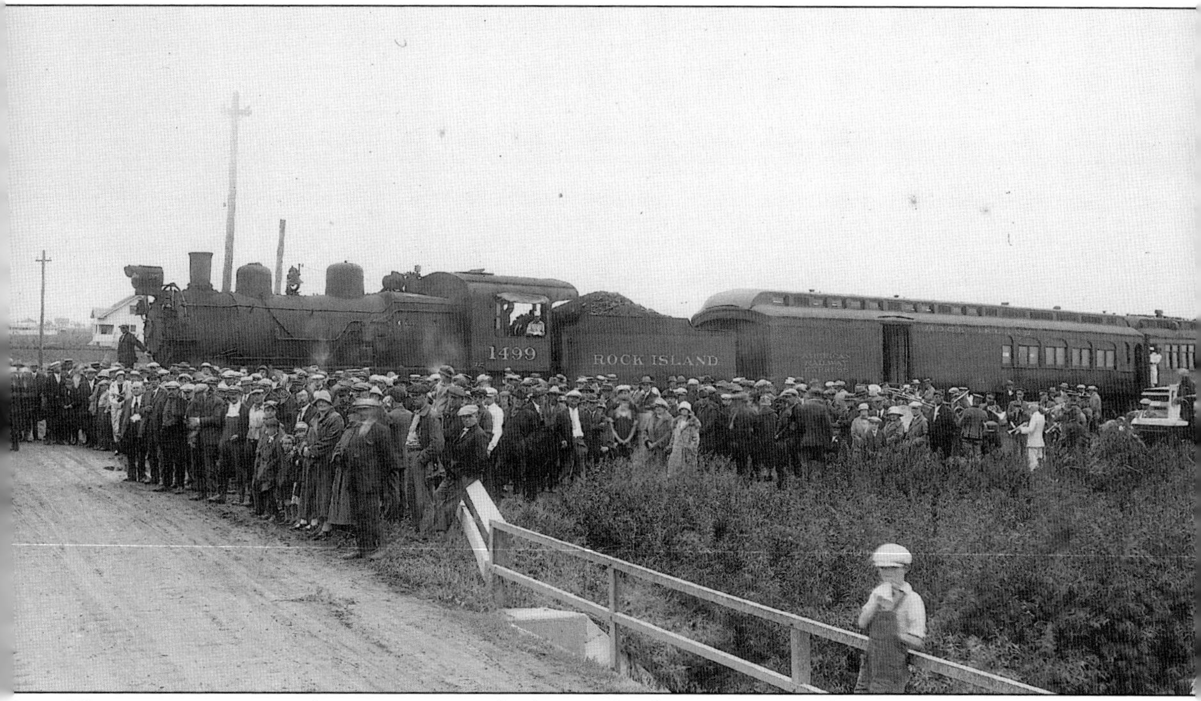

The association was also to go a step further and, when necessary, show growers how to get the most from their land. How well that job was done will be seen later. Even at the start, the value to top-quality crops was proved, when Hollandale seed potatoes commanded a premium of as much as 70¢ per bushel above the price of first-class table stock. Hollandale's tremendous production was such that, even at the start, it called for (and received) unique transportation facilities. These needs were satisfied when the Interstate Commerce Commission issued permits for two railroads (the Chicago, Rock Island, & Pacific and the Chicago, Milwaukee, & St. Paul) to build into Hollandale. The completion of that service was celebrated on September of 1926. The presidents of both of these railroads considered the connection of such importance that they personally attended the ceremonies of the opening of the line. It is said that no other tract of the same acreage in America is specifically served by two first-class railroads. Once begun, Hollandale was eventually destined to become a promised land for the farmers who came to participate in the benefits of the newly-opened acreage." (*The Community Magazine*, November 1949, an article titled "The Miracle Story of Hollandale.")

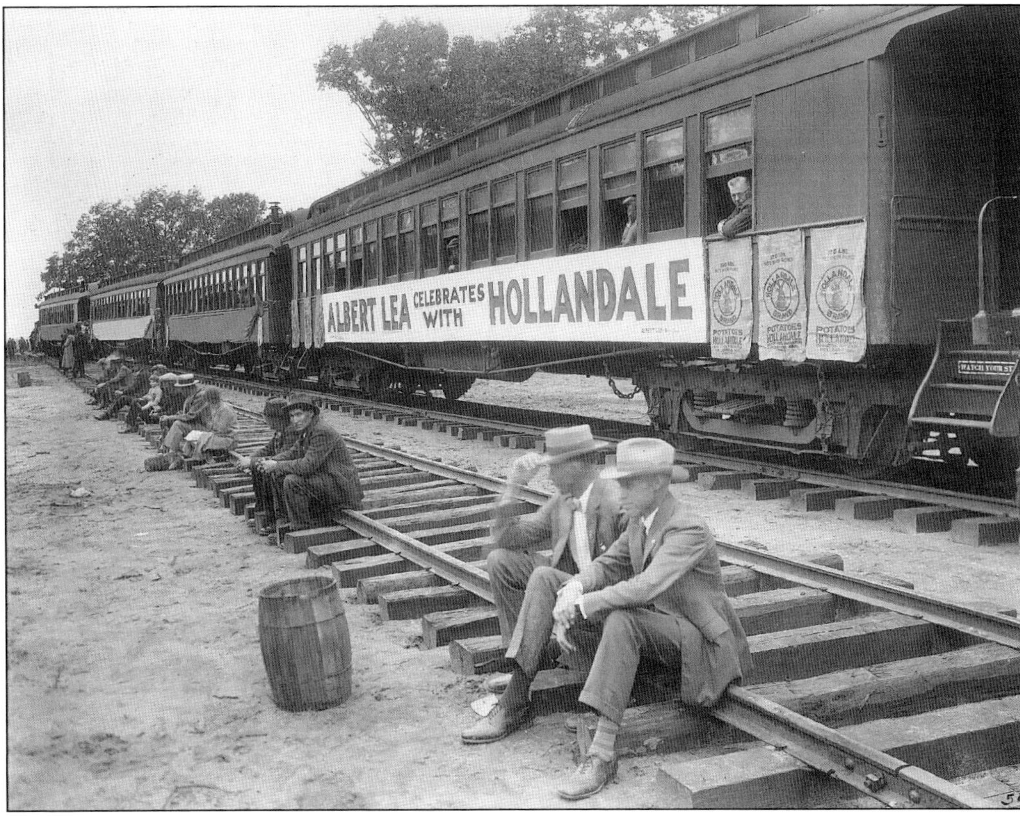

On September 4, 1926, hundreds of people flocked to Hollandale to celebrate the coming of the Rock Island and the Milwaukee Railroads and to recognize the entrepreneurial spirit and the hard work that made this dream a reality. Governors from two states, the presidents and officials of both railroads, the congressman from Minnesota's first congressional district, judges, lawyers, and ministers all joined with area residents to celebrate the event.

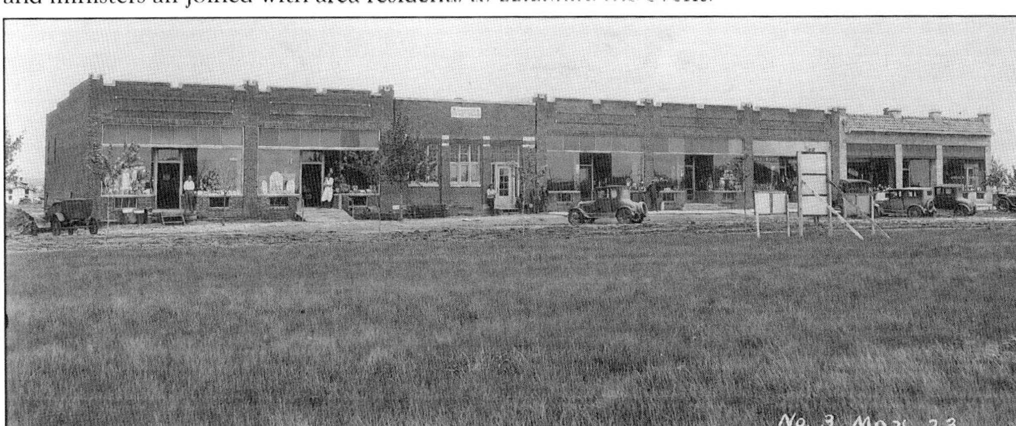

Hollandale was a planned community, developed according to the design of George Payne. His ideas on the homes, business district, and even the school showed a well-thought-out, balanced streetscape unlike any other rural Minnesota town. The view of Park Avenue West in 1927 shows the unique style of a business district built on a basic plan, rather than the haphazard growth of most urban areas.

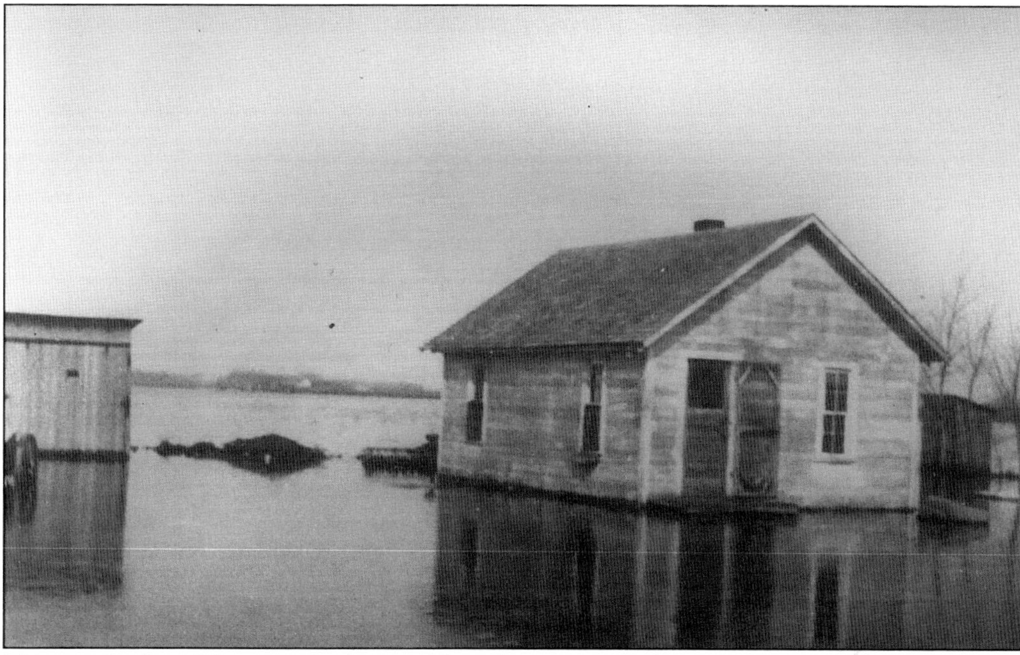

Miles and miles of drainage ditches could not keep up with the excessive rainfall in 1926, 1927, and 1928. It was as if nature was trying to reclaim her land. When the waters finally receded, the farmers found rotting crops in the fields. Many of them moved into Albert Lea and started new lives, giving up the dream of a prosperous farm life.

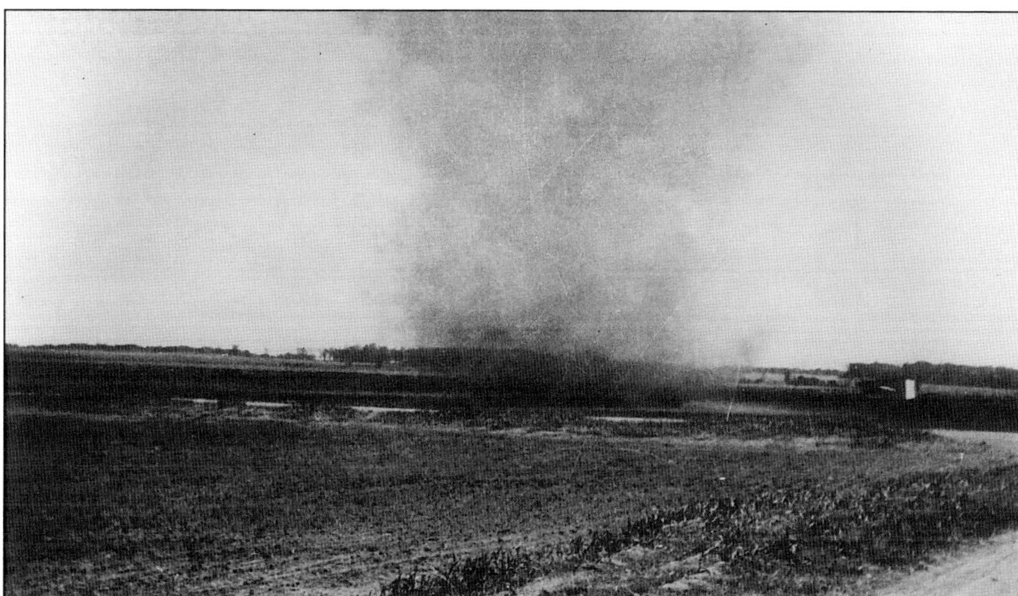

A strong wind and dry soil can be devastating to the farmer and frustrating to the farm wife. The fine, rich peat in the Hollandale area was formed by thousands of years of rank, jungle-thick vegetation decomposing in the swampy Rice Lake area. While it provides fertile soil for abundant crops, in the dry season it blows from the fields, settling in ditches and seeping into the finest cracks in buildings.

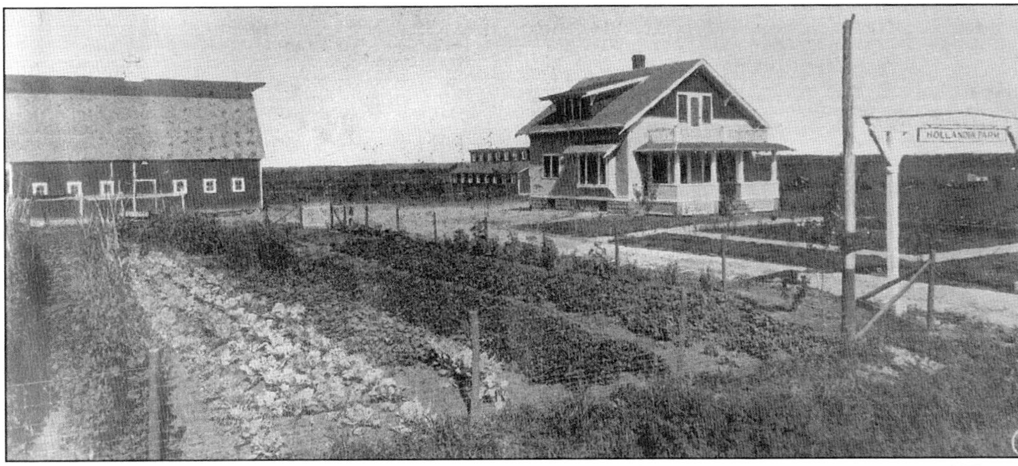

In 1921, because of high taxes and the possibility of another European war, Peter and Fenna Louters and their seven children emigrated to America. Stopping first in Iowa, in 1922 they became the first settlers in the Hollandale area. They purchased 80 acres of the newly drained land, farmed successfully on the Hollandale farm, and had the community's first church services in their living room.

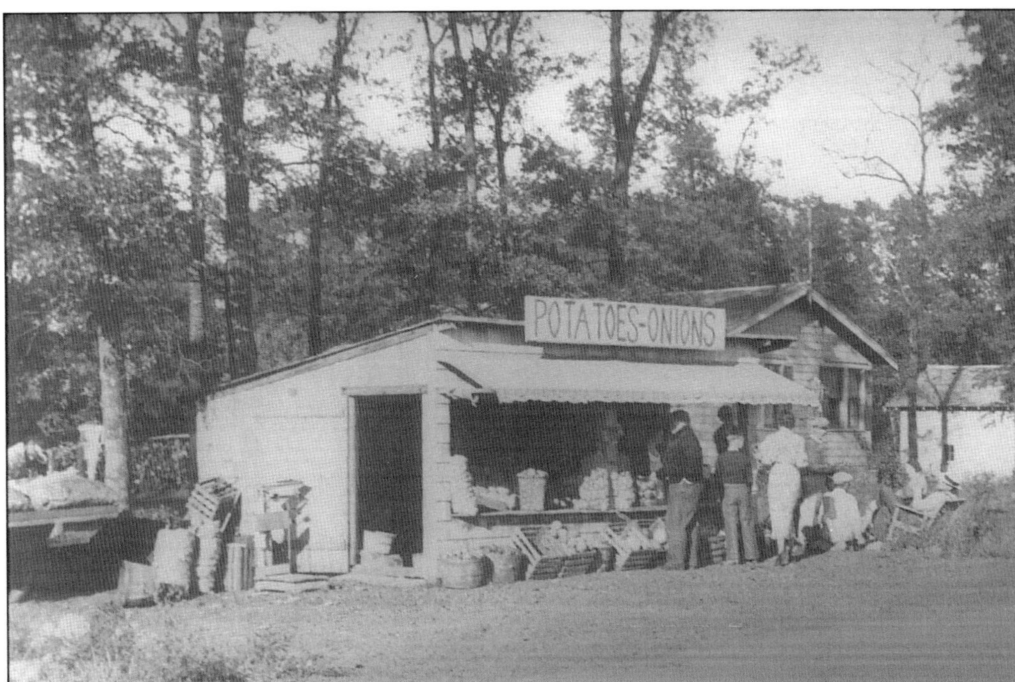

Cabbage, onions, celery, carrots, potatoes, asparagus, sugar beets—abundant vegetable crops that made dreams come true. Farms were paid off in five years, quality crops brought good prices, and success seemed assured for the Hollandale settlers. In addition to shipping vegetables to other parts of the country, city people from miles around came to the Hollandale/Maple Island-area to purchase fresh produce at road-side stands.

A Man in Hollandale Has 31 Acres of Muck Land

Just one acre of onions last year made him enough money to pay all his annual installments and interest on his purchase. 30 acres for himself—one acre for us

Another Has 160 Acres of Mineral Land That Cost Him $200 an Acre

40 acres of sugar beets made him $100 an acre clear profit after paying for seed and hand labor—think of making half the cost of an acre in a single year!

This 40 acres more than paid his annual installment and interest on the whole 160 acres. Will he pay for his farm?

Is There a Single Farm in the Whole State Where You Live That Can Show Such a Record? There are Many Like These Two in

Hollandale

Come and talk with the men who did it

WRITE FOR FREE ALBUM OF PICTURES OF HOLLANDALE

Albert Lea Farms Co.	**Payne Investment Co.**
Owners	Selling Agents
HOLLANDALE, MINNESOTA	OMAHA, NEBRASKA

These are promotional materials from Payne's *Hollandale Enterprise* magazine of May 1924.

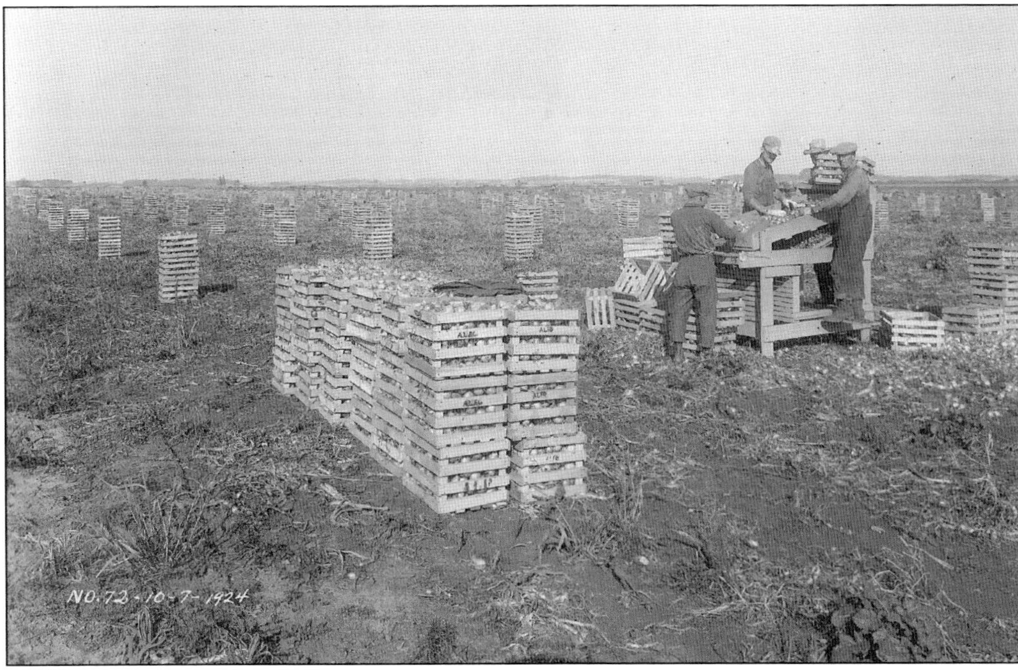

Onions were sorted in the fields by hand and then packed into wooden crates, each holding 50 pounds, before being loaded onto the truck to be taken to storage, or to the market. The size of this field and the number of crates gives you an idea of the amount of back-breaking labor involved in the planting, care, and harvest of a vegetable crop.

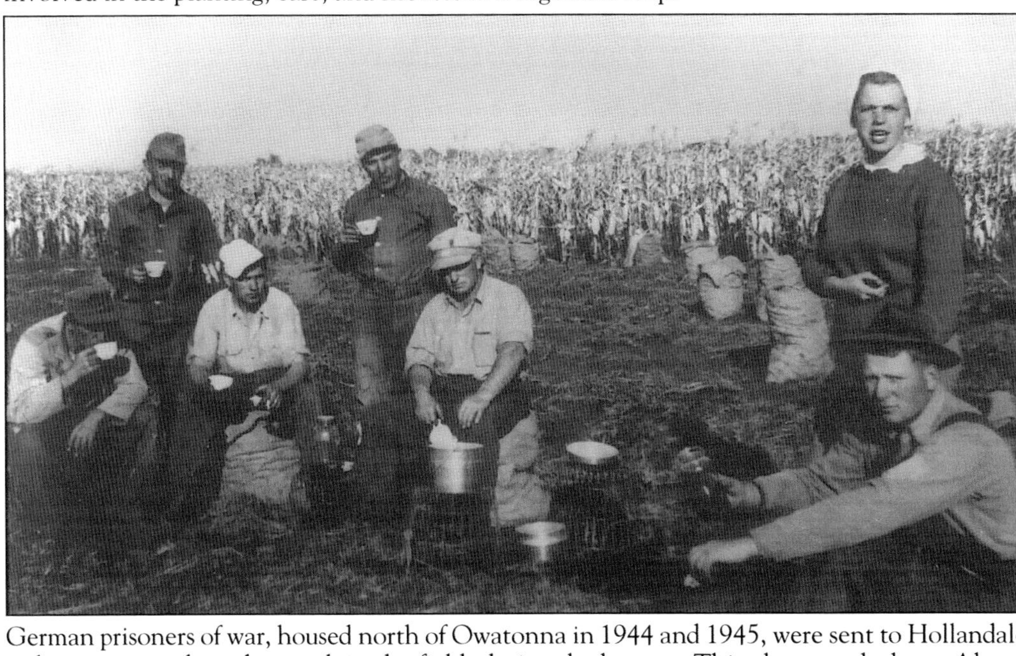

German prisoners of war, housed north of Owatonna in 1944 and 1945, were sent to Hollandale to live temporarily and to work in the fields during the harvest. This photograph shows Al and Doris Reynen, on the right, and five of the German workers. The Olin Hamer family also used the former members of the German military forces to help with the harvesting of sugar beets, potatoes, and onions.

Five

The County Seat

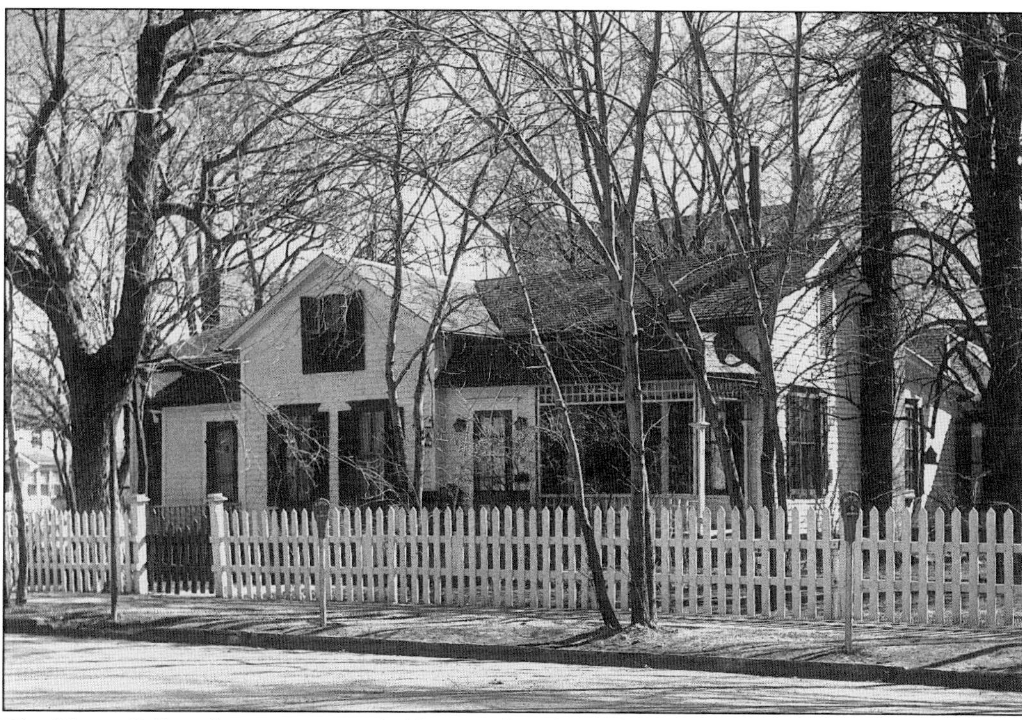

The Harry Gillrup house, surrounded by a picket fence, lives on in memory as a once-elegant home, owned by a prominent Albert Lea attorney. Located on the corner of Washington and Water Streets, the home, with its many additions, was built on the site of the Lorenzo Merry cabin, the first in Albert Lea. The Merrys called their place the "Strangers Hotel," and provided bread and sustenance for newcomers in the mid–1850s.

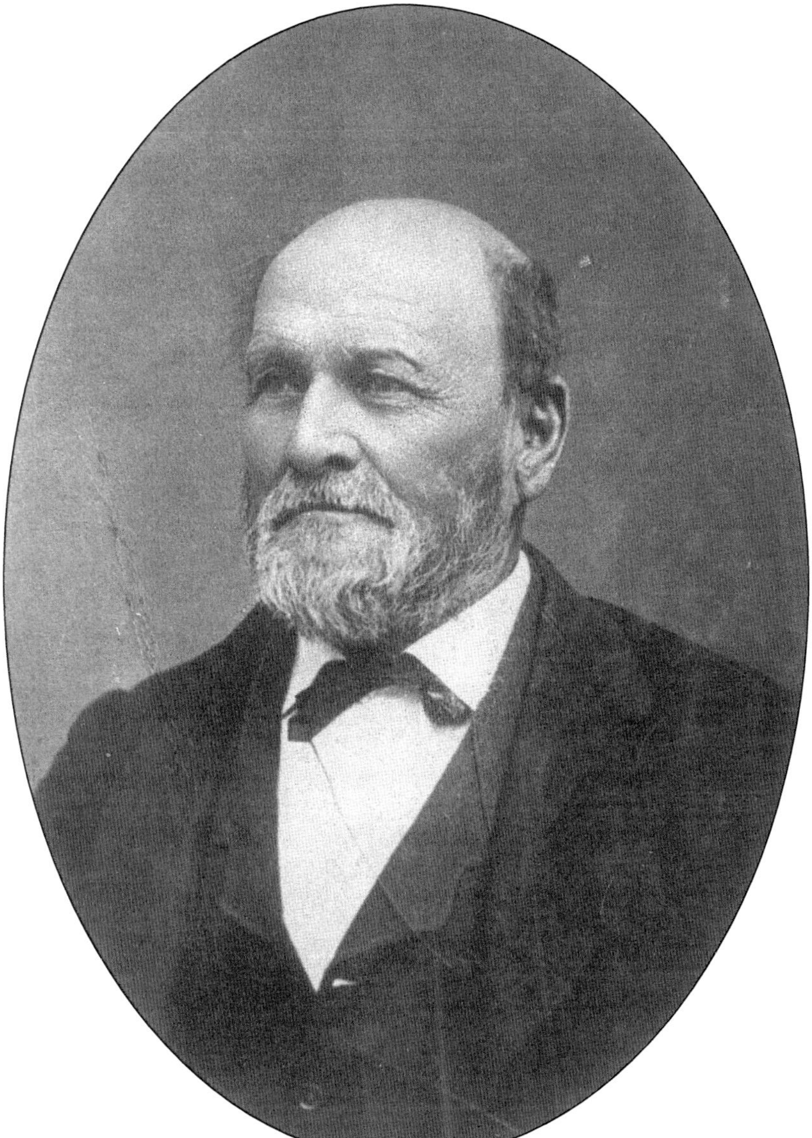

Albert Miller Lea was born in Richland, Tennessee in 1808. He planned to practice law, but because of his father's death, he left law school and entered the U.S. Military Academy at West Point. In 1835, Lieutenant Lea was a surveyor and a map maker with the U.S. Dragoons out of Fort Des Moines, Iowa, when they traveled through the area that was to become Southern Minnesota. Lea mapped "some of the most beautiful country he had ever seen." Though he named the largest lake in the area Fox Lake, the name was later changed to Lake Albert Lea by a cartographer in Washington, D.C. Twenty years later, the area's first settlers chose to name their village after the lake. When Tennessee seceded from the Union in 1861, Albert M. Lea served as a major in the Confederate Army. This caused much concern among the citizenry of Albert Lea, and there was talk about changing the name of the city. However, cool heads prevailed, and there was no name change. In 1879, Colonel (an honorary title) Albert M. Lea returned to Albert Lea, Minnesota to be honored at a celebration of the Old Settlers Association.

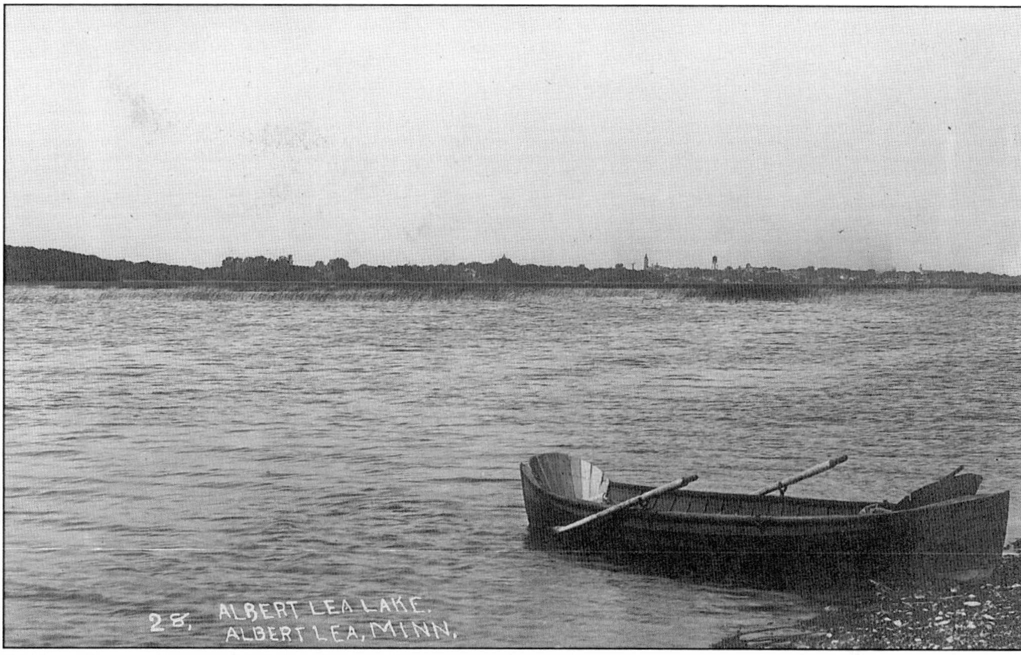

"Albert Lea, a beautiful lake about thirteen miles in length and varying in width from a quarter of a mile to three miles and situated in Freeborn County, Minnesota, is an attractive body of water to the sportsman . . . ducks, and geese visit Albert Lea in myriads. The elevation being great, the air is pure and the climate healthy. People seldom die there." (From the *Turf, Field and Farm*, May 22, 1874, New York.)

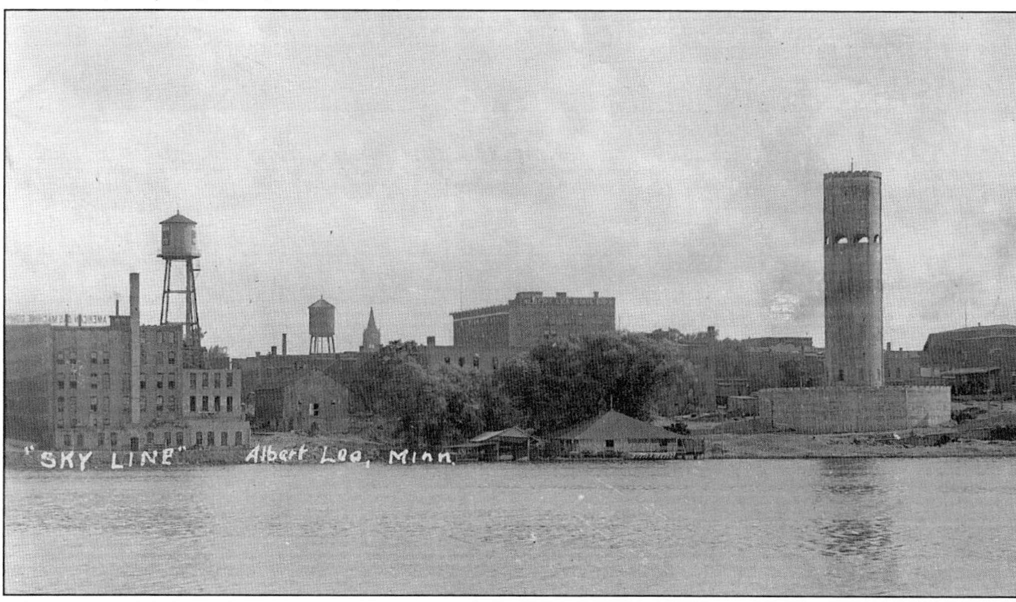

The City of Albert Lea surrounds beautiful Fountain Lake. This view shows the skyline as it looked prior to 1939. The cement water tower that did not hold water; the imposing six-story building, the Home Investment Building, which housed offices and stores; and the Casino/ Dance Hall and boat rental are all a part of the heritage of the residents of Albert Lea, the county seat of Freeborn County.

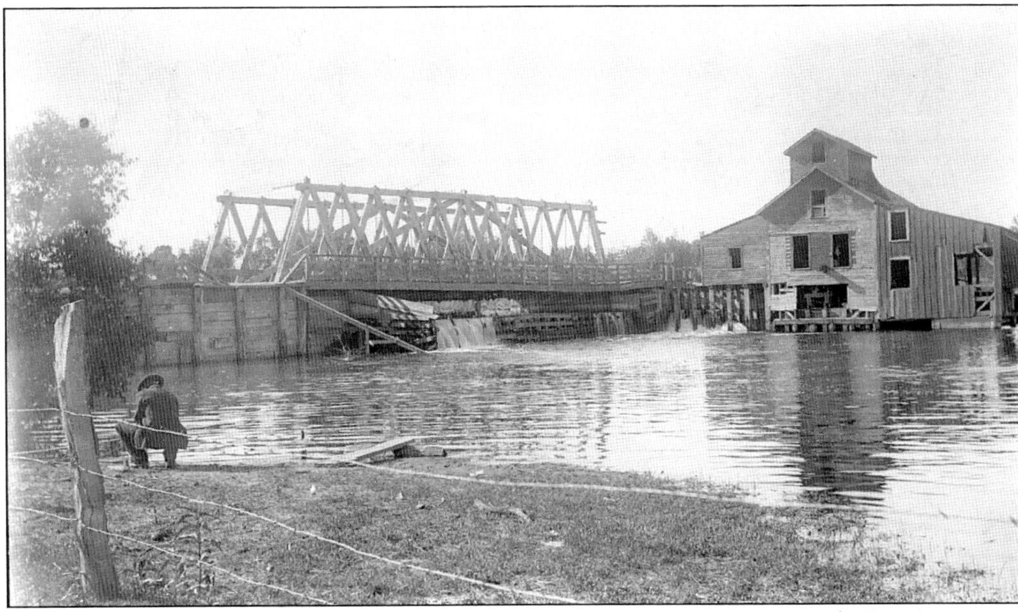

George Ruble came to Albert Lea in 1855 and made plans for building a dam between a wiregrass slough and Albert Lea Lake. He received permission from the Territorial Legislature to do so. A lumber mill was constructed, and a flouring mill was added. The site was destroyed by flooding in 1861. The photograph shows the Francis Hall flouring mill, built in 1867, north of the former mill.

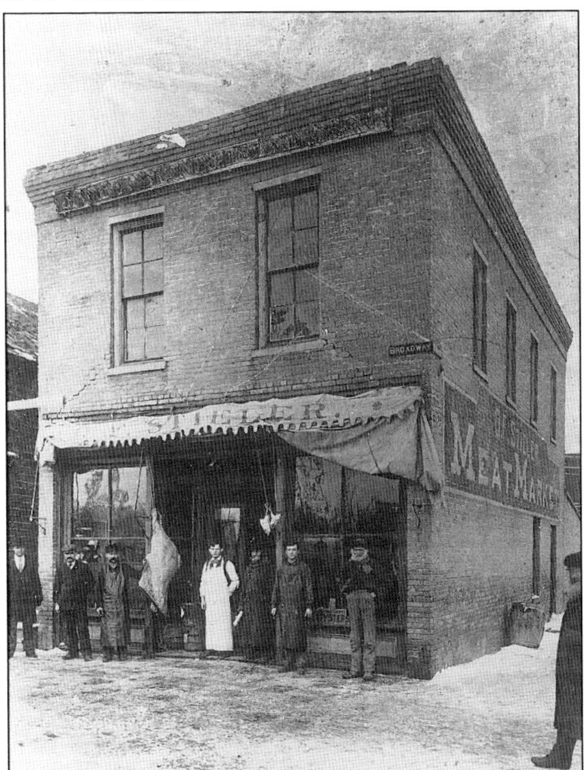

A beef carcass and two plucked chickens advertise the Stieler Meat Market on the southwest corner of Broadway and Main Street. The building was demolished in 1902. Before the meat market opened, Johnson and Nelson operated a grocery store in the building. Hugo Stieler is pictured here in the white apron. Among the others are D. Stieler, Helmer Kvame, and Dean Clark

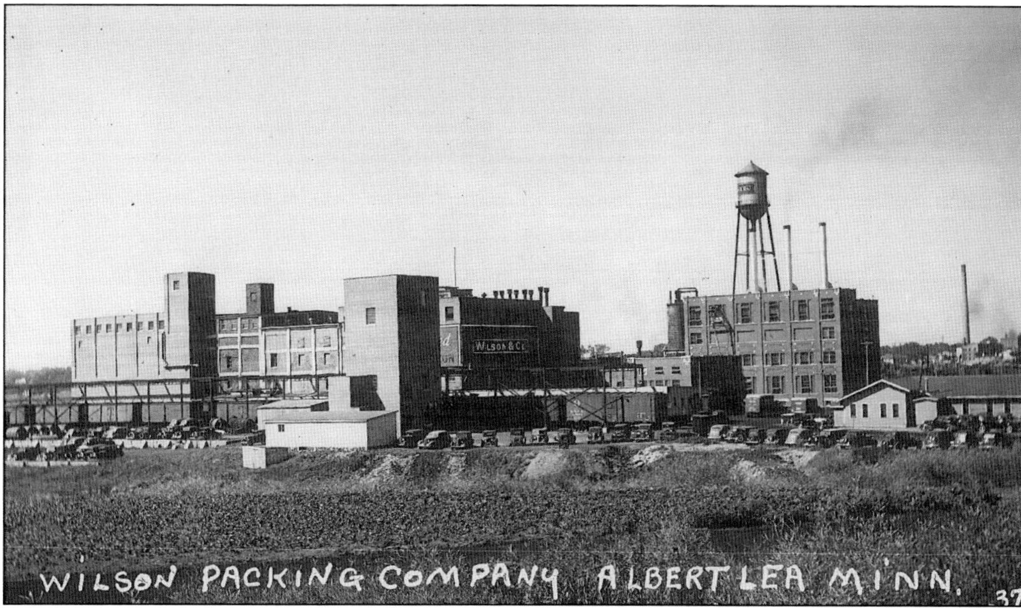

Wilson and Company looks busy and productive in this 1940s photograph. Early meat packing history in Albert Lea included such names as: Brundin Meat Packing Company, Albert Lea Packing Company, the Soth Packing Company, and Sulzberger & Sons Company. In 1916, the Wilsons decided to invest in the community, and thus began a successful expansion and employment pattern that continued almost 70 years.

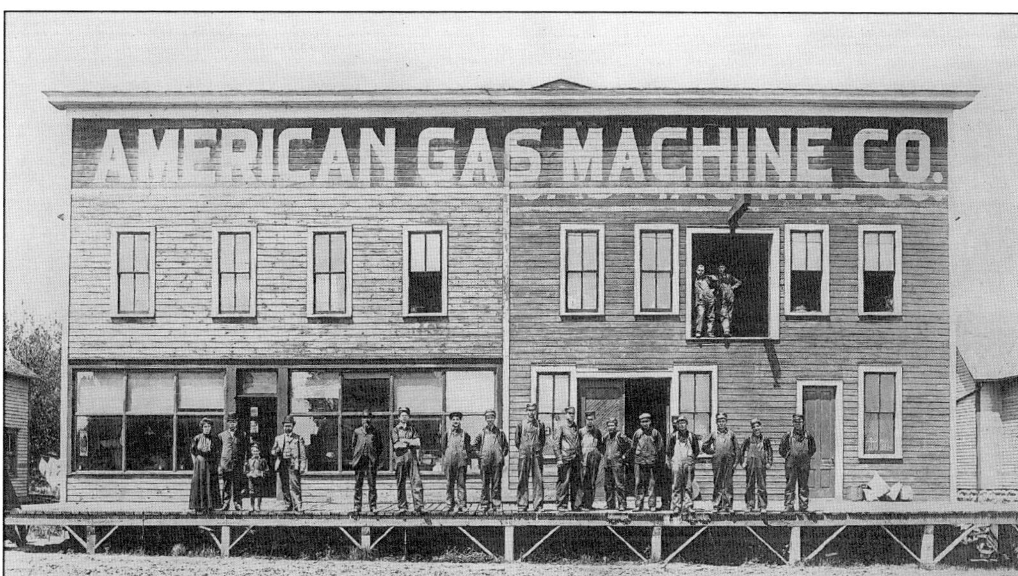

In 1894, H.C. Hansen began tinkering with gas lighting apparatus. With the help of local investors, his interest grew into the American Gas Machine Company, one of the largest employers in the city. This building on East William Street was soon outgrown , and in 1910 they moved to Clark Street, and in the 1920s to Front Street. Their manufacturing lines of items for cooking, heating, and lighting were sold world-wide.

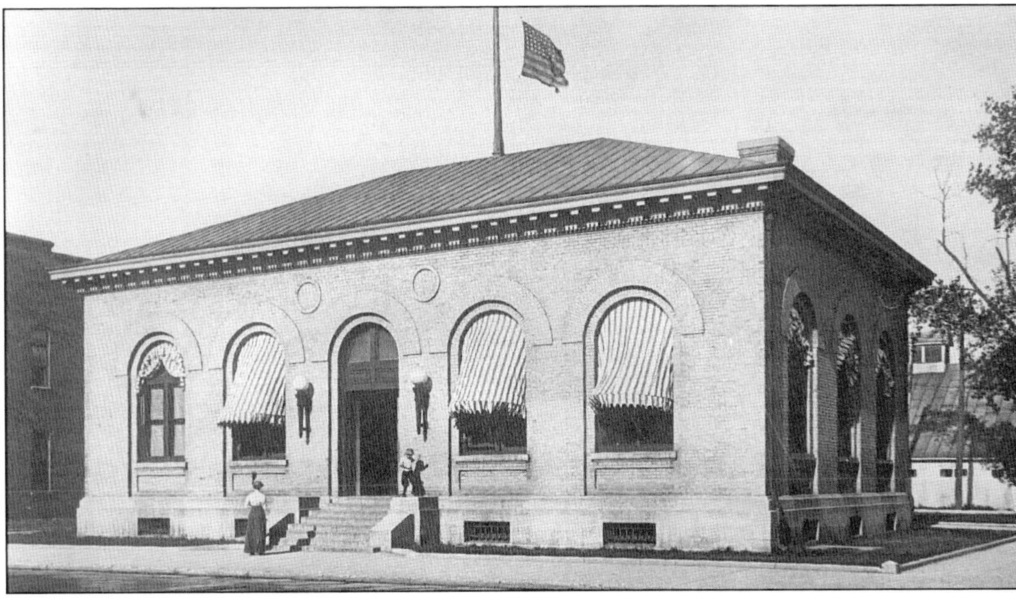

Between 1855 and 1905, the Albert Lea Post Office was located in several different buildings, each dependent on the current postmaster. In 1905, this building was erected on Newton and William Streets. It was of light-gray brick with a stone foundation and was 67 by 45 feet. The *History of Freeborn County* states, "An iron railing has been provided for hitching teams near the east door. The cost of the complete building and grounds was $36,000."

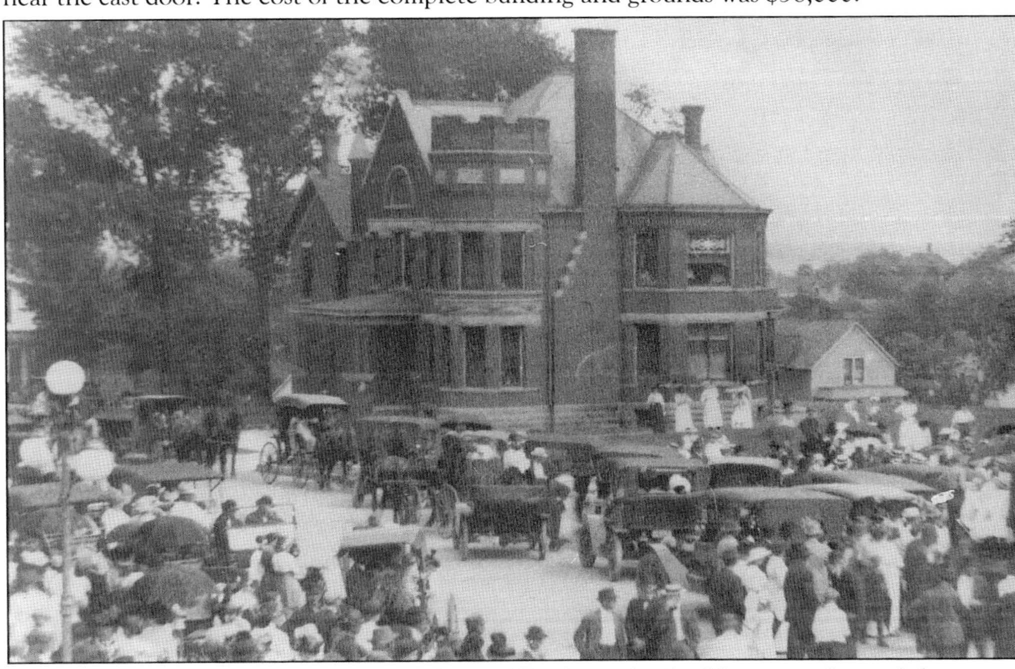

Looking like European architecture of the Middle Ages, this building once housed the county sheriff and his family on the first floor and the jail on the second floor. Built in 1875, it stood on the corner of College and Newton. In 1886, a new jail addition was constructed on the east side, and the home's second floor was remodeled for family use. Meals for the prisoners were made by the sheriff's wife.

The Richardsonian-Romanesque style of construction, with its massive shape used in the building of the Freeborn County Court House, was a great source of pride to the community. The total cost of this building, in 1887, was $75,000. In 1938, the courthouse custodian, when checking on the clock, was surprised to find the body of a man hanging in the tower. In spite of a thorough investigation, the dead man's identity was never discovered.

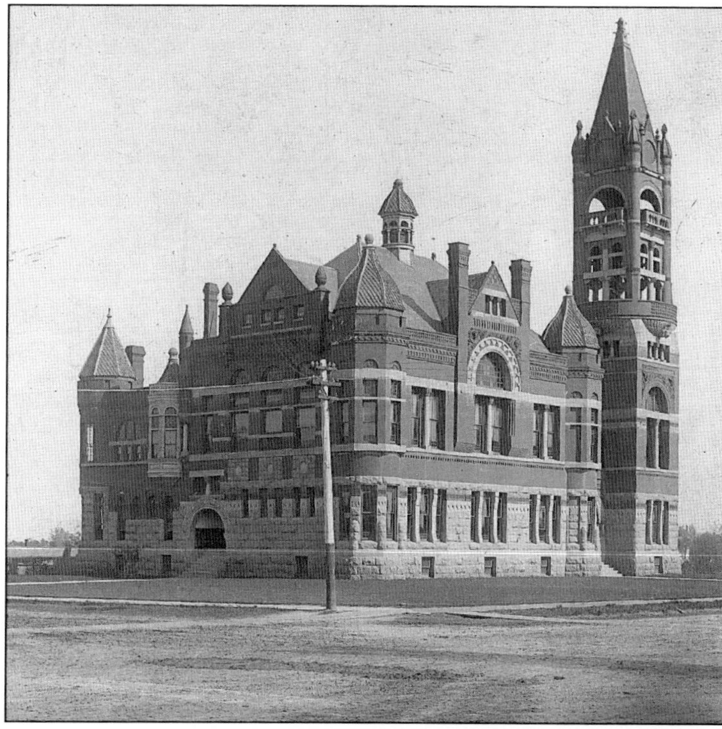

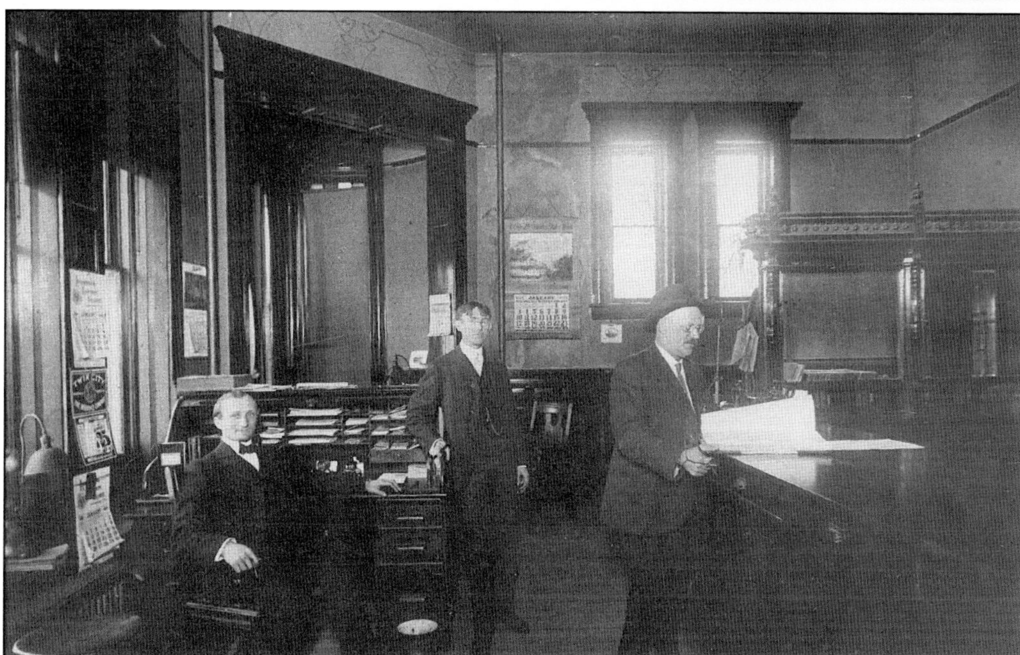

This photograph was taken in the county auditor's office in the Freeborn County Court House in 1913. The office was located in the northwest corner on the first floor. The auditor at that time was Charles E. Brainerd, probably the gentleman seated at the desk. He had previously served as city clerk. He was also active in many local organizations, was an assistant fire chief, and was an ardent Republican.

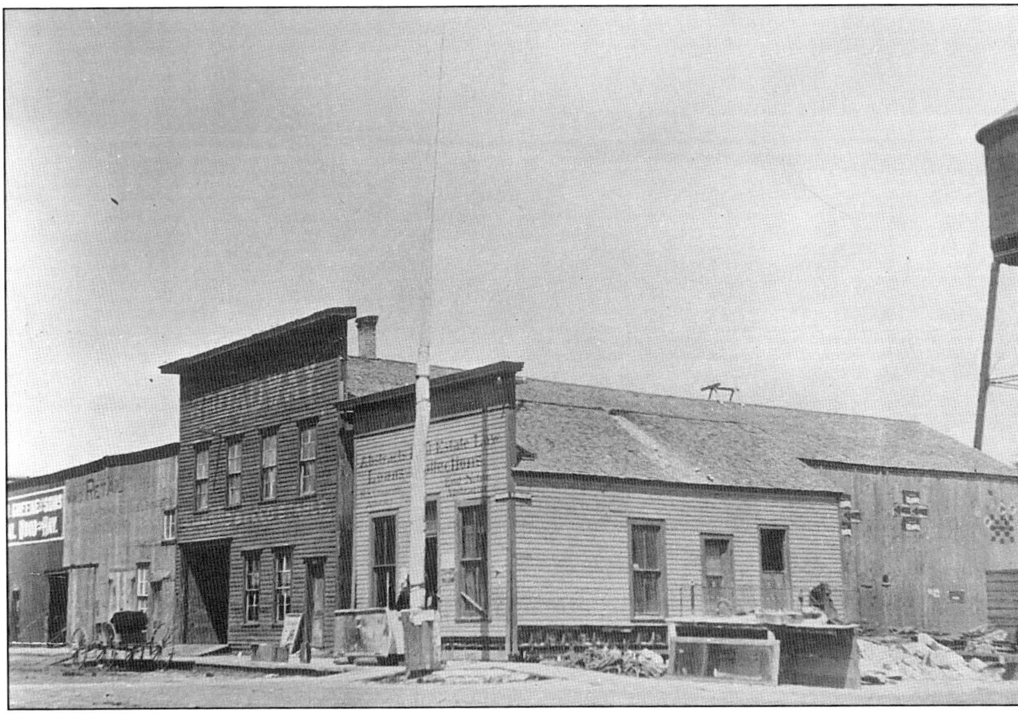

This photograph shows the northeast corner of Broadway and College as it looked in 1899. At that time, this was the site of Morin Law Office and Real Estate, and L.O. Greene & Sons Livery Stables. These buildings were then demolished for construction of the Hotel Albert. William A. Morin, whose father was one of the early successful financiers of Southern Minnesota, was instrumental in the development of the hotel corporation.

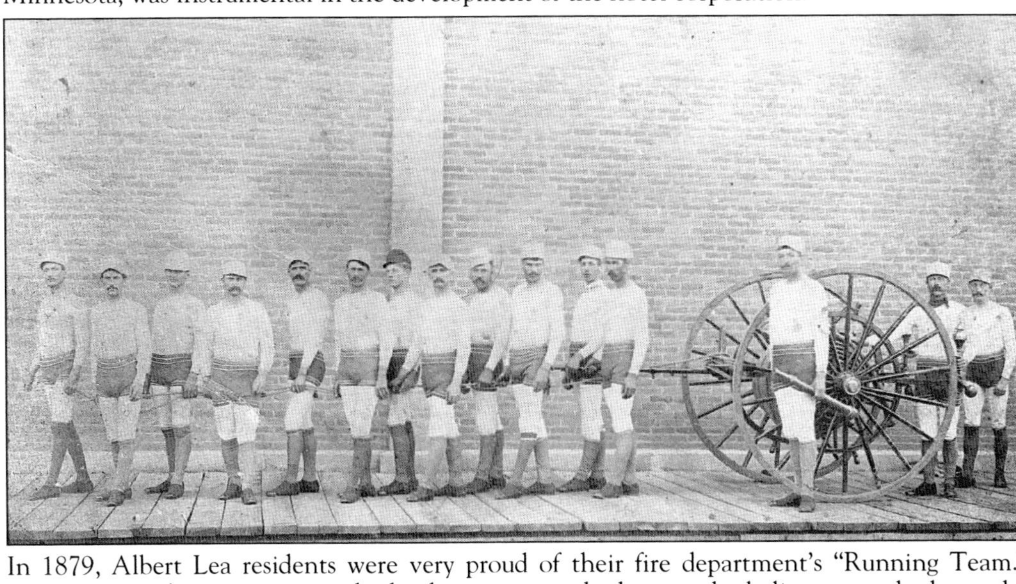

In 1879, Albert Lea residents were very proud of their fire department's "Running Team." They competed in an event in which a hose was attached to a make-believe water hydrant; the team ran 360 feet with the hose unreeling from the cart, and then a nozzle pipe was attached. The Albert Lea team came in second, losing only to the Red Wing team, whose time was 29 seconds, a United States record.

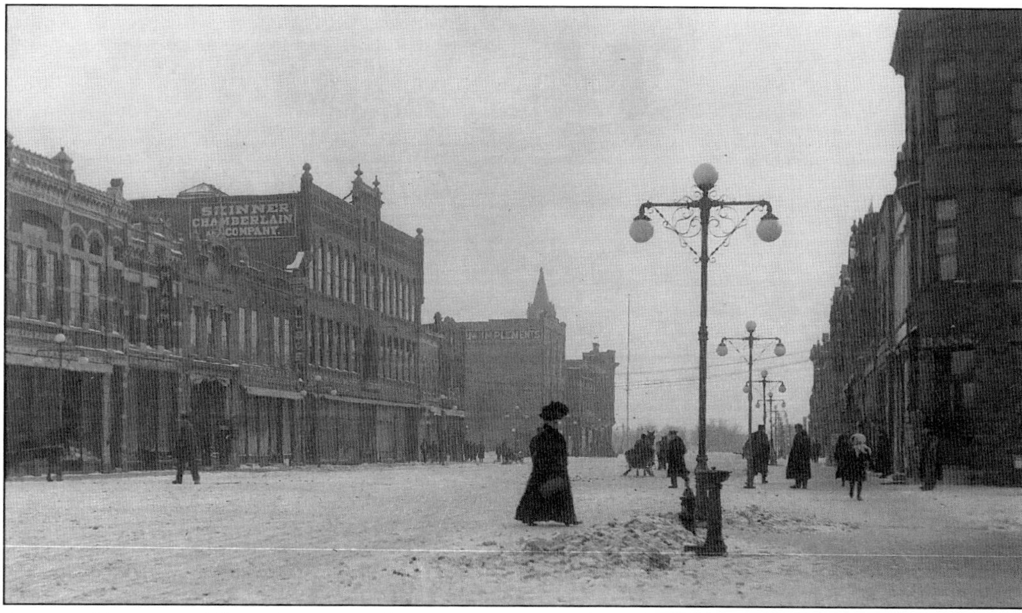

It looks like most Albert Leans on this winter day in about 1915 were home where it was warm, while a few hardy souls ventured out, intent on business. The lady in her broad brimmed hat, the ornately scrolled lamp posts, and the detailed roof tops of the buildings give a wonderful Victorian charm to the scene. The lady is crossing Broadway at the corner of William Street.

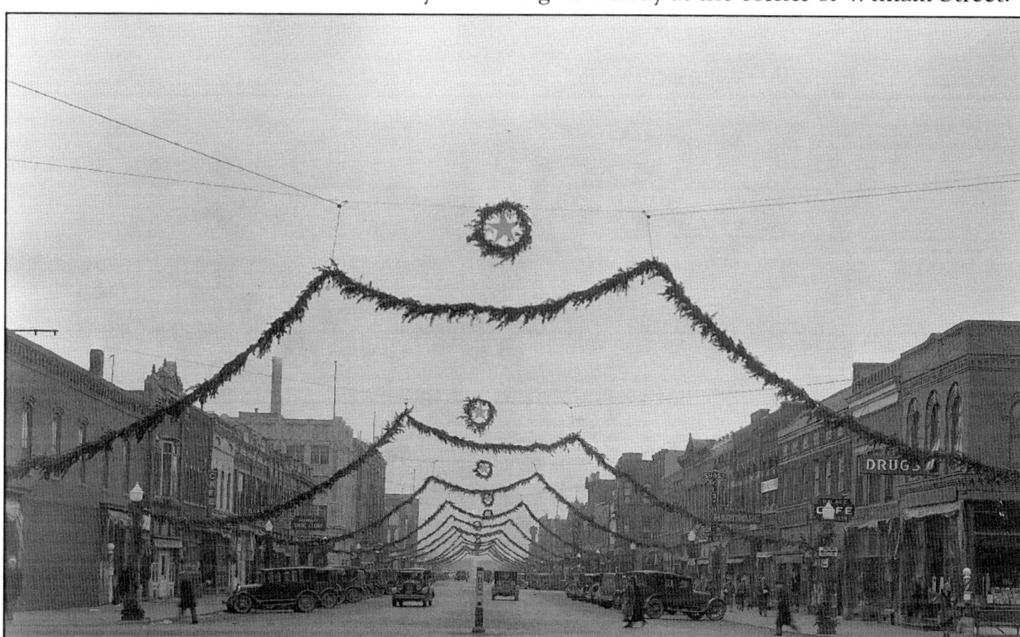

In the 1930s, national publicity was directed toward Albert Lea as a result of its Christmas display of wreaths. Each year, businesses and homes were decorated with streamers of green fir wound with colored lights, and wreaths were hung on the building tops and in windows. The number of automobiles and pedestrians seems to indicate a good atmosphere for business, as well as the holiday season.

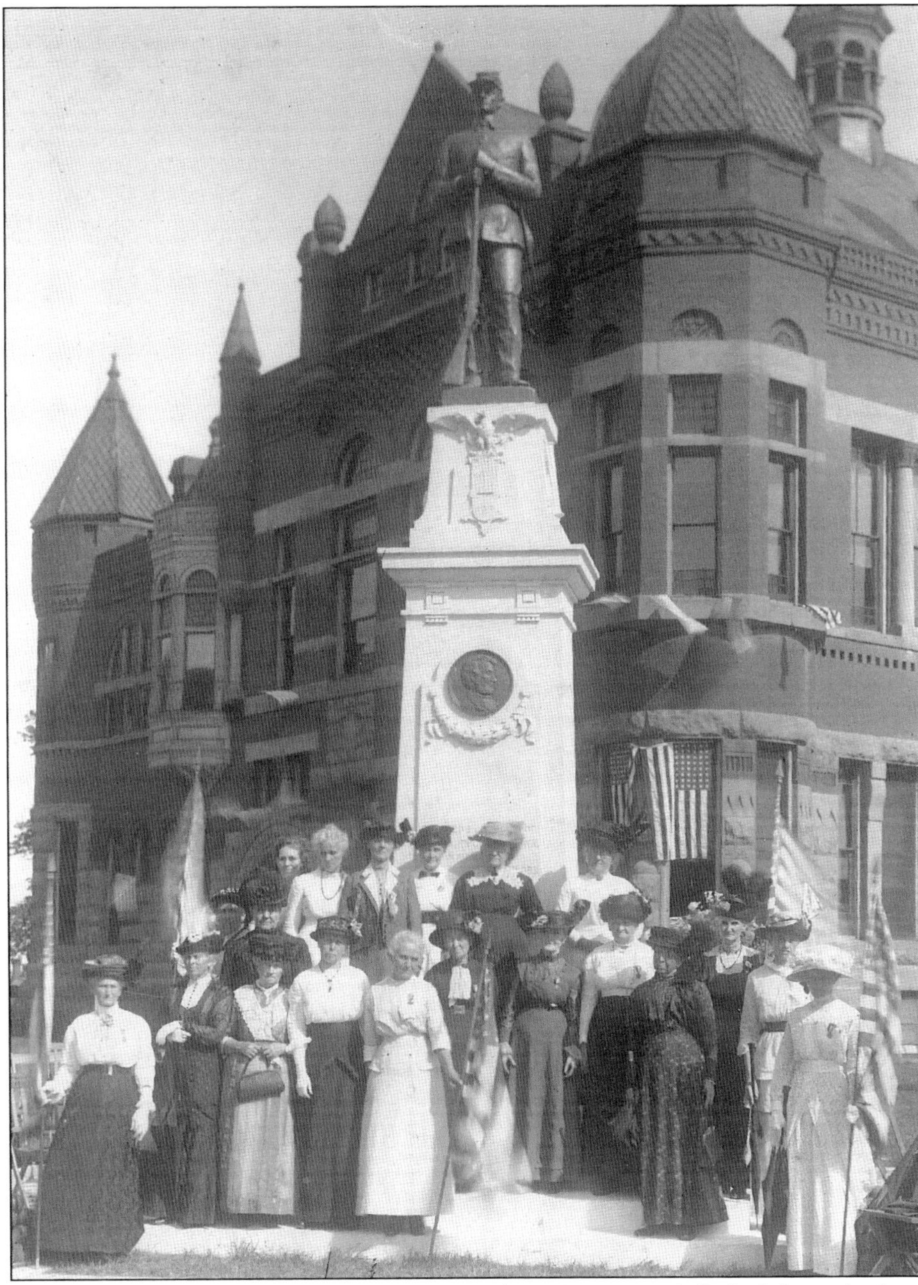

Formed in January 1894, the Robson Post, Number 93, Women's Relief Corps had a charter membership of 45 ladies. They assisted the members of the G.A.R.—Grand Army of the Republic—in visiting the graves of those who had served in the military, and they remembered those in the soldiers' homes with special gifts.

The W.R.C. members are shown in this photograph near the monument built to honor the memory of the Freeborn County men who had served in the Civil War. The photograph was taken May 30, 1914, and the monument was dedicated on June 11th that same year. The bronze soldier and his musket stood atop a granite column on the northwest corner of the courthouse square. It was moved 100 feet to the south, in 1953, to make room for the courthouse addition.

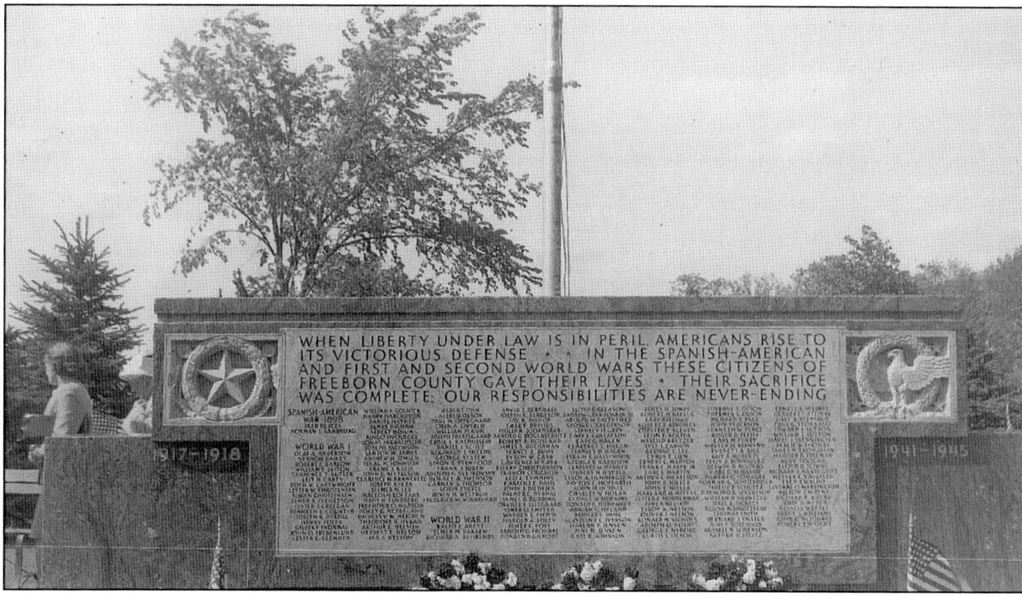

Memorial Day services at Graceland Cemetery in 1947 included the dedication of a new monument honoring the Freeborn County men who gave their lives in the Spanish-American War, World War I, and World War II. Funds for the monument were raised by members of the American Legion, Veterans of Foreign Wars, and the Disabled American Veterans. Several years later, names were added of those who died in the Korean and the Vietnam Wars.

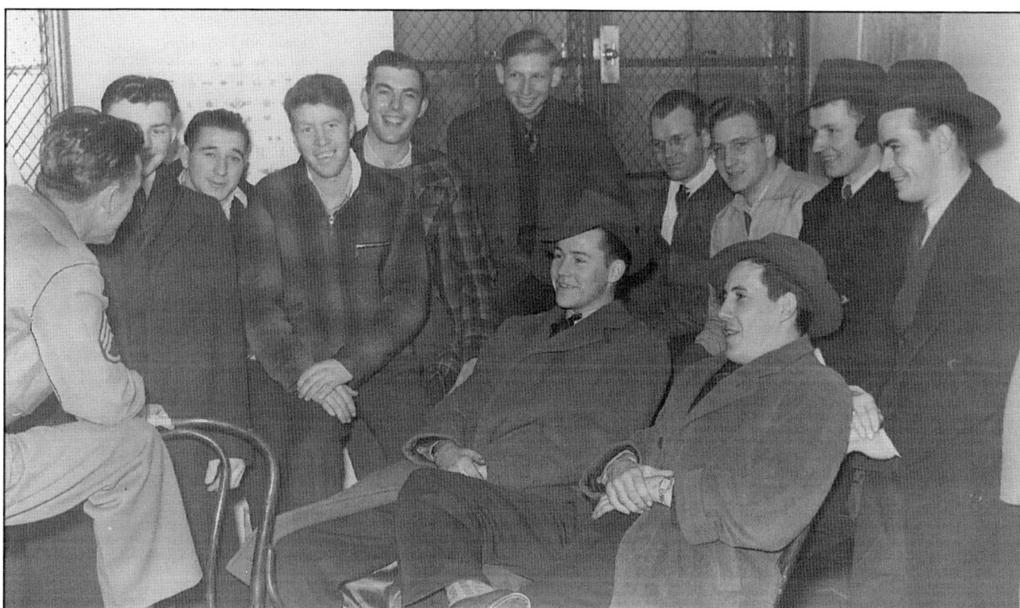

With determination and enthusiasm, these men left Albert Lea on a Rock Island train on December 27, 1941, for Fort Snelling and their training quarters. They are, from left to right: Harold Mork (Albert Lea); Damon Schulenberg and Orville Miller (Wells); Steven Prochniak (Fairmont); Gerald Weerts, Warren Shields, and William McClaim (Winnebago); Kenneth Jacobson and Kenneth Anderson (Albert Lea); Charles Bias (Wells); Leslie Brimacond (Austin); and Bernard Staubor (Fairmont).

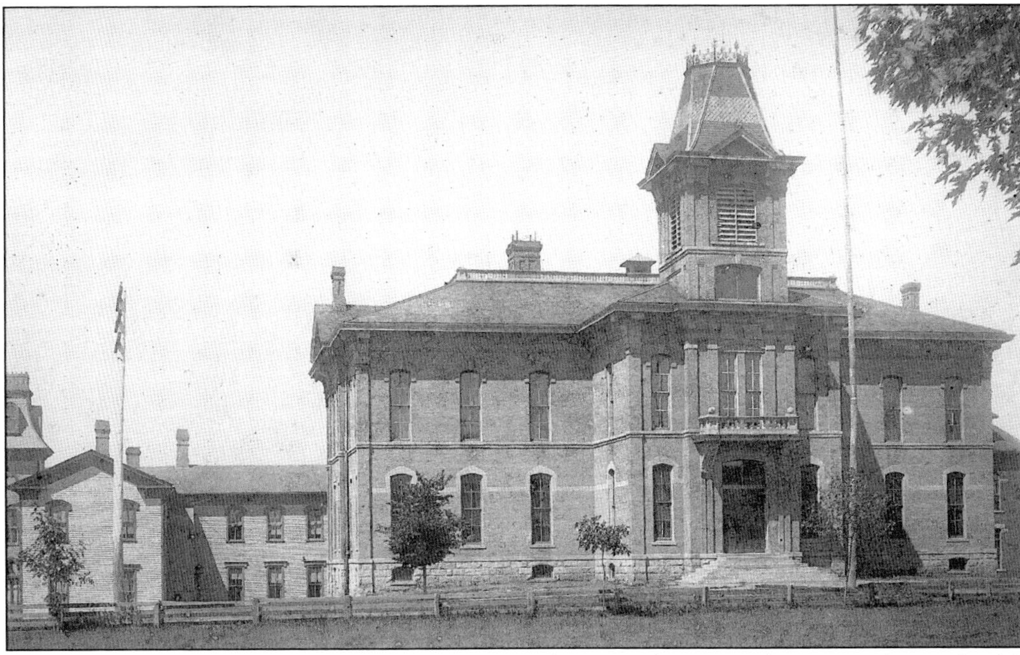

Beginning in 1857, school buildings, their sites, and their architecture, have varied considerably in Albert Lea. Central School was built in 1881 at a cost of $15,000. It was on West Avenue facing Central Park. In 1895, another brick building for high school classes was erected to the north, near Water Street. The wooden building on the south, on Clark Street, served as an elementary school.

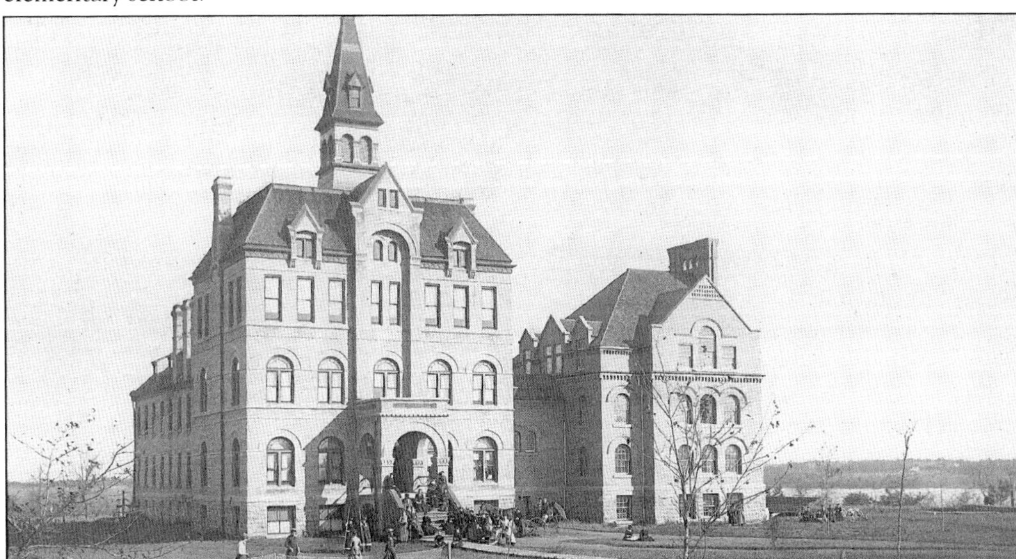

The Albert Lea College for women opened its doors on September 8, 1885, with an enrollment of 51. The building was designed to be constructed in three phases as expansion was needed, and was supported in part by the Presbyterian Synod. Classes included: German, French, Latin, history, science, mathematics, Bible study, sociology, English, physical culture, music, art, and home economics. The college closed in 1916.

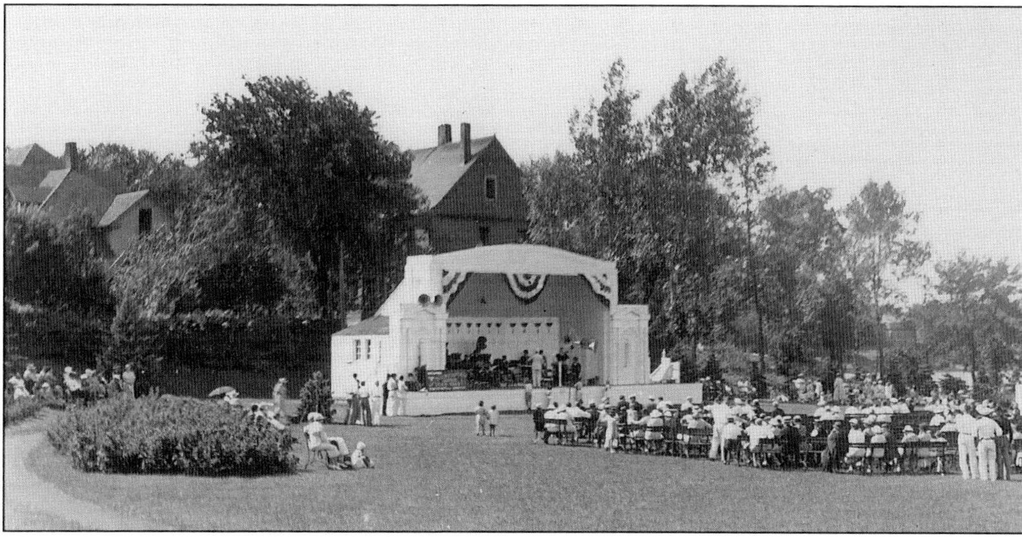

On the former location of the livery stable and an ice storage building, these 3 acres of lakeshore were transformed into a lovely park, dedicated in 1937. In 1933, the city purchased the Greene property and, later, a federal employment project—the Works Progress Administration (WPA)—provided the finances and the labor to build the park, bandshell, lakeside observation deck, and a turn-around lane on North Broadway next to the park.

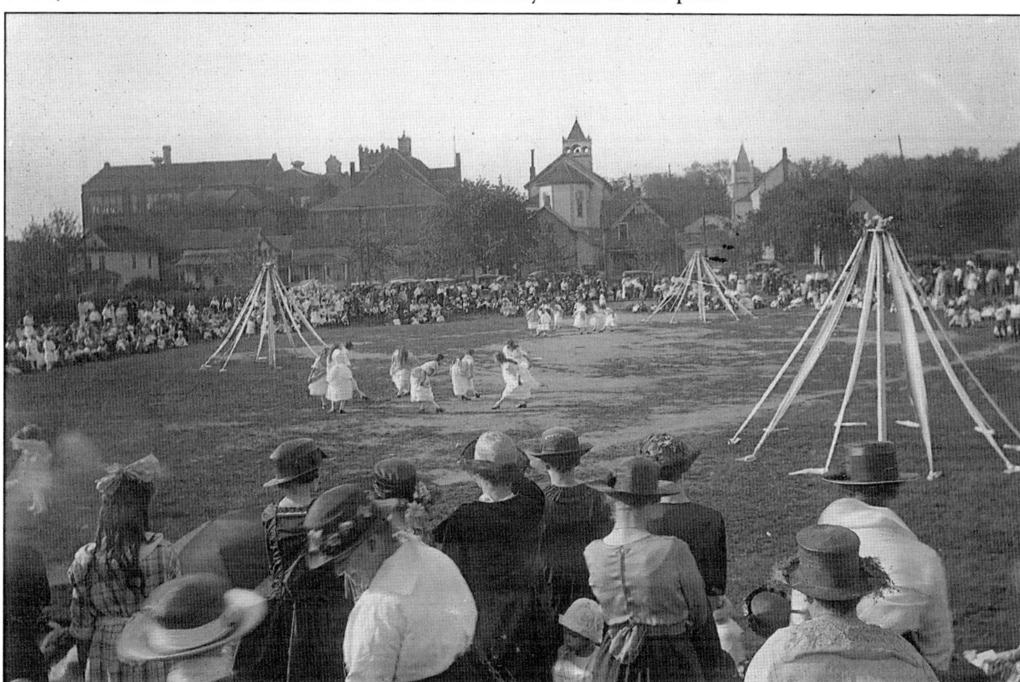

In this lovely park where maidens dance among the May poles, a shallow lake once existed where city residents tossed garbage and where it was said that "a team of horses once drowned." Around 1881, the lake was drained. Plans were later submitted to the state for suggestions on park and playground features. The name was changed from Spring Lake Park to Morin Park to recognize the donor.

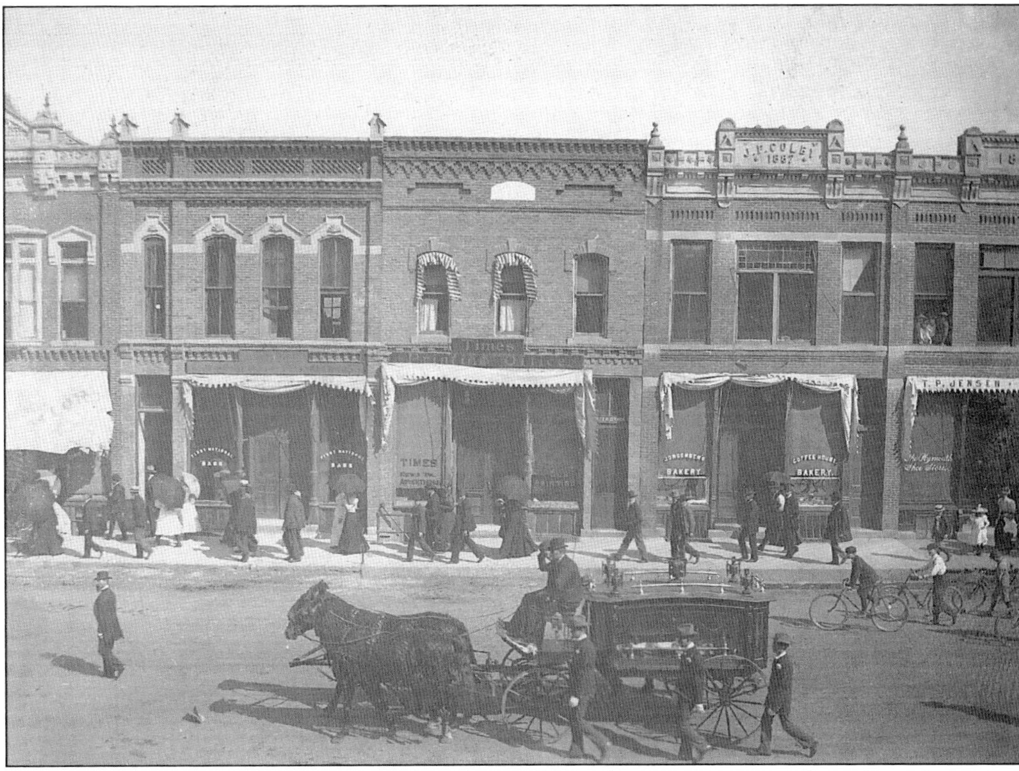

As the townspeople go about their day, a horse-drawn hearse moves north on Broadway. It is accompanied by six pallbearers walking alongside and one in front. The buildings in this 1898 scene are, from left to right: the First National Bank, Times Printing Office, Charles Jorgenson Bakery (J.P. Colby building), and T.P. Jensen's Boots & Shoes (1895).

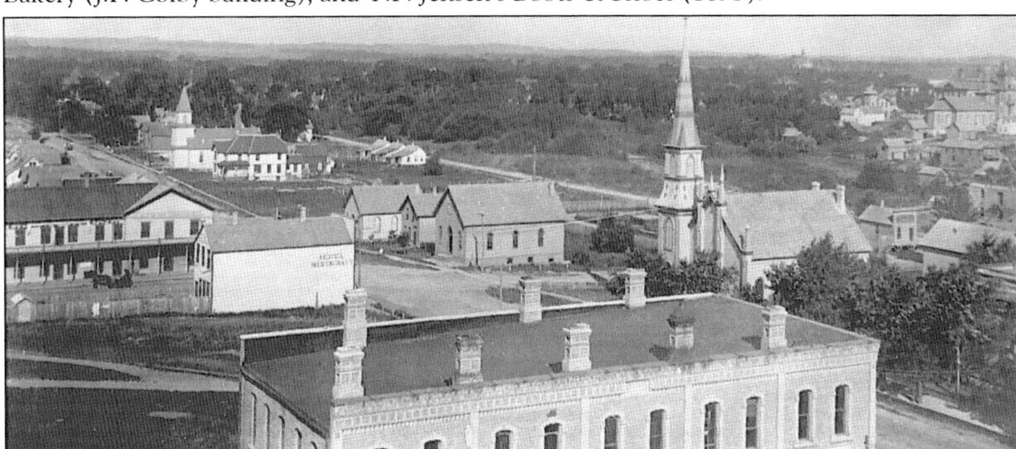

This aerial view of Albert Lea was probably taken from the courthouse tower. Looking to the northwest, we see in the foreground the Albert Lea Tribune building, and to the left the Gilbert House and the Central Hotel Restaurant. The street angling through the picture is West College, intersecting with South Washington. The four churches, as listed in the 1895 plat map, are, from left to right: Trinity Danish Lutheran, Swedish Baptist, Methodist, and Trinity Norwegian Lutheran.

Elizabeth D. Stacy was the first woman to graduate from the University of Michigan Medical School, thus being the third woman in the nation to become a doctor. She moved, with her husband, Judge Edwin C. Stacy, and their children to the Minnesota Territory in 1856. During much of the Civil War, she was the only physician in Freeborn County, riding all over the thinly-settled county helping the settlers with their medical needs.

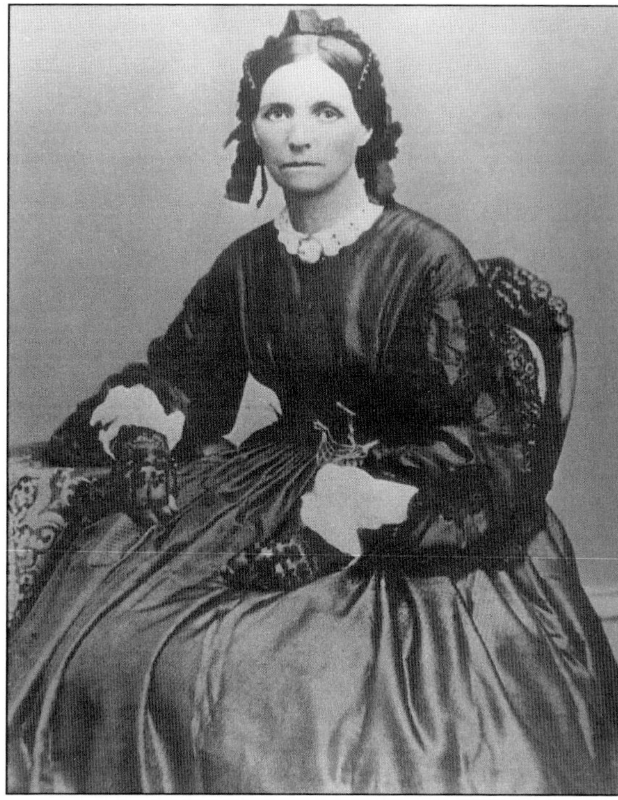

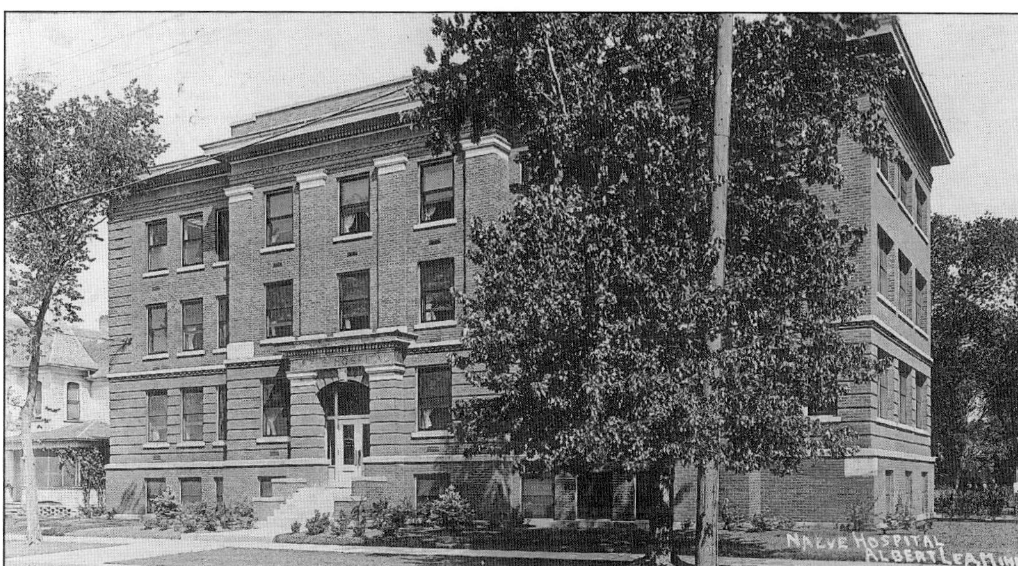

Hospitals in private homes, owned by doctors or medical associations, provided care in Albert Lea prior to 1910. While the need for a large, modern hospital was often discussed, it was not until the City and County Hospital Association was formed, and a sizable donation of land and funds was received from the Naeve and Soth estates, that the planning began in earnest for Naeve Hospital. The cornerstone was laid in May of 1911.

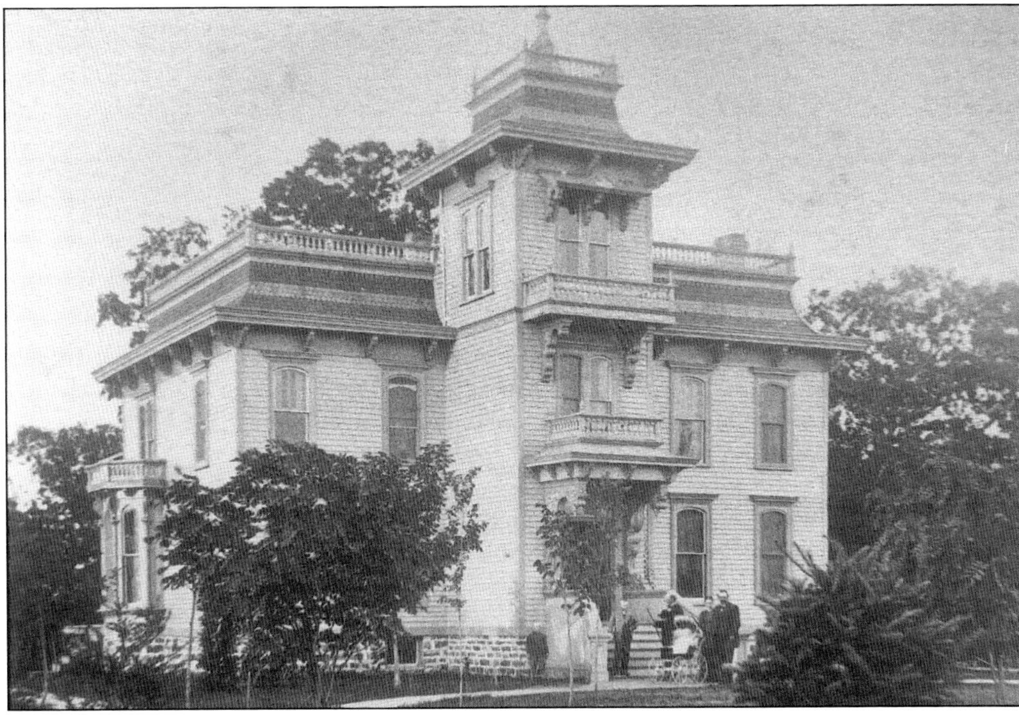

This image of the W.P. Sargeant home on Grove Street was taken from a stereopticon photo card. Sargeant and his family came to Albert Lea in 1871, where he purchased a lumber yard and a farm. In 1882 he was elected to the state senate. An earlier owner of this home was William W. Cargill, who operated a warehouse dealing in grain, hogs, and hides.

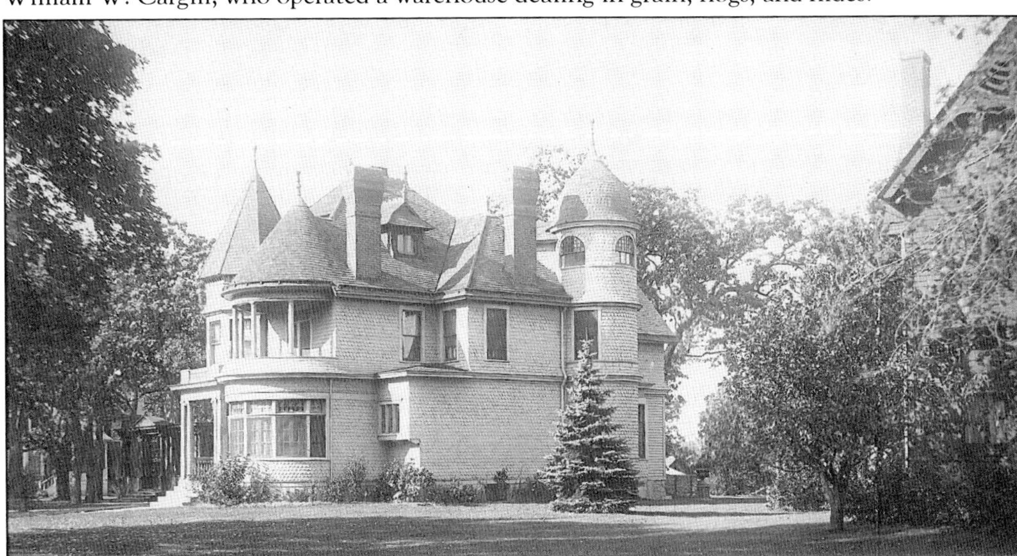

Built in 1889, the Charles Jorgenson-A.O. Watland home on Grove Avenue was an excellent example of Victorian Picturesque architecture. The Queen Anne style home was sided in both clapboard and shingles, and had several corner towers, dormers, and bay windows of leaded and stained glass. The home's interior contained several ornate fireplaces and a cherry wood buffet in the dining room. Jorgenson was a prominent businessman in Albert Lea.

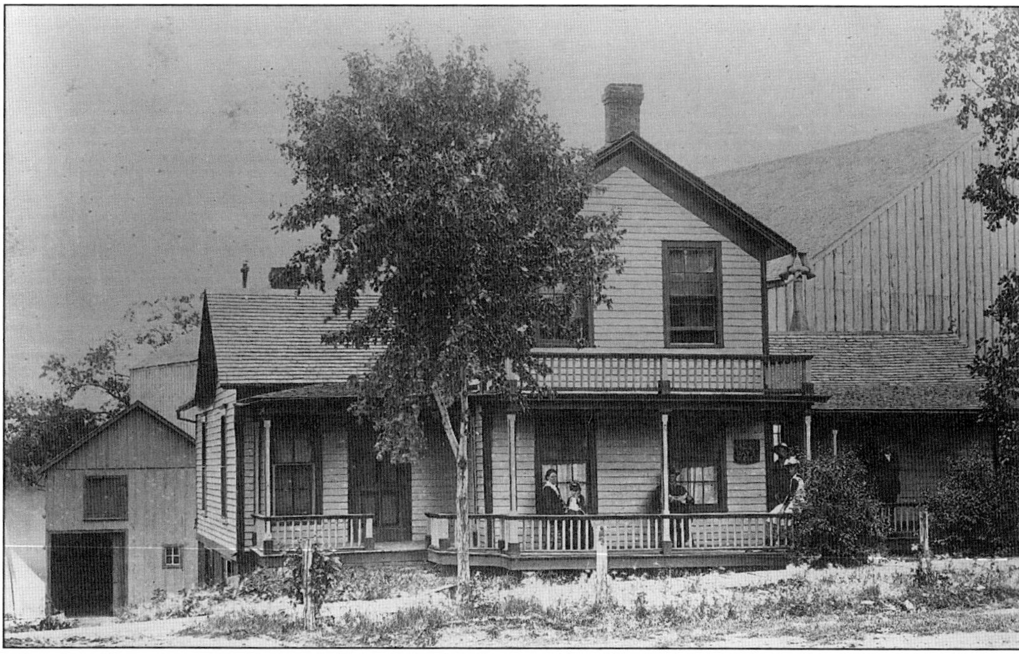

This residence on North Broadway was the home of the Reuben Williams family, and later the John Wing family. Both men had served in the Civil War, with Wing being one of the honor guards at the funeral of Abraham Lincoln. This photograph shows the Wing residence, *c.* 1890, with a sign on the house reading, "Boats for hire by day or week."

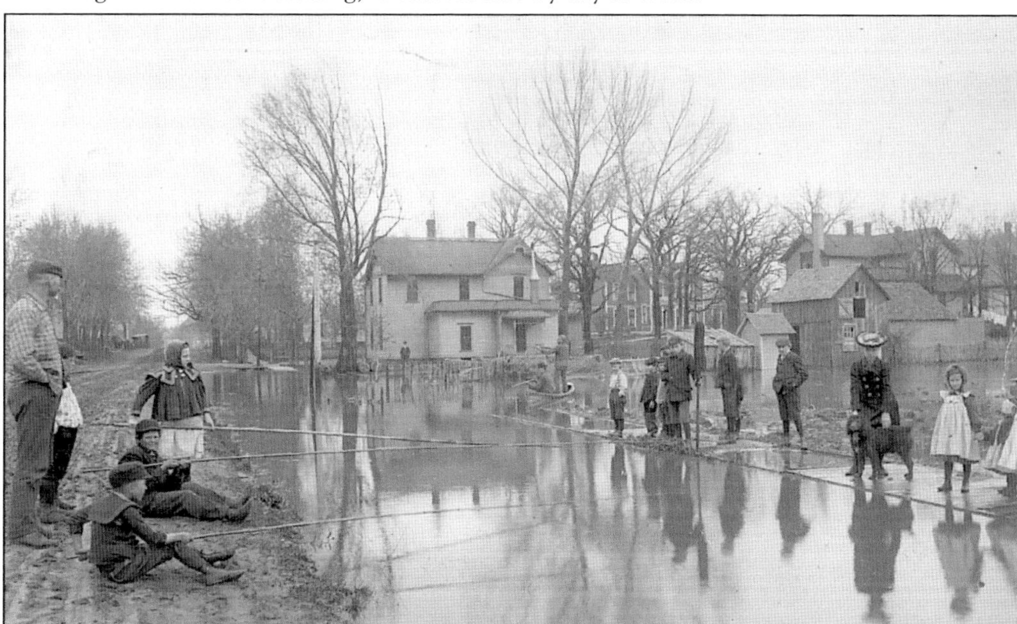

A warm spring day, with the accompanying muddy streets and flooding, must have brought frustration for the adults and joy for the youngsters in this scene at the corner of Euclid Avenue and Court Street. The children with cane poles, and the others standing on the sidewalk, seemed to enjoy posing for the photographer, *c.* 1912.

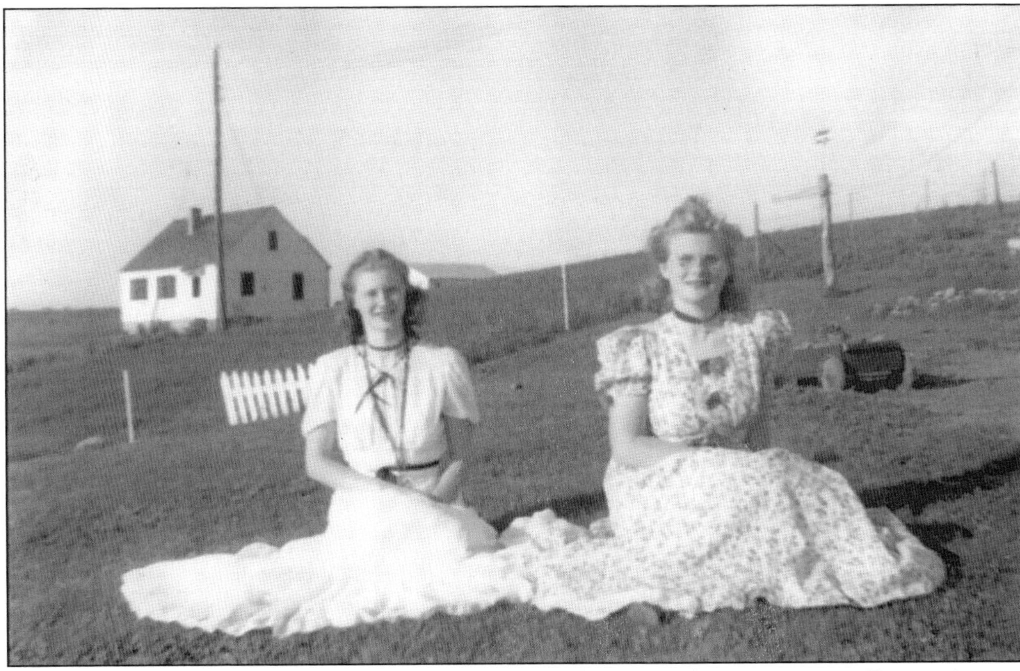

In the mid–1930s, Edward and Elsie Peal purchased a home on the Government Project located east of Albert Lea. One of Franklin D. Roosevelt's plans to help the U.S. out of the Depression, this homestead project provided 5 acres and a small home to qualified buyers. Daughters, Dorothy and Lois, are all ready for the Colonel Albert Lea Days celebration, which took place in 1940.

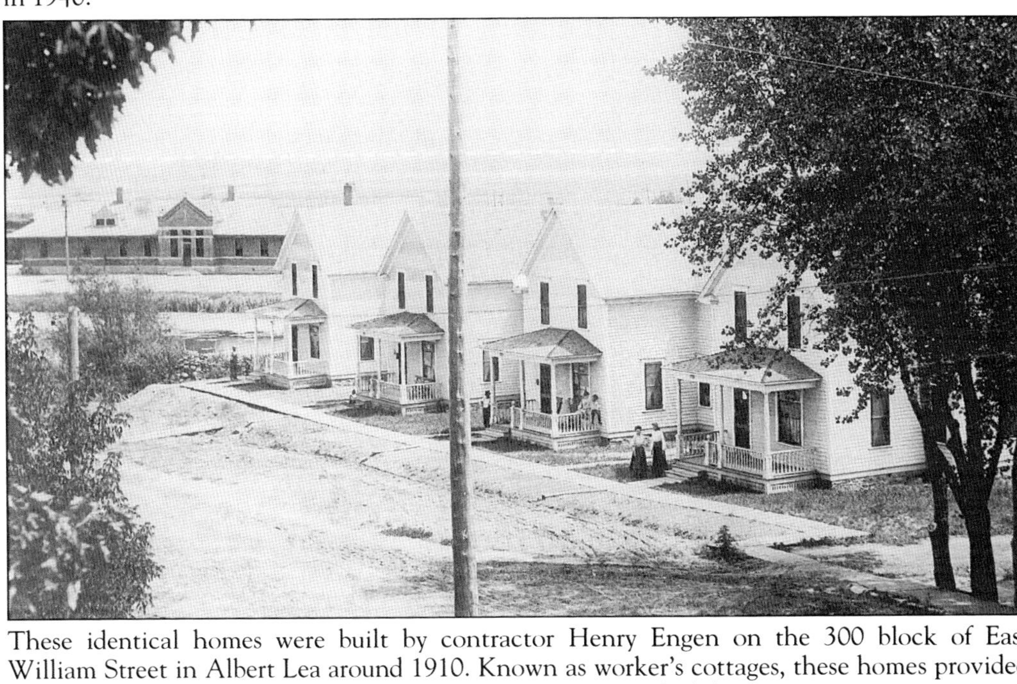

These identical homes were built by contractor Henry Engen on the 300 block of East William Street in Albert Lea around 1910. Known as worker's cottages, these homes provided inexpensive housing for families. The front porches were ideal for enjoying summer evening breezes and neighborhood visits. The Rock Island Railroad depot is in the background.

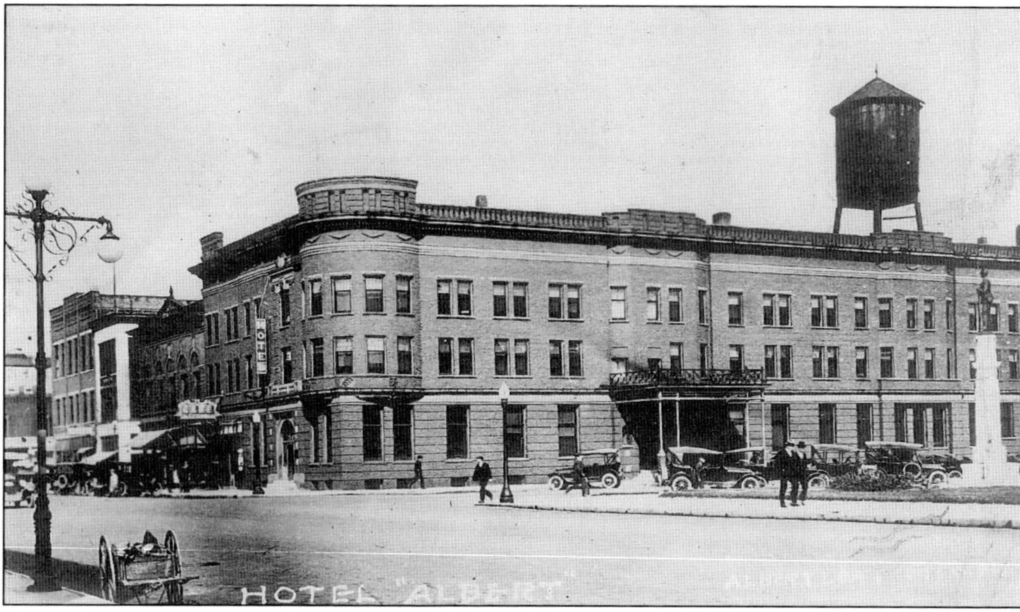

In 1899, the Hotel Albert was built by the Albert Lea Hotel Company. Shortly after, Charles Jorgenson bought out the other two stock holders, and within 20 years, it was the largest hotel per capita in the United States. Its 225 rooms, Spanish dining room, coffee shop, lounge, and elegant atmosphere provided respite for thousands of guests, including movie stars and prominent politicians, who traveled the Jefferson Highway.

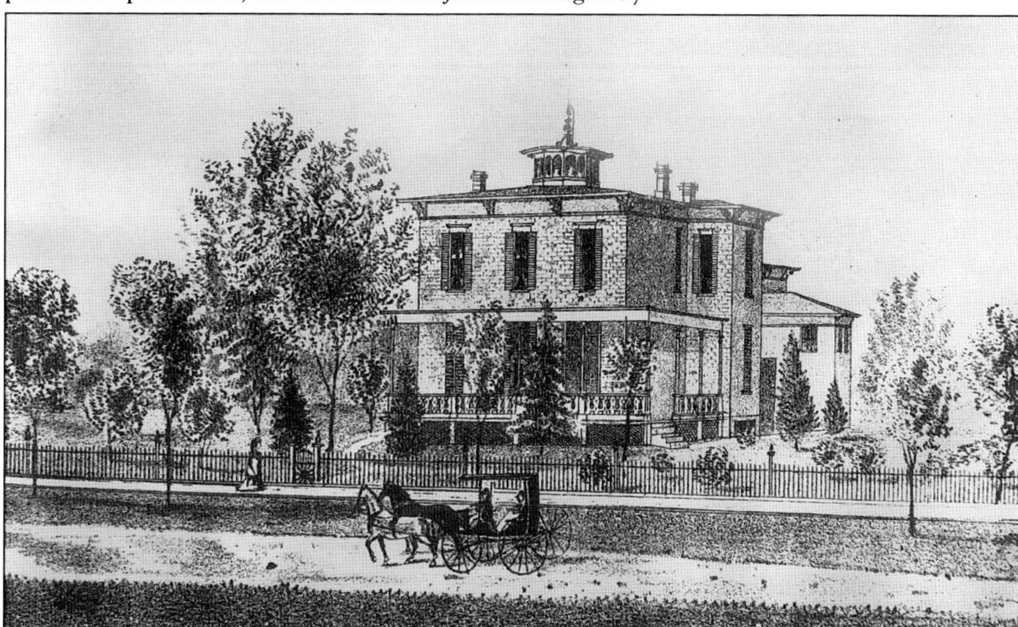

On October 14, 1865, Frank Hall wrote his purchasing agent to obtain the best lumber, window caps, door sills, and other materials. He knew the best materials would cost more, but he wanted to build a quality home. Hall served as Albert Lea's mayor, but he was a bank president and a merchant by trade. This home on East Clark Street eventually became the Hall House, later known as the Freeborn Hotel.

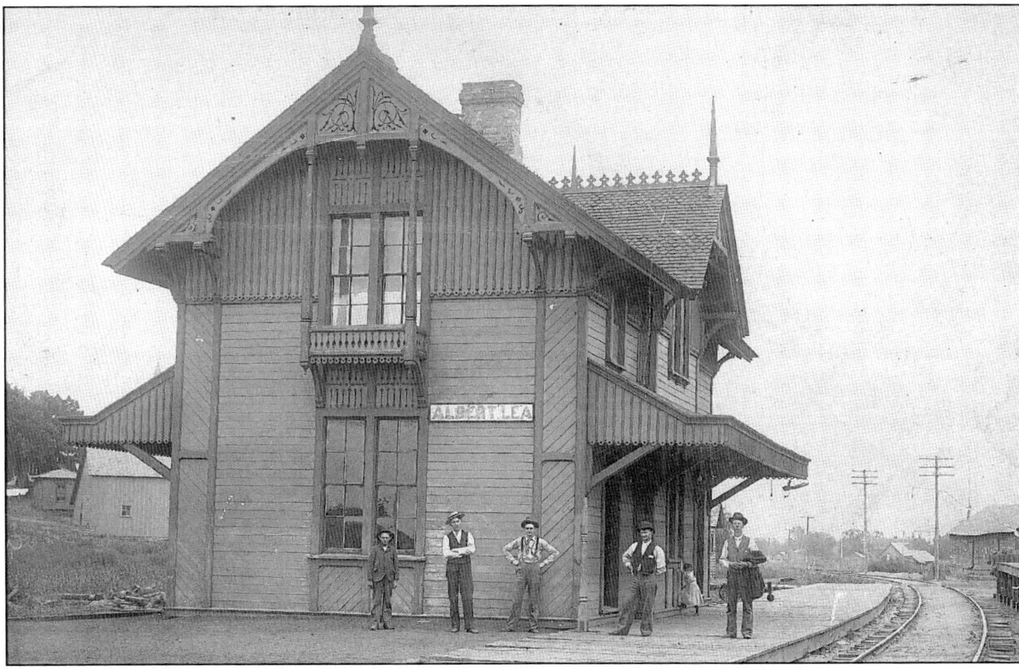

The Southern Minnesota Railroad reached Albert Lea in 1869 as the first railroad into the city. It was purchased by the Milwaukee Road in 1880. The depot just west of South Pearl Street, a good example of a Swiss Chalet style building, burned down in 1890. A new depot was built two blocks east, nearer Broadway.

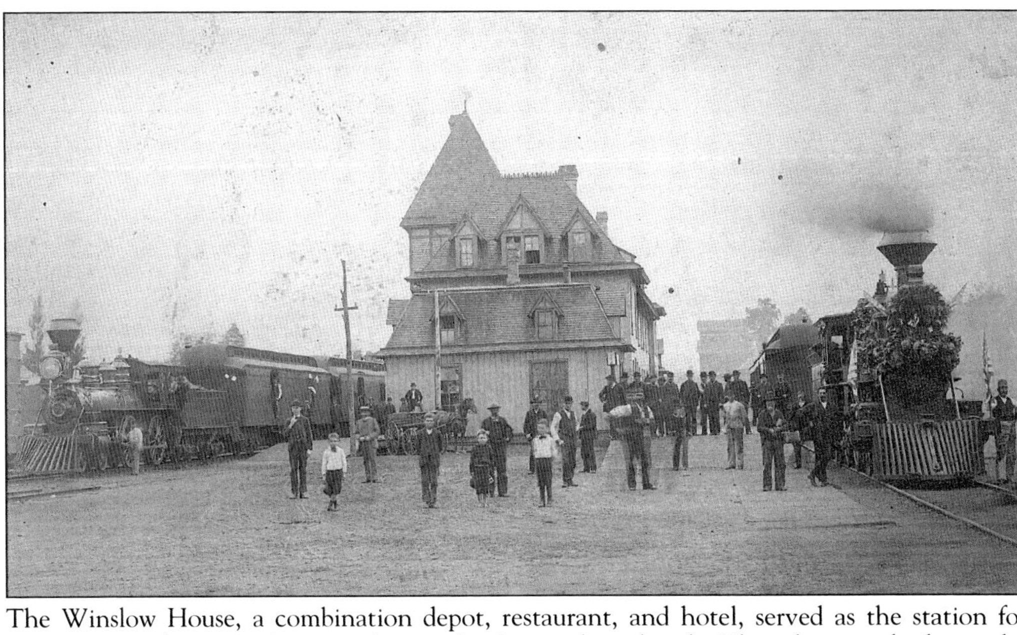

The Winslow House, a combination depot, restaurant, and hotel, served as the station for the Minneapolis & St. Louis and several other early railroads. This photograph shows the celebration in 1877, marking the arrival of two railroads, the M & StL and the Burlington, Cedar Rapids, and Northern, into Albert Lea. In 1880, there were about 40 arrivals every 24 hours, including eight passenger trains.

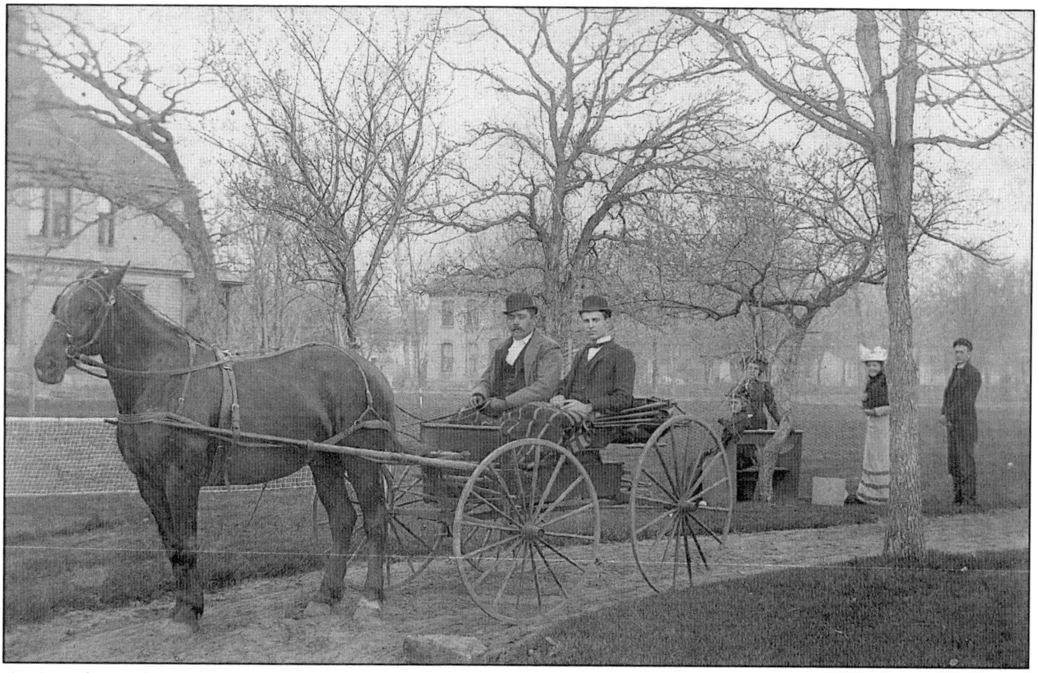

A Sunday afternoon drive and a visit with good friends—what a wonderful ending for our trip through Freeborn County! The folks in this photograph hope that you have enjoyed your journey, and that the bits of history that we have shared bring you a greater appreciation of our heritage and our home.

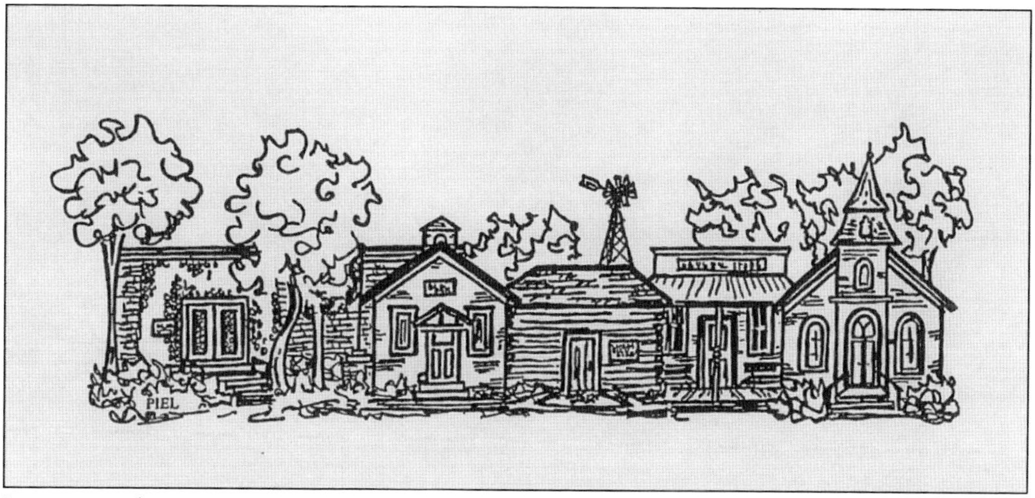

Interest in the preservation of Freeborn County's history surfaced periodically, with the Old Settlers Association in 1875, the Territorial Pioneers in 1899, and the Freeborn County Historical Organization in 1948. This effort led to the incorporation, in 1959, of the Freeborn County Historical Society. The community, generous with its volunteer hours, historical artifacts, and resources, has built a museum , library, and pioneer village complex at 1031 Bridge Avenue, Albert Lea. It is recognized as one of the leading historic sites in Minnesota. Shown in this sketch are, from left to right, as follows: FCHS museum, Big Oak School, Livdalen cabin, general store, and Norsk Evangelisk Luthersk Kirke. (By Beverly Piel Jackson, 1996.)

FREEBORN COUNTY TOWNSHIPS

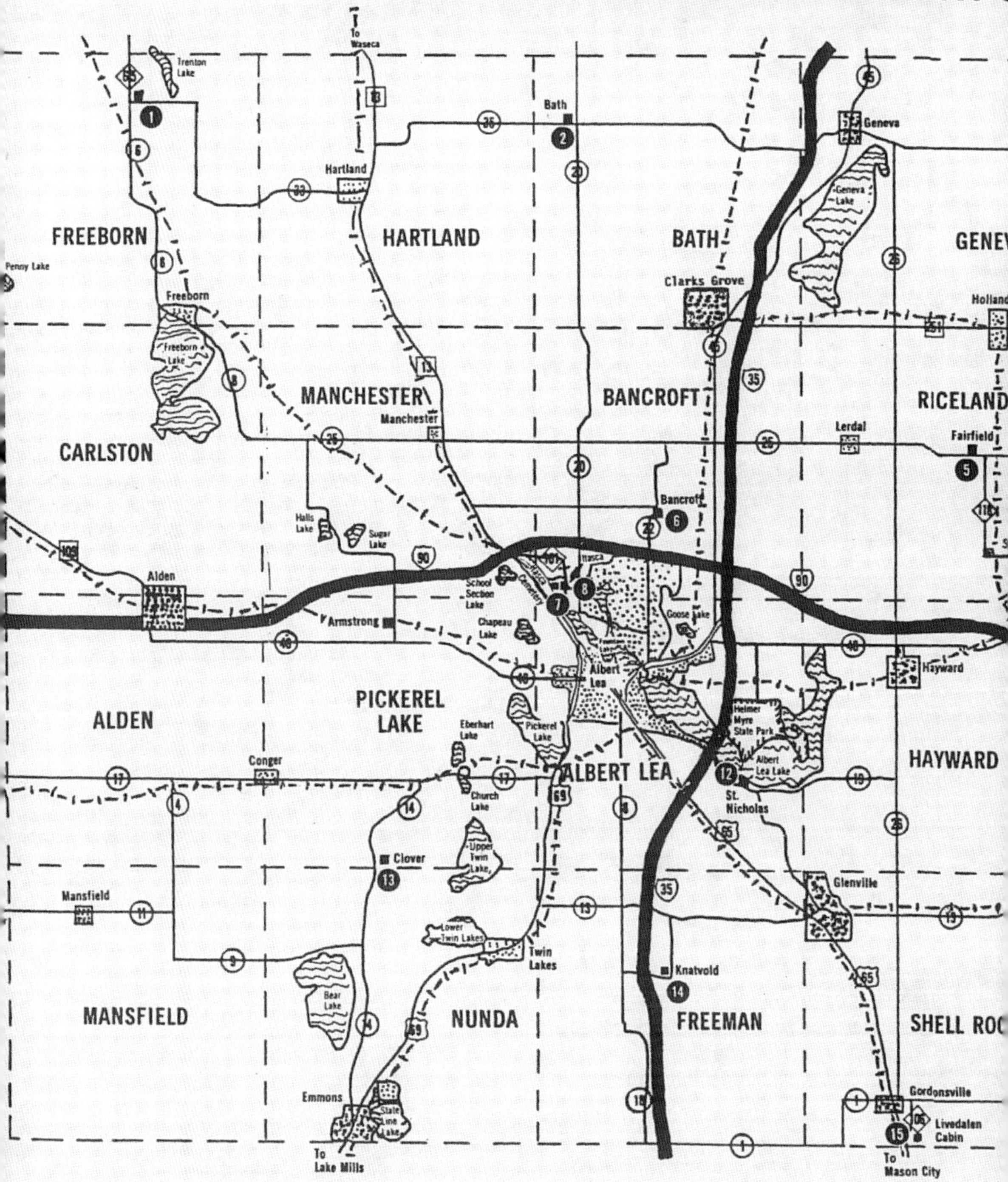

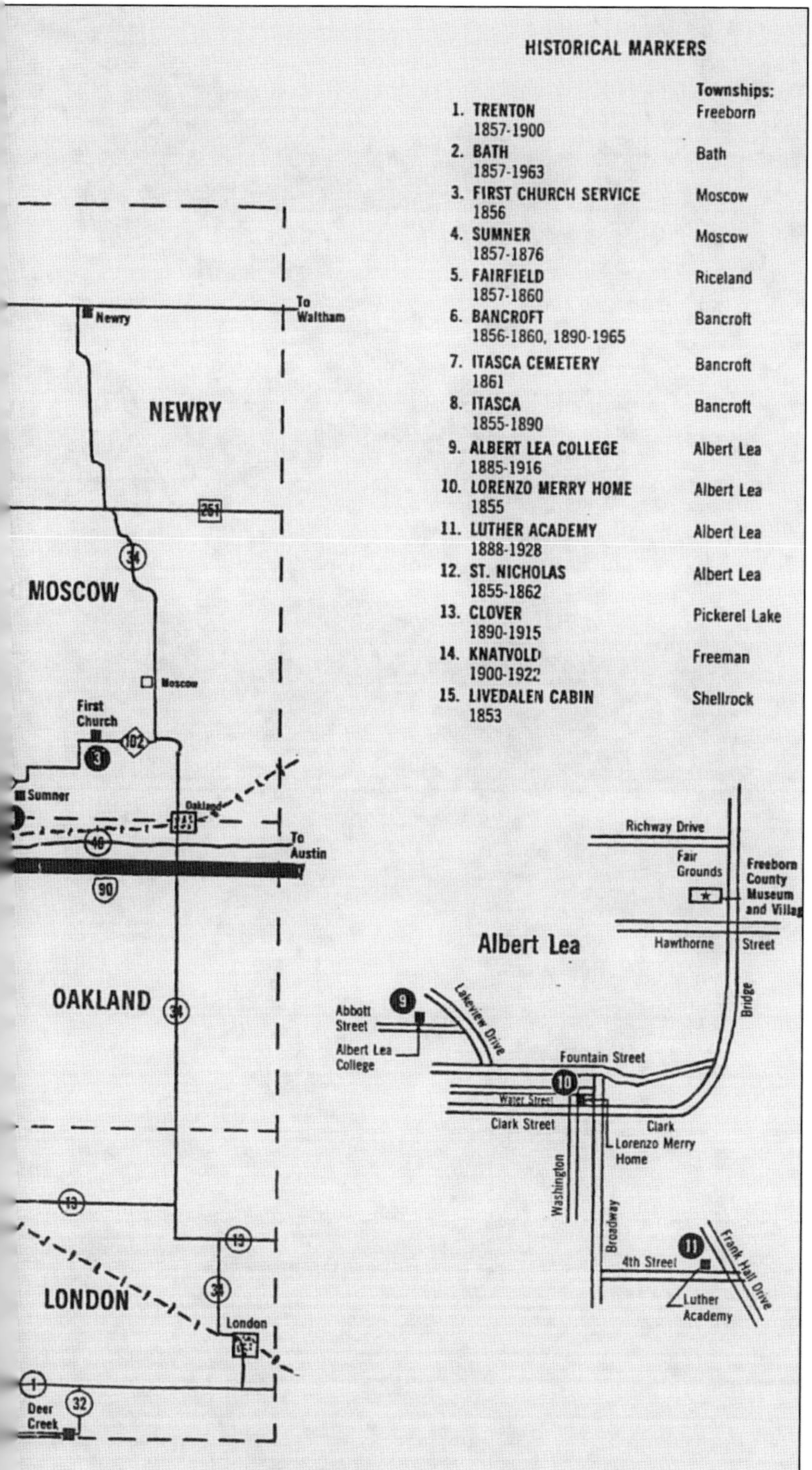

This is a map of Freeborn County, Minnesota.